THE
INSIDERS'
CALGARY

Is there life after the Stampede?
At last, a book about Calgary, by Calgarians,
for Canadians everywhere.

THE INSIDERS' CALGARY

Edited by Penny Williams

Key Porter Books

Canadian Cataloguing in Publication Data
The insiders' Calgary
ISBN 0-919493-03-3
1. Calgary (Alta.) — Description —
Guide-books.
I. Williams, Penny, 1943-
FC3697.18.158   917.123'3   C82-095122-6
F1079.5.C35158

Published by
Key Porter Books
59 Front Street East
Toronto M5E 1B3

Cartoons by Vance Rodewalt.
Designed by Wendy Pease.
Cover design by Ken Rodmell.
Cover photograph by Steve Dunwell.
Typography by Canadian Composition Limited.
Printed and bound in Canada by Webcom Limited.

It seems only fitting to dedicate this book to the city of Calgary itself, and to everyone who shares the insiders' enthusiasm for it.

Acknowledgements

The following deserve more recognition for their part in this very collective effort than a few lines of type can convey: Minette Robinson, who with grace and generosity brought me this opportunity; all the contributors, who provided the knowledge and ability that made the book possible; *Calgary Magazine* and its publisher, Ronald Stern, who provided me with a pleasingly rigorous training-ground and a chance to come to know this city and its insiders; Gayle Herchak, who did the copy-checking with her usual care for detail; Lynda Hodges and a few other deep-throats who murmured extra tidbits in my ear; all the Key Porter people, who put some fine Toronto production skills to work on behalf of Calgary opinions; and, at the risk of sounding mawkish, everyone who has ever reinforced my belief that words matter.

The Time Warp

You will notice, in a few instances, that we refer in the future tense to something that at some point in the life of this book will move triumphantly to the past tense. Since the only way these events could stay in the future tense would be never to take place, we prefer to accept the consequences of their successful completion, and trust that you will too.

Contents

Introduction

It is time for a book about Calgary, by Calgarians, for Canadians everywhere—a guidebook to living here, visiting here, and just plain thinking about here. Calgarians have felt this way for a while, but until very recently the rest of Canada hardly agreed. You could talk about the Stampede—but then what?

Calgary has not exactly dominated the national consciousness over the years. For decades, there was Ontario. Then came the sixties and the Quiet Revolution, and national (read, Toronto) media voices felt impelled to explain Quebec. Then came the seventies and OPEC, and those same voices started explaining Alberta—especially Calgary—as well.

Some of those explanations read very strangely indeed.

This is not the result of a malicious eastern plot, nor even of incompetence or bone-laziness. The true reasons are much less dramatic. Two of them are so obvious that they seldom receive the respect they deserve.

I remind myself of the first by thinking about my two world maps. One is normal, but the other—which I acquired while living on a small island in Indonesia—is somehow askew. It takes a moment to puzzle it out, and then you see that, in addition to being labelled in Indonesian, it puts *Indonesia* at the centre of the world. "Amerika Utara" is shoved off to one side. These maps amount to a salutary lesson in perspective, a lesson that has grown on me during my travels—from Montreal to Toronto, to Pakistan, to Peru, to Toronto, to Montreal, to Indonesia, during years of Third World activities and (in 1977) to Calgary.

Vocabulary changes along with perspective. When I lived in Toronto, "the East" meant the Atlantic provinces and "the West" meant everywhere west of the Ontario-Manitoba border. "Canada," practically speaking, meant Ontario—though of course we knew there were peripheral bits of geography strung out on either side. Now, for me, "the East" means Ontario and Quebec; the Atlantic provinces are referred to as such or by their individual names; and the term "the West" excludes British Columbia, which is known as "the Coast." And "Canada" has become a much more complex reality than it used to be.

The second main reason for the bizarre turn of some Toronto analyses of Calgary is, I think, sheer unfamiliarity. Furthermore, the unfamiliarity—and this is central to Calgary today—isn't all in the East. It is right here in Calgary as well. Because people have been flooding in at a rate of up to twenty-six hundred a month. Because Calgary has been exploding. Because old-timers, as a result of the newcomers and the boom, don't much recognize their city any more.

So there are old myths and new myths and old truths and new truths that, virtually by the time they are acknowledged, have to be filed away, victims of Calgary as quick-change artist. But there is a constant in all this flux, and it is this: Calgary has become interesting to (though not necessarily beloved by) an enormously wide range of people—federal cabinet ministers; Eastern Canadian motorists; friends and relatives all over Canada (and the world) of people who have upped stakes and moved here; all those newcomers themselves; prospective newcomers; and the old-timers who view recent events with a volatile mixture of pride and apprehension.

I am now western enough that when eastern (*sic*) friends beg the main question to ask instead, "When are you moving back?," I bridle at the assumption. I explain why Calgary is so interesting today—first, because of the economic-political power struggle being waged with Central Canada and, second, because living here (like my Indonesian world map) teaches me that Toronto's view of Canada is not the only valid perspective on our country.

But Calgary is also interesting in and of itself. Allan Connery's wonderful creation, "The Old Man On The Bus," is right when he grumps: "Pay attention to where you actually are." That is exactly what my magazine and broadcasting work here has allowed me to do. First as assistant producer of the local CBC morning radio show, then as a freelance writer and documentary-maker, then as editor of *Calgary Magazine* for almost three years, now working independently once again—all this has most satisfyingly required me to pay attention to where I actually am.

Furthermore, it has brought me into contact with many Calgarians who are just as fascinated with this city as I am. Indeed, some of them number among the insiders contributing to this book. For we do not attempt to bring you one monolithic Calgary, filtered through one mind to be described in one voice. We bring you twenty-one Calgary minds and voices, all of them rooted in the city and sufficiently experienced in certain areas to be entitled to offer subjective analyses along with their factual reports.

Each piece was written independently, each stands on its own. And yet, tellingly, cross-references abound. Echoes build up: through this spontaneous repetition, certain places, people and attitudes acquire a multilayered reality. A composite Calgary emerges, with the overlapping dimensions that always result whenever knowledgeable, opinionated insiders settle down to discuss one subject.

Welcome to these insiders' Calgary—myths, realities, places to go and things to do. Read, cross-reference and add our Calgary to the one you already carry in your mind.

Penny Williams

PART ONE:
Myths and Realities

The Newcomer

"The poor devil doesn't yet know what he has found, but he knows what he has lost. He is unquestionably an expert on that topic, and very eloquent."

By Allan Connery

"I had lunch with a newcomer today," said the Man On The Bus. "He doesn't like it here."

"How very unusual," I replied.

"Isn't it?" said The Man. "I hadn't heard that opinion expressed in, oh, it must have been several hours. It was a stunning revelation, my boy, stunning. Challenged my whole understanding of the universe. Not since Einstein . . . think of it: an observer leaves Toronto at noon and travels westward for four hours at five hundred miles per hour; when he gets to Calgary it is only 2:00 P.M. *and he doesn't like it here*. Gad. Not since Einstein have I encountered such a mind-boggling idea. Well—maybe since Einstein, but certainly not since lunch."

"Astonishing. Doesn't like our pretty little city, eh?"

"Not a bit," said The Man.

"The usual bill of particulars?"

"Essentially," said The Man. "Grasping rednecks, vulgar materialism, no cultural life, no night life, no bookstores, no good restaurants, no picturesque minorities, no quaint neighbourhoods, no elegant shops, no beautiful women, no park benches, no fire hydrants for the dogs, no trees outside the houses, which are all made of ticky-tacky and cost too much, AND the city looks as if it's just been uncrated."

The Man drew a deep breath. "Sorry to sound like an auctioneer, but I find it best to cover familiar ground quickly."

15

"Yes. Since a point-by-point rebuttal would have been tiresome, I assume you expressed the customary hope that he would find happiness on the next plane east?"

"No, no, no, my boy." The Man rapped his cane on the floor. "Good Lord, no. When you have been patronized as long as I have, you will learn that neither defensiveness or aggressiveness will avail you anything. Listen patiently, nod sympathetically, suggest modestly, and wait. Given time, a few of the poor, simple bastards will learn to like the place."

"Uh-huh. How long has your pal at lunch been here?"

"Two months," said The Man, "but wait. The poor devil doesn't yet know what he has found, but he knows what he has lost. He is unquestionably an expert on that topic, and very eloquent. Even I felt a pang for his loss of the Kensington Market, back home in Toronto, and I have never wanted to buy a live chicken."

"I should hope not. You could have directed him to the Calgary Public Livestock Market, but I suppose a live steer would have been a bit unwieldy. Did you give him a nice lunch?"

"I must admit," said The Man, "that I had heard so much of his conversation—he works in my office—that I wanted, vindictively, to give him the canonical Calgary lunch."

"Oh, dear."

"Yes. So I fetched him at half-past eleven and took him to a nearby place where the red carpet runs up the wall, and there fed him three Bloody Caesars and a steak sandwich."

"Eugh. That's no way to make a convert."

"I ate the same thing, my boy, and I am suffering for it already. The way of the satirist is hard."

"You could have taken him out on the mall and fed him take-out souvlaki in the sunshine."

"Out of the question," said The Man. "It would have looked like special pleading. He would have treated me to an ear-batch about the comparative urbanity of The Danforth and the more genuine Hellenism of its denizens. No, no. Never apologize, never explain. Caesars, steak sandwiches and a straight face."

"Sounds defensive to me, or maybe aggressive. I suppose you dragged him back to work at one o'clock sharp?"

"Five to, actually," said The Man. "Lacking an American Express card, I was forced to snap my fingers at the waitress and brandish a fifty-dollar bill."

"Lovely. No doubt the portrait on the bill inspired you to make a remark about Mackenzie King?"

"Need you ask?" said The Man. "This fellow had signed up for a Calgary lunch, and that's what I gave him, full strength. I could have done no more had he worked for the *Toronto Star*."

"Welcome to Calgary," I said.

"Welcome indeed," said The Man, "but when you are welcomed, pay attention to where you actually are. I marvel, truly I do, at the people who spend three days in Istanbul or Amsterdam or Calgary and come away with glib explanations of the place and its quaint customs. I marvel, but also I tire of being understood too quickly. A city, any city, offers mysteries that are open only to those who are willing to pay attention for long enough."

"Calgary has mysteries?" I asked.

"The principal mystery is that anyone would want to live here," said The Man, "but what is mysterious is not necessarily incomprehensible. Any fool making wishes could name a dozen better places to live, or a hundred. Tahiti and Venice would figure prominently on many wish-lists. Of course the difficulties of getting to live in either place are nearly insurmountable. It's hard work getting what you like; liking what you get—without being slavish about it—is more practical.

"Speaking of practicality," The Man went on, "Calgary is a brisk and practical place, and that is one of the things I like about it. At the turn of the century, or so my father told me, local boosters proclaimed that Calgary would become the Chicago of the north. Commercially we have fallen short, but spiritually—in the sense one would use the word about Chicago or Calgary—I think we have succeeded."

"Surely we're friendlier than Chicago," I said.

"Well, perhaps," said The Man. "I can't speak for Chicago, which I know only by cliché, as so many people know Calgary. This is a much harder-headed city than most people want to believe. Remember what we are: this is a Canadian city, founded by a police force and populated by successive waves of newcomers from all kinds of backgrounds. We may be civil in public and helpful to strangers (helpful, I say, not charitable), but we stop a long way short of indiscriminate chumminess, let alone automatic friendship."

"Oh, come on," I said. "In Calgary the latch-string is always out."

"Pull on the string," said The Man, "and you will find that it has been untied from the latch. Don't believe in the myth of the Old West, propagated by Old Hollywood: 'Howdy, stranger, and welcome to the friendliest doggone little town in the whole darned universe.' Nggggh." The Man shuddered. "Talk like that turns my guts. No, no, no. This is getting to be a big, hard, commercial city. Civility, thank heaven, is still nearly automatic, but we spend a lot of time looking each other over before we make friends in any real sense of the word. As a result, it's a long time before newcomers feel at home here, if they ever do.

"This is Calgary's special misfortune: it has so many citizens who would rather be somewhere else. They are here only to make a living. Naturally, the more thoughtful among them deplore the city's materialism."

"All right, where would *you* rather be?" I said.

The Man raised his left eyebrow and his right moustache. (I don't know how he does that.) "Love it or leave it, my boy? Piffle. I was born here and I will die here—probably under the wheels of a pickup truck driven by one of the bozos who infest our streets nowadays. However, I will come back and haunt the first son of a bitch who suggests that my fate was paradigmatic of life in Calgary.

"Now, then, as to your question. I have always had a soft spot for Vancouver. Time in that gentle climate seems like time out from real life. In fact—just to give you an example of the inconsequential things that make us love a place—the thing I remember best about Vancouver is the way it smells in autumn. I suppose the smell is composed of ocean and mist and rotting leaves. Whatever it may be, for me that smell is infinitely nostalgic."

"Uh-huh. Very mellow, Vancouver."

"Hmmmm," said The Man. "A few things bother me about Vancouver though. One is the feeling that the vegetation is about to take over. I prefer a climate that keeps the living side of nature in its place. Much worse is the plague of life-stylists—those wretches who know the only perfect place to buy an avocado and drive for half an hour to get there, then come home to complain about air pollution and the ravages of heavy traffic in fine old neighbourhoods. They are a monument to the phenomenon of disposable income. If there were an appliance called an income-disposer, they'd buy one—though I suppose governments do what they can in that direction. But I digress."

"You do," I said.

"We have life-stylists in Calgary, too," said The Man, "though they're not happy. This fellow I entertained at lunch bemoaned our lack of outdoor cafés. I don't know why he'd want to eat quiche on the sidewalk, but I suppose he's entitled to. He's a nice fellow, essentially, but he suffers from the delusion that a city should be a Disneyland for grown-ups. Some cities are; most aren't; this isn't."

"But you were going to say something nice about Calgary, weren't you?"

"Well, yes," said The Man, "but it's not personal. You and I have the good fortune to make a living where we were born. Many people nowadays aren't as lucky. Forced mobility and endless media harping on city life-styles—do I sound like a sociologist?—have caused a lot of fussing about places to live. Too many people now act as if they were required to buy their clothes from a store that never has their size.

"As for Calgary, you have your memories, and I have mine. I still remember a night in December twenty years ago when I went outdoors to greet a chinook, smelled its warmth, felt it on my face. And a Sunday afternoon in October, downtown, yellow light slanting down those lonesome avenues, and the sky. The sky—that deep, dry, heart-breaking blue. And think of the way the hills and the river and the city fit together. Not long ago I saw the city from the east on a clear morning—that clump of arrogant towers rising out of the valley, standing against the mountains, every window flaming orange. At times, you know, it is possible to love the place.

"Well, here's my stop," said The Man On The Bus, reaching up to ring the bell. "I must admit, my boy, that I don't entirely love Calgary for its mind. Mostly, I'm afraid, it's physical."

Early Calgary

"I find that looking at Calgary now, product of this recent period of explosive growth, is like looking at something through a telescope, first from one end and then from the other."

By Jack Peach

When I was born in an upstairs bedroom of a rather handsome house on the rim of town, Calgary's population was fifty thousand rather than the six-hundred thousand of today.

My father, a building contractor, had built this small mansion because times were good and it seemed the prestige move to have a house with a parquet oak floor in the kitchen. The house stood (as it staunchly does today) on a seventy-five-foot strip of south slope prairie overlooking a small hillside creek that nattered past the front gate on its way down a winding coulee of its own making to the Elbow River, one of the two rivers flowing through the town.

Father had chosen this twenty-five-dollar piece of land, roughly an acre and a half in area, because of the creek. To prairie settlers, running water was a spiritual magnet that somehow added an assurance of continuing life to an otherwise landlocked and fairly arid prospect.

The land was situated impractically on the outskirts of the quite newly incorporated city that still had to boast a trifle loudly of its status and prospects. Communication was chancy and primitive, land plentiful and neighbours few. In retrospect, I admire my mother for having agreed, reluctantly I suspect, to the launching of a frontier life in so remote a place.

But Calgary was spreading at a phenomenal rate and before

many years had passed my parents found their 1912 outskirts house was to be part of a new residential development.

The centre of Calgary had been started a rather bleak five miles to the northeast of their house. On the banks of the glacier-fed Bow River, less than a mile downstream from its junction with the Elbow River (then called the Swift), courageous pioneers seeking freedom from whatever had constricted them had pitched tents and laboured over raw lumber in order to build a settlement. They hoped it would become a stopping place for the railway that was laboriously inching west toward the mountains.

A few years earlier, in 1875, when the weather was pleasant enough to reveal the bowl wherein the two rivers met, a group of North West Mounted Police encountered a haven in a stretch of almost treeless tableland wilderness. The riders, known as F Troop, crested the north rim of the Bow Valley and gazed across a quite awesome panorama. Far to the west, filling the horizon like a theatrical backdrop, was a chain of the Rocky Mountains, blue ice, white snow, stabbing at the wide and crystal blue sky. Out from the southwesterly hills at their feet wound the Swift River, sparkling as it rambled around curves of woodland or momentarily spread over gravelly shallows.

From the more forbidding ramparts directly to the west emerged the larger stream, the Bow River, in a darker and more determinate path, having carved a severe, definitive passage through the rocky hills in its headlong rush to the prairies.

Around the courses of these two rivers stood, in a noble ring, treeless prairie hills, shores of a prehistoric lake that had been fed by the primeval ancestors of the two rivers and an almost extinct third one that still meandered out of habit from the north.

Constable George Clift King, who became the "first footer"—the first mounted policeman to set foot upon the prairie tongue of land edged by the rivers—wrote this in his diary:

> *"Never will I forget the scene that met our eyes—
> the confluence of the two winding rivers with their
> wooded banks, the verdant valley, and beyond, the
> wide expanse of green plain that stretched itself in
> homage to the distant mountains. After the barren
> march . . . at last we had received our reward, that this*

*was the 'Promised Land'! A wonderful country! A
Garden of Eden! A place to live forever! My home
ever since. We descended the hill to the river ford.
As there were no boats or ferries we quickly improvised one. We tied our tarpaulins, which were closely
woven and fairly waterproof, underneath the wagon
box, and with the aid of some long poles rowed
ourselves across the river in safety. I was the first out."*

Far out on the flatland between the rivers was a lone white
tent. It was the stopping place of two intrepid Roman
Catholic missionaries: Father Léon Doucet, O.M.I., and
Brother Alexis, known variously as Alexis Cardinal and
Alexis Ninaskoto. The pair had demolished a log mission
established twenty-five miles to the west in 1872 and were in
the process of rebuilding it at the junction of the rivers.
Where for years Indians on Nose Hill had seen nothing but a
bowl of empty land, a new, little white settlement had begun
to take shape.

The mounted police were soon to find two other men of
the land had arrived before them. One was Sam Livingston,
an Irish-born adventurer who had settled on a homestead
south of the future site of Calgary in that same year of 1875.
Livingston, who was an imaginative, determined and progressive farmer, and the other newcomer, John Glenn (who
was Irish too), were to be recognized as the original residents.
John Glenn, like Livingston, had been lured by the prospect
of Klondike gold and then disillusioned by Klondike reality.
In 1873 he had arrived in the area that was to become
Calgary, staked a homestead, devised a way of irrigating his
foodstuffs crop and won the draw to buy the first plot of land
in the newly surveyed townsite when the railway arrived.

Soon these enterprising sodbusters were supplying the
police post with such food and dairy treats as could be
grown in what was purported to be an inhospitable and
barren wilderness.

The railway inched its way across the prairie, which rose
steadily toward the base of the foothills that led in tiers to
the Rocky Mountains, spine of the continent. At last, in
1883, the rails reached the Elbow River, which after a share
of not too unexpected mishaps was then bridged. The
railway-building crews girded themselves to tackle the mountains that were already being assaulted from the western
side, inland from the Pacific Ocean.

The CPR made Calgary one of its stopping places, then set about changing the geographical pattern of the tiny community by placing its Calgary station (at that time merely a box car) on railway-owned land a couple of miles *west* of the original townhouse. It then entered into, and won, a bull-headed contest to lure settlers away from the original site and onto its holdings, centred upon its new station.

Shortly after that victory my father arrived in Calgary, an immigrant from Britain who had already taken a stab at settling in South Africa. He arrived a single young man whose cash assets of fifty cents were augmented by a seemingly limitless reserve of energy, determination and enthusiasm.

In due course I entered the picture and, over the ensuing years, inherited from him by example and a certain measure of goading encouragement, a similar attitude toward this foothills city. He insisted that survival in the obviously competitive atmosphere of the city depended largely upon one's ability and willingness to use one's hands as well as one's wits. Hence, during an old-fashioned, stern apprentice-ship as a carpenter, I had many first-hand encounters with the growing city and its people.

Father also passed on to me his love of books and his keen ability to view and assess the passing scene. In turn I found myself squirrelling away a hoard of clippings, books, pamphlets, anecdotes and personal notes as the years passed. Out of this, I suppose, grew and ripened my own crop of vividly remembered details of my formative years and of the people and events that shared and shaped them.

I have as a result kept up a running commentary in print, radio and television over the years of the city's early days, its changing face and its irregular pace of development as a Canadian community.

I find that looking at Calgary now, product of this recent period of explosive growth, is like looking at something through a telescope, first from one end and then from the other. Observation from the usual viewpoint reveals a burgeoning city of almost undisciplined expansion. Viewed through the other end of the telescope, though, the entire history of the place appears to exist within my own living memory. For example, in my enthusiastic days in high school—when life was a triumvirate of unsavoury book learning, exciting girl discovery and blood-pounding love affairs with the year's eye-popping crop of exotic and unattainable automobiles—I had a brief puppy love encounter with a little blonde girl whose books needed to be carried to and from classes. On a small handful of occasions I was invited into her parents' home. An elderly man who seemed to be as old as the foothills themselves was a resident of that house. I didn't realize at the time that this bright-eyed, white-haired and wonderfully articulate man was George King. Here, well within my lifetime, was the man who had gazed upon the prairie bowl when its only occupants lived in a single tent.

Not long ago I received a telephone call from a small-town woman who said a certain Beatrice Whitehair was listening to me daily on radio and would love to see me and talk of old times. I was astonished that the old lady was still alive, for she and my mother had been newlyweds and neighbours, both recent arrivals from overseas, when Calgary had only just graduated from town status. I met "Mother B"—as I felt I had to call her, for even though I had long since grown up I still recalled her as a mother figure, disciplinarian and teacher during successive summers spent on her farm north of Calgary.

Her spry memory of details, her endurance of a very bumpy life that had included the loss of a husband and two of three children, her self-reliance nurtured by years of survival on a farm of marginal worth, had made this pioneer Calgarian a person of remarkable stamina, wisdom, optimism and humour. As we crossed the small town where she now lives, I found myself walking quite briskly in order to keep pace with this woman who had just passed her one hundred and second birthday!

One of my most enjoyable companions today is Bell Renard, one of seven children of a pioneer farmer. Bill is a horseman who from early schooldays knew and loved horses and cattle. With his father, grandfather and brothers he trailed three hundred head of horses north from Montana to Okotoks, just south of Calgary, in the hope that they would be suitable mounts for cavalrymen in World War I. The trail riders' ages ranged from eight to seventy-two and the ride took fifty-five days at a pace of twelve miles a day. He is now one of the few remaining cowboys who can break horses, shoe them, midwife and doctor them, and who still trains them for trail riding and cattle cutting. He is a crinkly-eyed outdoorsman who, like me, has seen Calgary grow from an awkward, self-conscious little town to a sky-scrapered metropolis. Our lives almost bridge the entire history of the city. The earliest span is provided by the memories of people we know who are older than ourselves and were here virtually from the beginning.

One Calgarian I would have enjoyed meeting for myself was Daniel Webster Trotter. He lived and worked a fair distance from the town centre and, in his own way, helped shape it as much as did my father. Trotter was a salty-tongued giant, an ex-colonel in the United States Army, who always dressed in khaki above his mirror-shined boots.

In 1904 he established himself on the southeastern edge of town on a farm distinguished by electricity, black and white wooden buildings, manicured flower beds and lawns and sturdy fences. The land supported herds of horses and Jersey cattle as well as scores of hogs and chickens. He ran the place like a military camp, determined to prove this western land could be a top-notch farming area if managed with discipline.

There, on Calgary's outskirts, Trotter toured the prairie village of Ogden recruiting boys who, for a dollar a day, slowly advanced across his fields in line abreast picking weeds. He had them march, whistling, to and from their "Weed Gang" assignments, and in the process won their respect and affection even as he provided many of them with a sense of discipline that would last a lifetime.

All was not discipline in early Calgary. There was also, for example, a man with a strange sense of humour stoked by his pet kinkajou. The two of them would arrive at the busiest intersection in the small downtown core. There the man would disengage the furry little beast from his favourite resting place around his neck and, with a curt command, send the kinkajou scurrying up onto the nearest trolley wire. The little animal would dart along the wires and completely disrupt all streetcar traffic until reluctantly ordered down by his picture-of-innocence owner.

We had a tinsmith who amused himself by appearing in the city centre at the height of the tourist season clad in fringed buckskin. As a stone-faced, grey pigtailed "Indian," he fooled thousands over the years into having their photos taken with him. It's as well he maintained his stone face for had he ever spoken he would have revealed a well-defined English accent!

We had Bob Edwards, who became nationally known for his wit, philosophy and maverick personal observations — as well as for his capacity for alcohol — all of which sharpened the editorial style of his sporadically issued newspaper, the *Eye Opener*. And there was Ernie King who, one day each year when the sun began to warm the winter-frozen land, would appear on 8th Avenue impeccably clad from head to toe in white. We looked forward to this event every year, our own dapper and unmistakable sign that spring had arrived.

There are many newcomers who dismiss Calgary as a cultural wasteland. There are many who miss the sense of age and maturity in the centres they have left in order to move here. There are others who find our people and our geography equally rough around the edges. But then, there are many who find this young part of our nation a challenging and exciting place, free of traditional fetters and possessed of a hint of the maverick. What the first group calls disadvantages, they see instead as advantages. They enjoy Calgary as headstrong youth, as the Canadian pacesetter.

But inevitably, newcomers see Calgary in the present tense. We who by birth call Calgary home — who remember it from its dusty bronco days, through the early waves of boom and bust, through the depression and the heady post-World War II oil discoveries — we see the city's whole history as well. It is a brief history, by most standards . . . but what a history. In our lifetime, Calgary has grown from infancy to rank as one of our nation's great cities.

Calgarians

"There's little question that Calgary has become
a haven for risk-takers. People are not measured
by who they are. They're measured by what they've
achieved."

By Gordon Legge

Giovanni De Maria has always been a busy man. For
instance, in the late sixties De Maria was not only working
with Sheik Abdul Aziz Al Sabah, a member of the ruling
family of Kuwait, he was also a consultant representing
several European countries in the Middle East and he ran a
thriving import business in electronics. Nonetheless, active
as he was, De Maria felt he had reached a plateau in his
career. He yearned for new challenges and fresh horizons. In
1975, following many far-flung journeys in search of a new
home, De Maria settled in Calgary. He liked the city's
climate, its wide open spaces, and the boundless enthusiasm
and opportunity that seemed to emanate from the energy
industry.

Needless to say, the transition wasn't easy. Despite his
experience and credentials—including two knighthoods, a
rare one conferred by the Pope and a second granted by the
Italian government—De Maria found himself returning to
school.

True to character, De Maria, an Italian raised in Egypt and
educated in French and Italian schools, plunged headfirst
into a master's degree program in international relations at
the University of Calgary. At the same time, to alleviate
homesickness and ease his adjustment, he immersed himself
in the community.

Today, he operates an active consulting company, accom-

27

panying government and industry tours to the Middle East and leading Middle Eastern businessmen around the province. He's a member of the Calgary Immigrant Aid Society and the Alberta Cultural Heritage Council, and he assists the Calgary City Police Race Relations Unit. In fact, with a proficiency in seven languages—French, Arabic, Italian, English, German, Japanese and Spanish—he's become a self-appointed ambassador to Calgary's burgeoning ethnic communities. Sitting in his modest but comfortable home in northeast Calgary, De Maria says, "This house will always be open to those who have nowhere to go." De Maria feels a duty to bring a measure of humanitarianism to the city's materialistic "boom" environment. "I want to be able to promote friendship among neighbours. That is my ideal. If I am able to reach that, I will be proud of my existence in Canada and in Calgary."

Not all newcomers necessarily react quite like De Maria— indeed, he and the other people mentioned here are "typical" Calgarians only in that they illustrate the new diversity of the city's population. Still, De Maria is typical in this: there's little question that Calgary has become a haven for risk-takers. In Calgary, people are not measured by who they are. They're measured by what they've achieved.

At last count, there were 623,000 Calgarians, with 2,600 more arriving each month. One native Calgarian, Alan Singer, typically attired in blue jeans and clogs as he presides over United Management, one of Western Canada's largest private developers, was asked to name a few people who have come to Calgary and are helping to shape and define its personality. His reply: "Where shall I start? They're all from somewhere else." It's true. If you've been in the city longer than two years, you're an old-timer. If you were born here, you qualify for the Glenbow Museum.

Until very recently, Calgary was a homogeneous city, with the bulk of its citizenry either from Great Britain or of British descent. Even so, there have been waves of immigrants since the turn of the century. There were the Chinese, brought in to build the railroad, who settled in Calgary and created the second largest Chinese community in Canada, after Vancouver. Italians, Germans and Central and Eastern Europeans who arrived in the early 1900s formed the city's working class. In the fifties, a wave of professional people, primarily from Holland and Germany, came to Calgary.

There are many transplanted Americans, some of whom arrived with the United States oil companies throughout the forties, fifties and sixties; others, more recently. There are internal waves of migration as well, people from Ontario, Quebec and the Maritimes. "Goin' down the road" no longer means heading for Toronto. It means moving to Calgary.

All these groups have been assimilated virtually unnoticed. It wasn't until the mid-sixties, when South Asians began arriving (mostly from India, Pakistan, Sri Lanka and Bangladesh), that the city began taking on a more cosmopolitan flavour. The seventies saw the arrival of many East African Asians, expelled from their adopted country; exiled South Americans; and South Vietnamese "boat people."

As in any other city, these people have become everything from shopkeepers to civil servants, chief executives to office cleaners. Many of the unskilled have found work on the construction projects that have dominated the cityscape for the past half decade. Other newcomers are members of the corporate managerial class transferred here from eastern head offices.

In many respects, Calgary is a city of specialists and technologists—engineers, accountants, geologists, geophysicists, academics, doctors, lawyers, computer programmers and systems analysts (Calgary is one of the largest data-processing centres in the world). Nonetheless, it is the entrepreneurs who really thrive in Calgary's booming climate. All risk-takers, yes, but it is this last group, more than any, who is giving the city a distinctive personality in every field, be it the petroleum industry, retailing or the arts. These men and women bridle whenever they come into contact with the type of government or corporate bureaucracy that is increasingly commonplace elsewhere. With guts and raw energy, they have used their expertise to transform their ideas into reality. For them, the dusty prairie city that was Calgary a decade ago, catalyzed by a petroleum bonanza, provided a free and fertile ground for their efforts. Capturing the city's palpable currents of energy (not to mention its money), they have transformed Calgary from a friendly, spirited town into a dynamic, gangling metropolis and pushed it toward maturity like a strip of time-lapse photography.

Each Calgarian, regardless of his origins and place, makes his own unique contribution. Walk around the city and you'll find descendants of the first families, the Crosses and the Burnses, still influencing its direction. Many Calgarians have become familiar names on the national level and first among them is Alberta Premier Peter Lougheed, whose roots stretch deep into Calgary's history. There's the oil patch royalty: "Smiling" Jack Gallagher and Bill Richards of Dome Petroleum; Bob Blair of NOVA, An Alberta Corporation; and Jim Gray of Canadian Hunter. There's Ralph Scurfield of NuWest, the home builders; and Ron Southern of Atco. Others, like Frank King who with diplomatic flair and astute politicking earned Calgary the 1988 Winter Olympics and Mayor Ralph Klein who told the East's "bums and creeps" (read, thugs and muggers) to stay home, have found their place in the Canadian catalogue of current events.

Still, there remain many others, less visible, who through their leadership are sculpting the city with their ideas, plans and ambitions.

"Calgary is a north Texas boom town," says merchant banker Bob Wisener. Cradling a glass of wine in his hands as he stares out from his lair overlooking the Bow River west of Calgary, Wisener says, "It's a frontier town whose God is business. People come here to work." Like the seemingly endless vista of mountains that stretches in front of Wisener's home, Calgary induces a state of mind that is as boundless and uninhibiting as the geography, one of unlimited ambition.

Wisener first set foot in Calgary in 1950 after rolling through Trinity College School, the Royal Canadian Naval College, Royal Roads, and the University of Toronto. His family have been investment dealers on Toronto's Bay Street since 1917. And he soon discovered that even with an engineering degree, his talent lay in handling money, particularly other people's. Wisener left Calgary in the mid-fifties and didn't return for twenty-one years. In 1978, soon after his return, he established the city's first merchant bank, the MerBanco Group (of which he is co-chairman) and, in 1981 made well over $100 million-worth of deals. It's indicative of Calgary's place in the country that a guy like Wisener—one of the best-connected people in Canada—should open up shop here.

At the other end of the entrepreneurial spectrum is Bill Yarrow. He arrived in Calgary in 1974 "broke and with half an education." A native of Montreal, he had grown tired of working for someone else. So, at twenty-five years of age, he quit his job in the soft goods business on a Friday and landed in Calgary the following Monday.

Before long, he began purchasing old properties, renovating and reselling them. He still chuckles when he recalls his early, naive appearances before city council, a kid with hair halfway down his back and drywall dust clinging to his jeans. His bankers called him the "capitalist revolutionary." But he managed to take on former Calgary Mayor Rod Sykes as a partner and at one point he was the largest landowner in Mission, one of Calgary's oldest districts (originally settled by the French but now peopled by the nouveau riche). Today, when he talks about Alberta and Calgary, it's with unabashed enthusiasm.

"I'm in Alberta forever. I love Alberta. There's a true immigrant mentality here. All the people who want something better come here. And they work twice as hard and get twice as much." Likening Calgary today to the frontier times of 1882, he adds: "Everybody who comes here wants to do something. People here are enjoying their lives." And he's helping them enjoy it—he designed and originally owned one of the city's trendier restaurants, 4th Street Rose, before selling it to its present owners. Much of his philosophy, not to mention energy, is poured into a two-minute commentary each weekday evening at 5:42 P.M. on CKIK-FM, Calgary's newest radio station.

CKIK, which features the "new music," is operated by Robert Whyte, another expatriate Montrealer, who left his wife and family to move to Calgary in August 1980. He quickly established a one-man advertising agency, nestling into a tiny office (three hundred square feet) in a posh location (Mount Royal Village). With no furniture or filing cabinets—but a supply of peanut butter and jam sandwiches—he immersed himself in the city, taking on volunteer work with the Calgary Centre for the Performing Arts and Alberta Theatre Projects. When it came time to apply for his FM licence, Whyte had 163 letters of support. He became the youngest person ever to receive an FM licence in Canada, and his station is the only one in town that is independent and Calgary-owned. (And, incidentally, his ad agency now employs fourteen people.)

But it doesn't take a newcomer to realize the city's potential. When Rick Orman was growing up in his family's Memorial Drive home on the north side of the Bow River, he could gaze out his second-floor bedroom window and see, between the tall cottonwoods that line the river, all the way to the Robin Hood flour mills located on 9th Avenue at the far edge of the downtown core along the CPR railway tracks. The mills were a dominant part of the Calgary skyline in the fifties; now they have been demolished (after a furious debate) and when Orman looks out from his parents' home, he's hard-pressed to find even his own tenth-floor office in the Trizec building that stands amid the soaring mini-Manhattan maze of glass and concrete that is downtown Calgary. Orman, now in his mid-thirties, is a third-generation Calgarian who grew up with the city.

Resting his feet on the bottom drawer of his immaculate, blonde desk, Orman tells how he went to the University of Eastern Washington on a football scholarship and came back in the early seventies to a job as a novice petroleum landman with Red River Oils. A chance encounter on an airbus to Edmonton led to a job as an executive assistant to the then energy minister, Bill Dickie (now retired from politics but working hard as a development lawyer). That led to a job in the premier's office in Calgary as a government-industry liaison on energy matters. After a few years, Orman left government to start his own firm. Today, he is president of PLM Resources Ltd. and a participant in a joint-venture company called Signalta Resources. In 1981 Signalta drilled 150 exploratory wells in Alberta, making it the most active exploration company in the province.

Orman is also involved in one of the city's most popular and innovative restaurants, Cafe Calabash, a Casablanca-style restaurant in the trendy Hillhurst-Sunnyside area, across the river from downtown Calgary. And about a year ago, after another chance encounter—this time in Caesar's Palace in Las Vegas—Orman took a partnership in what was to become the Michael Richard Gallery, the only gallery in Western Canada authorized to sell limited edition serigraphs by LeRoy Neiman.

Like Orman, Lee Richardson, who is now director of the premier's office in Calgary is a native of the city. He did a degree in commerce at the University of Calgary, then spent a year at Oxford. Soon after his return to Calgary he was working for Peter Bawden, a prominent member of the Calgary oil establishment. When Bawden went east as a member of Parliament in the early seventies, Richardson accompanied him to help set up an office. Richardson soon found himself working with John Diefenbaker, assisting him with his memoirs, *One Canada*.

By the mid-seventies, Richardson had returned to Alberta, first to Edmonton and then back to Calgary to his present position as head of the government's listening post here. Richardson is also actively involved with the Calgary Stampede, is a member of the Southminster United Church and quietly admits to owning a few race horses. Like almost everyone who is making it in Calgary, he loves the city's energy level: "I think the thing I find most exciting about Calgary is the upbeat, aggressive style of the city. I travel a lot, and I see a lot of chins on the chest, but not in Calgary, even with this recession."

Another individual who's involved in government, but at a different level, is Brian Lee, a local alderman with a populist touch, a taste for the good fight and a reputation for being someone to watch. Recalling his childhood years spent selling *Liberty* magazines in front of the 9th Avenue liquor store, Lee brands himself an overachiever. But one with foresight. Lee led a crusade concerning the transportation of dangerous and hazardous goods that eventually resulted in Calgary's adoption of the most comprehensive and progressive contingency plan in the country—long before the Mississauga disaster.

Perhaps his greatest strength is an acknowledged ability to tap into the city's ethnic communities. Lee has a working knowledge of twenty languages—and he uses them. "I know of no other politician who stays in such good touch with what's going on," says Tom Kirkham, a retired city hall administrator who sits on Lee's informal breakfast council that meets at the Westgate Hotel every second Friday to discuss civic issues and give Lee hell. (Kirkham, known for years around city hall as "the chief shit disturber," now spends his retirement days travelling across Alberta taping oral histories with native Albertans for the provincial and Glenbow archives.)

A group with which Lee sometimes touches base is the South Vietnamese community of which there are seven thousand members in Calgary, almost all recent arrivals. One member, Vu huu Quang, spends most of his spare time working with those immigrants as president of the Calgary Vietnamese Association. Vu, a Canadian-trained engineer, remained in South Vietnam after the American evacuation and Communist takeover. He hoped a reunited Vietnam would be able to forge a strong, vibrant new country out of the wreckage of the old. But it didn't come to pass, so in 1979 he purchased a boat, constructed a large keel along its base and made an escape attempt. Unfortunately, the keel grounded in the mud where he was to rendezvous with his wife and family. The police nabbed and jailed him. Four months later he used the last of his savings to bribe his way out. His second attempt was successful, and after three days in a tiny fishing boat—thirteen children, six adults—he arrived in Malaysia. Fortunately, he spent only one month in a refugee camp before a Canadian immigration officer cleared the way for his passage to Canada. A week after he arrived in Toronto in June 1980, his sixth child was born. Three months later he took a job with the Montreal-based engineering firm of Lavalin and moved to Calgary. One of only a few dozen Calgary Vietnamese who can speak English fluently, he works diligently to help his countrymen adjust to the new culture and society.

In addition to their language problems, most are unskilled. And many are here with only half their families, having had to leave a husband or wife behind. Others face the loneliness of a single person caught in an unfamiliar, unconcerned society with no prospect of returning home. Says Vu: "Our bodies are here but our minds and hearts are back there."

The private and public support network for immigrants has been growing in response to this kind of need. One important part of this network is the Calgary Immigrant Aid Society. Executive director Yvette Knott graduated as a psychiatric nurse from the University of Manitoba, arrived in Calgary in the mid-sixties and soon found herself working as a childcare worker at the William Roper Hull Home for emotionally disturbed children. It wasn't long before she was the chief childcare worker and personnel supervisor. She left Calgary in the mid-seventies to travel the world with her husband, Bill, a community worker in Airdrie (a booming bedroom community north of the city). When Knott returned, she went back to school to obtain a master's degree in social welfare.

In 1980, she joined the Immigrant Aid Society. She rapidly expanded its outreach services and began educating the public about the new arrivals in their midst. With her whiskey voice and straightforward manner, Knott has gained a certain visibility with her crusades, and she's one of the women now beginning to break through the city's chauvinistic veneer.

Many others have also seen a good opportunity and seized it. One of them is Joanne Hedenstrom. With a master's degree in English, she has taught at the University of Calgary, the University of Alberta and the University of Lethbridge. Back in the sixties, long before it was fashionable, she pioneered the fight to improve pollution controls and limit sulphur-dioxide emissions from Alberta's natural gas processing plants. While in Edmonton, she became a strong advocate of the public-hearing process and a vocal member of a transportation task force in the city's west end. Today, she's busy establishing a sawmill business in northern Alberta, Hedenstrom Wood Products, based on a revolutionary sawblade designed by her father, now in his eighties.

She's also busy rebuilding her home in Inglewood, one of Calgary's first settled areas. "If there's a Calgary, this is it," she says. Every day at four o'clock she wanders down to the corner store for her newspaper and a chat with the local Chinese grocer. "It's an old community that's alive and fighting. Very rarely do you pass someone without speaking to him. I'm starting to take on this neighbourhood like a second skin."

Sandra LeBlanc is just as active. Though she is not establishing a business, she is helping to construct an institution whose impact will endure for decades. Since the mid-sixties, LeBlanc has been pushing to see a performing arts centre built in Calgary to serve the city's overcrowded cultural needs. After many lengthy battles, it is now underway—"I can show you the bruises from the past fourteen years"—but that isn't the end of LeBlanc's commitment. She can remember touring her beltline neighbourhood as a teenager, circulating a petition to save the area's many old homes and mansions. Later she helped reclaim Fort Calgary, now a large civic park. A former long-time member of Calgary's Junior League (a women's group devoted to providing professional training in volunteerism), she's now a member of the Calgary Stampede's grandstand committee, the Calgary Olympic Development Association, the National Ballet School and the Calgary Regional Arts

Foundation. In 1979 she was named to the Canada Council.

What does she like about the city that has been her home all her life? Without hesitation, LeBlanc answers: "The people. I love their enthusiasm for doing things, their ingenuity, their energy, their ability to gamble and to give it a try."

What more can you say?

The Boom

"The true prairie sailor knows just what to do when the boom swings back and threatens to remove his left ear: duck and wait for the rebound."

By Catherine Ford

Only new arrivals, wearing cowboy boots still stiff and shiny, greeted the economic downturn in Calgary with predictions of doom and gloom. In the spring of 1982, when the whole economic structure across Canada seemed to collapse within itself, the native Calgarian knew how to handle the bleakness of the future. He treated it like he treats the Calgary weather: wait five minutes, it'll change.

I'll tell you a secret: the native Calgarian is no more pleased about the crummy economy than the native Torontonian. But here in the province of free enterprise, where the economy is based on oil, agriculture and tourism, them's the breaks, pardner. When your good times depend on something as impermanent as natural resources, when the quirks of the weather can mean the difference between a bumper crop and an agricultural disaster, when the third leg of the economic tripod is the fickle tourist dollar—why, you can accept setbacks with equanimity. At least, we *should* be able to accept those setbacks—it's not as if they haven't happened before.

In the thirties, economic depression coincided with drought and savage winds to turn the prairies into a dust bowl. We fought back. In 1932 an Ontario-born Calgary high school principal who was also head of his own Prophetic Bible Institute became convinced that a new economic doctrine could cure the depression. His name was William ("Bible

Bill") Aberhart, his doctrine was Social Credit, and in 1935 he led his new Social Credit Party to power and became premier of Alberta.

There was a downturn in the early seventies as well, when the bottom seemed to drop out of the exploration market. Engineers and geologists who had spent twenty years with one company suddenly found themselves looking for work. Calgarians hunkered down and went headfirst into the storm with the stolidity of farmers facing a prairie blizzard when the cows have to be milked and the chores won't wait for a break in the weather.

The true prairie sailor knows just what to do when the boom swings back and threatens to remove his left ear: duck and wait for the rebound.

To understand how Calgary has weathered, is weathering and will weather the dents in the Canadian economy, you have to understand the Calgary psyche. And "weather" (verb) is a good word, because "weather" (noun) is a case in point. People who have seen snow cover the peonies in July, who have sat on their front lawn in shirtsleeves on New Year's Day, who have watched relentless August hail beat the heavy heads of wheat and barley into the ground, are not going to be deterred by a flattening of "the boom." It's just another cyclical swing in a city where nothing much is permanent, except the Calgary Stampede and the myth of the cowboy.

Anyway, as swings go, it's the best one available. In comparison with the rest of the country, this is *still* Boomtown, Canada. A tad retrenched, maybe, but we're only up to our ankles, not our asses. And, after all, this is Next Year Country. Next year . . . when a chinook may melt the winter snow to promise spring in December, when the oil business will be back in the black, when you trade up from Mercedes to Rolls Royce. And we know there is wealth literally under our feet—vast reserves of oil, natural gas and coal and all that they promise. So we're not only resilient, we're optimistic.

We're also something different from the Calgarians I remember. This latest boom, the post-OPEC boom, has changed the city and it has changed us as well. It has given us a new voice—a loud one, at that—and a different, more worldly, outlook. Our self-esteem has risen, and so has our desire for revenge.

As usual, what we want revenge for is a mixture of things

others have done (or not done) plus things we have done to ourselves. We were responsible for our own civic inferiority complex, for example. A few years ago, years I remember vividly, anyone who crossed the Ontario border heading west (particularly if he could claim a Toronto address) was routinely interviewed by all the Calgary media. Pencil in hand, notebook open, we'd scribble whatever wisdom we could drag out of the visitor, including his response to the inevitable: "How do you like your visit to Calgary?" Of course, the answer would be some oft repeated platitude, but we kept asking and kept dutifully recording the answers. Yeah, it rankled. And so, unfairly but humanly, part of what we resent is what we did to ourselves.

The other part, though, is the reaction elsewhere to Calgary and to Calgarians. All through the sixties, we played hinterland hick to eastern sophisticate. Some of us moved to Ontario and spent ten years realizing that in Toronto the world ends at a line drawn from Manitoba to Quebec through Ottawa. (Actually, to the *true* Torontonian, the world ends at Eglinton Avenue. Anyone north of there lives in "the country.") Montreal was a nice place to visit, but you wouldn't want to live there.

Calgary was nowhere. Like the American who has to succeed in New York, if he's to succeed at all, Canadian success was Toronto-based.

Then, in 1971, came Peter Lougheed's Conservatives. And, in 1973, OPEC. And, in May 1976, the Heritage Savings Trust Fund—the piggy bank for present wealth that was to promote a diversified provincial economy and so make future, postoil, wealth possible. It started with $1.5 billion and a thirty percent share of future provincial oil and gas revenues. By 1982 it stood at $10 billion—a figure that is expected to double by 1985.

It may therefore appear highly unreasonable to non-Calgarians that when we got money—lots of money, pots of money—we also got angry. How can we be so rich, and so angry?

I'll not go into specific disputes because this is not an economic account of the boom but a human story of assumptions and reactions. And, humanly, this is what I think has happened. You see, I suspect most Calgarians thought money meant everything would change. We thought that once we joined the ranks of the Haves, we would no longer be ordering our furniture from Toronto or Montreal, or our cars from the Vancouver port or the Oshawa and Windsor factories. We thought that once we shook the hay out of our hair and proved we could pay our own way, Eastern Canada would notice and let us join the big kids. We were noticed . . . but not exactly understood or accommodated.

When the hordes of eastern journalists came to town to do superficial "What's the West really like?" pieces, naturally they found rednecks and malcontents and separatists. We had to bear the light, bright thirty-second clip about "The West." We had to read shallow pieces about the male-only Calgary Petroleum Club, the women-in-the-side-door Ranchmen's Club and the frontier mentality, and pieces that purported to tell who had all the money, who wanted all the money and just how big did Alberta expect the Heritage Fund to get? When the boom was in full swing, the city was crawling with parachute journalists looking for the "real West." (You'd think none of them had ever seen a pickup truck with a bale of hay in the box and a shotgun in the back window.)

Much was made of the fact that Calgary wasn't Toronto. (Dear God, they wanted us to be Toronto?) Critics bypassed the fact that Calgary has just about everything Toronto has—just the numbers are different.

Much was made of the pluses of living in Alberta: the lowest income tax in the country; no sales tax; no provincial gasoline tax; the cheapest gas in Canada; bargain wine prices; a provincial economy so far in the black that we stuffed thirty percent of the oil revenues into a savings account and started lending out millions—$2 billion at last count—to other provinces. Sure, there was an underside: Calgary accounted for the highest housing prices in Canada; freight rates still meant that every single manufactured item coming in from Ontario was more expensive out here (so much for not paying sales tax, the total remained the same); life became a daily hassle of dirt, dust, noise and snarled traffic from construction . . . there's more, but then every city has good and bad points.

The city. That's the second change brought about by this post-OPEC boom. Not only are we different, our city is different. We react to that as well.

Calgarians watched Easterners crowd into the city at a

rate that sometimes hit twenty-six hundred per month. We watched housing prices climb out of sight and watched the renovation madness grip the stately and tree-lined streets of Mount Royal (and spread to the tree-lined but definitely unstately streets of Hillhurst). It wasn't necessarily bad and it wasn't necessarily all the doing of the newcomers. But change this city they did.

Those of us who had grown up here were left with a severe sense of dislocation. So few people to share our memories with. . . . Some landmarks are still there: some shabby, some in existence only because they were designated as heritage sites. In preserving the sandstone heritage of Calgary, so also has my heritage been preserved: the old sandstone Calgary Court House, where I tried on the judge's robes my grandfather wore; Central United Church, which still has that faint lemon oil and sun-warmed leather smell; the old Calgary Police Court, where I would sell Girl Guide cookies to father's co-workers; Sacred Heart Church where I made my First Communion; and the school behind it, where I objected to my first kiss in the cloakroom in Grade 1 by chasing the perpetrator all the way to 17th Avenue, tackling him in the intersection and trying to remove his face with my fists.

Today the house in Mount Royal, which was built in 1912 by my Ontario-born grandparents, no longer belongs to the family. The inside has been gutted and renovated. Somewhere on one of the lintels, the renovators had to sand down my first attempts at writing—I used a knife. The crab-apple tree on the side lawn has been removed to jam in another house, because the land always was two separate lots and the buyer recognized an opportunity.

This is the heritage from the boom that nobody mentions, except the old-timers—so many memories covered over with cedar decks and poured concrete and hot tubs. Maybe I notice it more because I see it in stages, returning always to the one city in Canada in which I feel rooted. After ten years in Ontario, in 1976 and on the leading edge of the real Calgary boom, I came back, only to leave again in 1979.

Moving back again in the summer of 1981, I found that the boom has made life in Calgary a question of learning how to cope. Calgary's seams are showing the strain, and the demand for every service the city needs to provide its residents starts to tear that invisible cloth known as the social fabric. While the crime rate booms and Calgary learns about sophisticated criminals, we also learn what life is like in an expanding economy. It's crowded.

It's a block-long lineup to get into a movie on Saturday night. It's going into a bar at 7:00 P.M. for a 9:00 P.M. show, because that's the only way to get a seat. It's standing in line for a table at lunch; at the bank; in the department store.

Life in Boomtown is also bored store clerks, ill-trained waiters, surly civil servants and payment for other people's irresponsibility. It's finding out that because the previous tenants pulled a midnight sneak, Alberta Government Telephones won't connect your number until they've checked you out; Canadian Western Natural Gas Co. wants a $125 deposit; the stores want to see a two-part, photograph-bearing Alberta driver's licence before cashing a cheque . . . this, too, is part of the boom.

But, let's put it in context.

Granted, Dallas North is a city of steel and glass and too much concrete; a city of potholes and dust and weekly wheel alignments; of brown grass and few trees, which struggle to bud and bloom; of too much money and too little time to spend it; a city that rushes through a day beginning at 7:00 A.M. because that's the time the Toronto Stock Exchange opens.

Hurry and catch it, because it will be different tomorrow. Another highrise will be uncrated and thrown up against the prairie sun, and by the day after tomorrow, only the old-timers will remember what was in its place last week.

But you see, that is just the point. Calgary is whatever you want it to be: all out there just beyond the doorway, ready for the asking. And if Vancouver demands Canadian mellow, if Montreal sells sophistication, if Toronto peddles cool, then find the Trans-Canada Highway, point the car toward the mountains, come to Calgary and remember what it's like to have a choice.

We have precious sights worth holding onto; sights available no place else. The mountains, of course, dominate everything. In the springtime—when the air is clear and sharp and the warming sun is dissipating the winter's snow— there is a moment in the morning when you can reach out and grab a handful of Rocky Mountain. Like a painted postcard, too jagged, too purple, too snow-capped to be real, there they stand, an hour and a half away. The Rocky Mountains looking over your shoulder. You may have to sit in a hermetically sealed highrise office and fight with accountants and business managers and creditors. But then you can turn your back on them all, look out the window and lose yourself in reality.

And Calgarians do lose themselves in that reality. Weekend after weekend, the trek begins Friday afternoon for the ordinary folk, every third Friday morning for the lucky oil company employees who get the added bonus of that day off (Golden Friday, it's called). Thousands of people stream into Banff (or Kananaskis or Waterton), into the mountains where the Calgarian knows he doesn't need expensive psychiatry to cure the city blues. All he needs is a backpack and faith that this week he won't run into a bear.

Turn back from the mountains, head north and east, and visit another century. The badlands, home of the dinosaur, land of summer heat that shimmers over the blacktop and the burned grasses, where horse and rider can wander for miles untouched by the reality of the city.

This, too, is Calgary, this escape from the confines of the city.

The disgruntled, the laid-back, the shy and retiring newcomers may well ask, "If Cain made the first city, then who in hell made Calgary?" What they're not allowing for are the growing pains of a city thrust into the limelight of explosive commerce and rapid growth. They don't know the city of my childhood; they weren't here when the fuse was lit under the city built on oil floated up to the surface by American money; they've come late to the city of cowboy boots and couturier jeans. The "little cowtown in the West" has grown up.

Not elegantly.

Not with style.

Not with class.

No, Calgary doesn't have the beautiful insouciance of Montreal women; the celebrity-at-every-table rush of Toronto; the straight-armed hustle of New York; the elegance of San Francisco. This isn't Paris or London or Rome.

But if you think that's an apology, a shame-faced admission, you miss the point. This is still Boomtown, we are still growing and becoming something more and other than we have been, we are not (as one Toronto friend said of her city) "sunk in supercilious torpor." We're still a bit gawky for some tastes? The reward for sharing this stage of our civic life is that you also get to share a sense of fun and adventure, one that is missing in other cities.

We'll weather this swing of the boom with the same traits that got us through previous ones—with optimism, resilience and adaptability.

And if newcomers adopt those same traits, they'll get along with Calgary—and we'll all get along with each other—just fine.

The Oil Patch

"Oil is no longer a homogeneous entity. The 'patch' has become a 'patchwork quilt,' a clashing, conflicting coat of many colours."

By Frank Wesley Dabbs

In order to understand what was once known as the "oil patch" (a term now as dated as "golly gee"), it is helpful to remember the longer commercial life of the city.

Before oil, before ranching and coal, before the railroad and the Mounted Police, back in the timeless time between the ice ages and the Europeans, aboriginal man came off the plains and uplands each winter to shelter in the thickets of the Bow River Valley at the confluences of the Ghost and Elbow, Fish Creek and the Oldman rivers. White fur traders and their Métis agents found these encampments nerve centres for a nomadic civilization, an ideal commercial marketplace and Christian mission site. Fort Calgary, constructed amid the tepee rings at the Elbow River, was founded by the federal government to bring one corner of the trackless Territories into the national economy by establishing the rule of law over the fur trade.

Nothing is new under the sun. The rage of the Montana whiskey smugglers who watched the Mounties bash their casks and confiscate their furs is today, one hundred years later, echoed in the rage of the moguls of Exxon and Amoco as they watch the Trudeau government force march its troops, Petro Canada and the Petroleum Monitoring Agency, into the city on a different crusade. Now it is oil that is being saved for the national economy—Canadian ownership, consumer price protection and revenues for the government being the current national purposes.

After Fort Calgary came the railroad, built by British-backed investors of the Dominion to allow the development of agriculture and the settlement of the land. The initial fortunes made in the area belonged to a few powerful families who ran cattle into Texas, mined coal for the railroads and built everything that had to be built to subdue the land and make it prosper.

In the first half of the century, wheat and beef sustained the commercial development of the city, a slow and plodding growth scarred by recession and depression.

Oil changed all that.

One can make comparisons between the battle for federal control of oil and the battle for Canadian control of the fur trade: more subtly, one can seek to understand the petroleum industry by contemplating its similarity to archaeology.

The archaeologist peels back history, layer by layer, as he excavates a modern city to find cities of the past. Similarly, each new economic phase of Calgary's development has overlain the last: ranching and coal are still present, surpassed but not supplanted by oil and natural gas.

So it is with the local history of oil itself. Successive generations of oil companies have replaced one another; successive professions have dominated the boardrooms.

At the beginning of the century, oil belonged to the independent, speculative, high-rolling wildcatters. In the years before the Great Depression, these men found Turner Valley, the first great western oil field, and sold nickle shares in their companies on city streets.

The postwar years, starting with the discovery of Leduc's great oil reserves in 1947 and continuing with Redwater in the fifties and Swan Hills in the early sixties, belonged to the multinational oil companies, with Imperial Oil prominent in the oil fields and Shell Canada in the natural gas areas of the foothills.

The sixties brought a resurgence of independent Canadian companies and the cyclonic post-OPEC seventies saw the birth of the tiny junior exploration firms—and, paradoxically, the giant state-owned crown corporations.

Oil is no longer a homogeneous entity. The "patch" has become a "patchwork quilt," a clashing, conflicting coat of many colours. The main reason a successful, coherent oil policy has eluded governments in Canada and elsewhere is that they have failed to realize that oil speaks with many voices.

It calls to mind the Old Testament story of the men who decided to build a tower to heaven—and were then confounded by God, who created many languages so that the builders could no longer communicate with one another.

Their ambition overheated by the promise of easy and quick wealth, the dreamers of dreams in the Canadian oil industry have been confounded by conflicting interests speaking in conflicting tongues. This is a competition that no public interest law could ever create, the competition of irreconcilable entities in pursuit of the same source of wealth.

The various professions—geology, geophysics, engineering, accounting, law and finance—have in the same fashion struggled to control the levers of power within the business. Disciples of each profession from all over the world have been drawn here: French, Scottish, Japanese, German, American. . . . The list goes on and on, in a second wave of immigration and cultural diversity that rivals the first wave of dispossessed and poor who created agriculture in Alberta and elsewhere on the prairies.

The end result is a city rich in intelligent, lively, creative people, more serious-minded to be sure than Montrealers, Londoners or New Yorkers, but promising to bequeath to the culture a new energy and strength in arts and letters.

As to the corporate differences, some are obvious. The federal government's National Energy Policy of 1980 represents an attempt to divide the industry along lines of national purity: Canadian companies get more money than non-Canadian ones for their oil by earning grants for exploration and drilling.

The other great dividing line is the one between the state agency Petro Canada and its crown sisters (Canterra, Coenerco and Alberta Energy), on the one hand, and private companies on the other. A battle has been created over the issue of state ownership and neo-socialism versus private enterprise.

There are less apparent differences as well—for instance, between the large Canadian independents, such as Dome and Nova, and the small companies. National policies good for one are not good for another. Some of them are really natural gas companies, some are oil companies, some are heavy oil companies and some are exotic oil sands companies.

The resulting diversity is, by now, chaotic. Nothing is as it seems, and nothing is remaining the same. Not one category of companies has yet managed to devise for itself a corporate policy that will ensure survival, let alone prosperity. Small wonder, then, that government policy-makers are making little headway in their efforts to impose public order on the ferment.

But there is a drawstring that pulls this cacophonous babble into one place. The great Canadian dream of unlocking the vast wealth concealed in our rock and soil has no more visible manifestation in the whole nation than it has right here in Calgary.

Few cities, indeed, are more suited to harbouring a dream—although the brusque, macho tone of the petroleum business undoubtedly recoils from the affiliation of hard-nosed exploration and money with the stuff of dreams. Calgary was once called the "Jewel City of the Foothills," without a trace of self-consciousness, and there is indeed an ethereal quality to Calgary's loveliness. The blue skies, the clean air, the chinooks and the rich green mantle of the foothills below the glimmer of mountain snows visible from every corner of town. . . . If ever a place was built to the specifications of a public relations hack, this is it.

The commercial dream, once of cattle and coal and now of megaprojects and Swiss banking connections, is equally compelling. Thousands of Canadians have made the pilgrimage here in hopes of grasping the national brass ring.

You find them shoulder to shoulder on the LRT trains and the Blue Arrow buses—Newfoundlanders and Manitobans, secretaries from Swift Current and accountants from Toronto, all riding from the hillside suburbs to the city centre on the valley floor.

Many, many are Albertans: Harold Millican over at the Northern Pipeline Agency skinned his shins with his boyhood pal Peter Lougheed here. Arnie Neilsen, the chairman of Canadian Superior, grew up in a Danish-speaking community about twenty-five miles from the city and didn't come to town until he was a teenager.

Many others have come from Europe: Easton Wren, a Scottish geologist and geophysicist came via Libya; Tom Kennedy, long time Calgary oil journalist, is a Hungarian émigré (class of '56) who was educated in London and earned his way through school as a bus conductor there.

Down in Traders at the Four Seasons Hotel, Kenn Borek, the British Columbian oilfield construction magnate, strolls by the tables in his shirtsleeves and cowboy boots. One Friday night, Nova boss Bob Blair dances in the Chinese New Year at a "grass roots" dinner in Chinatown and wins the draw for a Chinese dinner for two.

In short, the image of Calgary as an American town, a dormitory for the oil multinationals, is as outlandish as it is outdated. The accents at the Petroleum Club, the symbolic repository of oil's corporate, financial and political clout, aren't nearly as often Texan and Oklahoman as they are East Indian or Francophone.

The resonances of Calgary—thanks to the way oil has drawn creative, enterprising dreamers who are also doers—are complex and rich. Because the desolate places evoked in his writings are known first-hand by Calgary's geologists and landmen and pilots, Pierre Berton has a better following here in Calgary, and draws a bigger, more appreciative crowd whose thinking he genuinely influences, than does Richard Rohmer of the oil novels.

If there is still a company town atmosphere about the place, it is because this interesting, colourful mob of citizens still hopes to become rich—or, at least, to associate with the commercial royalty who *are* rich.

The fact that designer jeans are more favoured by the new millionaires of Calgary than are three-piece suits is perhaps interesting, but it is deceptive. It is quirkily interesting, in a pop-sociology way: yesterday's millionaires were roughnecks who left their jeans behind as they clawed their way up from the drilling rig floor to the boardrooms. Today's millionaires, by contrast, are bright young junior executives who have liberated themselves from their three-piece uniforms after making a big score on the stock market. Behind the different threads of the two generations, though, beats the same heart.

However, to imply that the streets are paved with gold and everyone does well would be to perpetuate yet another myth.

In the words of John Stewart-Smith (a local rancher and Carl Sandberg-type exponent of the virtues of uncompromised free enterprise), the dream includes the right to fail.

For each of those who has succeeded, many have failed.

And many never do touch the rarified world of money and privilege. The disparities between wealth and poverty here in Calgary are as dramatic and sobering as they are anywhere else. Still, the glue that holds it all together is the Tomorrowland expectation that comes with the search for oil. Today's stock promoters are peddling the same dreams and running the same smoke-and-mirrors shows that the mud-spattered rogues of the Turner Valley oil discovery days touted half a century ago. The only difference is locale: curbs and gutters have given way to perfectly and expensively decorated offices.

We have recently come face to face with a dark side in this caravanserai. The richest and most powerful institutions in our society are today the governments. There hasn't been a respectable ambition since the invention of internal-combustion engines that hasn't included oil and, before oil, coal. Governments are now no exception to this rule. To the revenue-starved financial planners of Ottawa and Edmonton, Toronto and St. John's, oil is the light at the end of the tunnel of deficit financing.

Governments have, therefore, charted a course toward more income from oil, a course that has logically led to a hunger from equity ownership. In the resulting clash, bitterness, anger and even hatred have been let loose.

Certainly, government is not entirely to blame for the great difficulty faced by the petroleum industry in the middle years of the eighties. Inflation and fierce global competition for capital play an important part in the stifling of the dream.

Governments, all governments—both provincial and federal, conservative as well as socialist—have sopped up much of the oil revenues generated since OPEC ran up the price in 1974.

The reality is that, in the late twentieth century, oil is a national treasure. Our nation, however, doesn't yet know how to manage the treasury. The consequence of the new role government has taken in oil, be that role right or wrong, is that the oil companies have been rendered illiquid. We now have, in Calgary, the paradox of newly poor oil companies. The poorest oil companies, ironically and despite stated intentions to the contrary, are those started, controlled and run by Canadians.

In 1976, through a series of tax instruments in the federal budget, Ottawa inadvertently created a climate in which a generation of small, Canadian-owned oil companies could establish themselves and begin to grow. By the time the National Energy Policy was introduced, however, these companies had not yet reached the point where they could stand on their own two feet. On balance, the provisions of the NEP just as inadvertently destroyed the climate they still needed as the 1976 budget had provided it. Furthermore, the highly publicized grants for exploration by Canadian companies, while real, did not compensate for the damage caused: they amounted to replacing a dollar with a quarter.

The smart people cooped up in their Ottawa offices were full of good intentions but the NEP clearly demonstrates that they don't understand the realities of today's oil business. In 1976, they didn't realize they were making possible a whole new sector of small, Canadian-owned companies. Today, they don't know what to do with that sector. The government and its bureaucrats are still making policy as if oil were a monolithic entity composed of large corporations, a unified patch instead of a complex economic and corporate patchwork quilt.

The result of all this is that the Canadians who took the initiative to start those small companies and directed them to the point where they were drilling seventy percent of the discovery wells in Western Canada (and therefore leading the national search for oil self-sufficiency) have been goaded into incredible rage.

We have here the story of a marriage gone wrong, the story, therefore, of the makings of a great national divorce.

An anecdote. In the late winter of 1982, Charles Caccia, the federal labour minister and Liberal MP for Toronto Davenport, came to Calgary to help the party raise funds. He gave a speech at a dinner of the party faithful and asked for questions.

In the ensuing half hour or so, he was deluged with the anger and frustration of people who would normally be his political allies. Hurt and confused, he made as graceful an escape as possible under the circumstances and wandered through the streets of Bridgeland, an area in Calgary where immigrants have been starting life in Canada for eighty years.

I took it upon myself to walk with him, to try to explain to him why his friends, his fellow Liberals, could treat him so brusquely. It isn't easy to describe to as kind and gentle a man as one could meet in political life, the deep unhappiness he had just been confronted with in the meeting.

It is, I finally said, a divorce, a great divorce.

People in the oil industry, professionals in a business that short months ago represented the best opportunity they could ever dream of, now find themselves out of work because their companies are virtually out of business.

The relationship between Calgary and the rest of Canada is not one of "two solitudes" unable to reach across a cultural and linguistic gap. It is the history of a severed marriage, a ruined affection. It is compounded by a nagging sense over fifty years that the West has been losing out in its economic relationship to the rest of Canada.

Until now, the exact reason for this sense of unfairness has been intangible, something just out of sight on the periphery of vision; in the same way, a marriage breakup may begin with a sense of disappointment.

Now, with the creation of an energy policy that has hurt the very Canadian companies its rhetoric seems to venerate, the discontent has a touchstone, the marriage has its adulterous villain. A conflict embodied by the fracturing of the oil industry into new power blocs with conflicting interests has become a conflict with the potential to fracture the national marriage.

Since John D. Rockefeller built the Standard Oil Trust on the ruins of Pennsylvania's independent exploration companies one hundred years ago, oil has been notable for its wars and conflicts. It has never been a haven of brotherly love; too much is at stake, in both monetary and political terms.

The distance that has opened up between Calgarians and other Canadians is, however, not one of greed and power lust. It is born of a sense of opportunity stolen from a land that once stood for opportunity.

To be sure, the issues that have sundered the national relationship have also broken up a secure political camaraderie between Albertans and their own Ottawa-bashing premier, Peter Lougheed.

Let us state this reassuring truth: Calgarians are good, decent people, and there is a craving to be rejoined to the good and decent people of Peterborough and Sept-Iles and Dartmouth.

Nothing would befit the citizenship of oil people more

than to be reconciled to a larger national dream. As Calgarians accommodate one another's diversity, overlooking internal tensions for the greater good of oil, so we must learn to accommodate the contradictions, strains and even the injustices of nationhood.

But let us state this, too: the divorce will proceed unless the give-and-take needed to restore harmony is forthcoming from the other side of the dispute as well.

The Petroleum Club, Its Princes...and Reality

Oil makes people rich, and the rich are the royalty of an affluent society. In Canada, where for all practical purposes religion has been removed from public life, the rich are also the inhabitants of a pantheon around which the mass media shape social mythology. The hunger to know about the rich and their lives and to be able to point to their Olympian palaces is nowhere more evident than in the oil business.

The Calgary Petroleum Club, an insignificant-looking building on 6th Avenue S.W., is regarded by public opinion as the chief repository of the financial and political clout of the petroleum industry.

Inside it has the aura of masculine mystique: bronze cowboy sculptures, W. J. Phillips woodcuts, brass and glass and marble, heavy furniture, costly panelling, drive-in fireplaces and thousand-dollar card games. Women are still not admitted at lunch. That rule is so firm that a deputy minister of the government of the Soviet Union found her Kremlin membership wasn't enough to win her noon-hour privileges at the Petroleum Club—an embarrassment of the first order for her Canadian corporate host.

The myth of the Petroleum Club grew out of the golden age of the entrepreneur, which began in 1947 when the Leduc oilfield discovery put Alberta on the petroleum map and effectively ended in 1973 when the Organization of Petroleum Exporting Countries put the price of oil so high that governments moved in on the industry in Canada.

During those years, membership in the club (there is a ten-year waiting list) was evidence that you had arrived and were going to stay.

The reality of the club's importance as a broker of influence and opinion no longer squares with the myth. These days, it sometimes appears to be a kind of Elba where free enterprise in exile can remember the way things used to be and mutter less-than-sober imprecations against change in general and democratic socialism in particular.

Mention the club and the response now is often, "Who goes there anymore?" The question is asked either sorrowfully or derisively — that depends on the speaker — but it acknowledges this fact: the oil business is just too big and too complex, with too many competing forces, to speak with one voice any longer or to be represented by one social centre. Even so, the Petroleum Club is still the standard of excellence and achievement in petroleum, and the industry needs the club because oil is a success-oriented business.

Just as the public recognizes one palace of oil — the Petroleum Club — so too does it recognize a few select princes within the industry. The members of this small elite form the basis for constantly recycled stories about who's who in the business.

Some of those names have entered history: the Harvies, who founded the Glenbow Museum and the Devonian Foundation, and Carl Nickle, the deserving spokesman for oil to the rest of Canada. Other names come and go with their tenures as presidents of the Canadian Petroleum Association and the Independent Petroleum Association of Canada, or with changes in the editorship of *Oilweek* (the industry's self-acknowledged Bible).

The industry has its share of media darlings: Smilin' Jack Gallagher of Dome Petroleum, or James Gray and John Masters of Canadian Hunter. There are the public heroes — men like Robert Lamond, the free-wheeling president of Czar Resources, who promoted hundreds of Canadians into drilling fund investments; there are the enemies — Wilbert (Bill) Hopper, for example, chairman of Petro Canada and symbol of government intrusion into private enterprise.

But in the name-dropping game mythology and reality are two separate things, just as they are in discussions of the Petroleum Club. The industry is too big and changes too quickly now for a list of twenty names to embrace the totality of who's who and who counts.

People whose names never make the media list are nonetheless among those who really count. What outsider has heard of J. C. Anderson? Yet this geologist and corporate creator has launched scores of careers and companies. The cycles of investment that rock petroleum from time to time keep bringing new players into the game: recent examples are Sam Belzberg of Vancouver finance and development, Jack and Robert Cummings of the Montreal merchant banking family, and Frederick Walter Hill of Regina's MacCallum Hill.

Furthermore, as the pension funds, trust companies and insurance companies penetrate deeper and deeper into oil, major decisions and major successes belong to teams of faceless managers who work within walking distance of Bay Street in Toronto. And the czars of the bureaucracies in Ottawa and in the provincial capitals—Barry Mellon and Wayne Minnion, Ed Clark and Len Good and the rest—wield more and more clout along with their political masters, both the well-known such as Marc Lalonde and Merv Leitch, and the lesser-known such as Senator Jack Austin and Colin Thatcher.

We need the sense of a palace and acknowledged princes, for we need social mythology, but the reality is much more complex. And more interesting.

The Chinook

"Have you heard the one about the farmer who . . . ?"

By Alister Thomas

It is easy, in the depth of any winter cold snap, to tell the Calgarian from the newcomer or horrified passing visitor. The Calgarian knows what to say. First, he says, "It's a dry cold." This is meant to be reassuring. Once you find yourself repeating this irrelevant bit of folklore to others, in the same complacent tones, you will know that you, too, belong.

The second thing the Calgarian says is, "Never mind, there'll be a chinook soon. . . . " And he walks around with his gaze fixed due west, yearning for the sight of a chinook arch. He knows that once the arch has been spotted, a dramatic (if temporary) break from winter is on its way.

A chinook, rushing down from the Rocky Mountains, can raise the mercury through twenty-eight Celsius degrees in half an hour, make thirty centimetres of snow disappear overnight and lift icy winter-bound spirits immediately. Such is the power of the chinook.

It's not bad at making a tall tale taller, either. Have you heard the one about the farmer who is on his way home from town when he spots a chinook coming? Immediately he lays the whip to his horses but even so, he barely manages to keep the front runners of his sleigh on the snow during the long drive home. The sleigh's rear runners are dragging in mud—and the spare horse tied to the tail gate is raising dust at every step.

Then there's the man who goes out to the foothills for a

day's skiing. He laboriously climbs the mountain and turns around, set for the long run down. No snow. Seems a chinook followed him up, licking up all the snow as it went.

The wonder is that we bother to invent these tales—the truth is weird and wonderful enough. Trees, lilac bushes and crocuses fall for a chinook every time, budding as if it were June; threshing in southern Alberta can sometimes be started in February; and optimistic golfers keep their clubs handy throughout the entire winter.

But, much as we moan for a chinook every time a cold snap hits, there is another side to what some call "the wicked witches' wind." Gene Prozny, the officer in charge of Calgary's weather station, explains: "A strong chinook is distinctly unpleasant. The combination of heat and excessive dryness together with strong, gusty winds can cause physiological as well as psychological reactions, since irritability and headaches are quite common. The chinook also dries out the land and creates favourable conditions for forest fires."

Chinooks, however, while much-talked about have been little studied. We have to look elsewhere, to studies made of similar winds around the world—the *santa ana* in California, the *foehn* in the Alps, the *zonda* in Argentina and the *canterbury nor'wester* in New Zealand. In Israel there is the *sharav*, which brings with it heat, dryness and a surplus of positively-charged electrical ions. Dr. Felix Sulman has gained international recognition for his work on ionization and the fledgling science of biometeorology—the study of the effects of weather and environment on human beings. In an article in the *Financial Post Magazine* (April 1981), he details the consequences of the sharav: "The body loses fluids and gains potassium, thyroid and serotonin. The excess potassium is somewhat toxic and can affect the heart muscles; the extra thyroid can cause an assortment of symptoms including hyperactivity combined with exhaustion, while the serotonin can bring on irritability, giddiness, insomnia, depression and uncharacteristic behaviour."

While there is no scientific proof that chinooks have the same effect, Dr. Gordon Hodgson, director of the Kananaskis Centre for Environmental Research (and one of the key people behind *Chinooks*, a marvellous film on the subject), says: "It is generally accepted that there is an excess of positive ions in lee wave phenomena [chinooks]." Calgary weather station officer Gene Prozny will not comment on the role of ions in chinooks, but he does say that people with a history of migraines might suffer just before a chinook blows in because of the rapid pressure-drop associated with it.

Chinooks also cause the air pollution index to double. Since there is a very strong inversion ahead of a chinook and Calgary is in a river valley, the pollutants from automobiles (eighty percent of Calgary's total pollution), industry and home heating are trapped at city-level. The good news is that once the chinook itself arrives, its gusty winds quickly disperse the pollutants.

If we're not sure of all the chinook's effects, at least we know what it is: a warm, gusty, dry, westerly wind that causes a rapid increase in temperature and a dramatic decrease in relative humidity. We also know how the term originated: it is named after the Chinook Indians of the Pacific Coast. One of the earliest uses of the term was in Oregon, where a Hudson's Bay factor called Birnie claimed that a warm, westerly wind blew from the Chinook Indians' camp. (Chinook winds occur from the Yukon to New Mexico, a span of three thousand kilometres, but it is in southern Alberta and northern Montana that they are the most intense.) Indian legend says that Chinook was a beautiful maiden who wandered from the tribe and was lost in the mountains of the southwest. The bravest warriors searched for her without avail; but then one day a soft, gentle wind blew from the west and as the warriors gazed at each other they whispered: "It is the breath of our beautiful Chinook."

The wind does indeed begin on the coast. A Pacific (low) air mass comes across the Rockies counterclockwise, warms as it drops on the plains (three to four Celsius degrees for every three hundred metres of descent) and displaces the existing cold air to the southwest. Since the chinook blows in in waves, it is accompanied by strong, gusty winds (we talk about "chinook winds"), and it affects some parts of the city more than others (live in southwest Calgary if you want to maximize your chances for chinook warmth).

This wave effect also produces the spectacular chinook arch, which precedes the chinook itself. The arch appears in the western horizon, running parallel with the mountain range. It looks as if the sky has been sliced in two, with a solid grey bank of cloud above and intense blue beneath. The wicked winds of the chinook flow eastward beneath the arch.

The arch infallibly predicts a chinook but, beyond that, all bets are off. Weathermen struggle to be specific about where, how and when the chinook will hit, but they know it may well touch down in one place and skip another only kilometres away.

We do have *some* hard data, however. (Trivia freaks are encouraged to memorize the following.) One winter in eight there will be no chinooks, but there will be more than one hundred a year for the other seven (yes, summer too). Calgary averages 13.5 chinooks a month from October to March, each one lasting seven to eight hours. They are most likely to occur between 7:00 A.M. and noon, least likely between 3:00 P.M. and 9.00 P.M. One in two raises the temperature more than five Celsius degrees; one in four, more than ten degrees; one in twenty is the stuff of which tall tales are made and brings at least a twenty-degree rise in temperature. And those gusty winds indeed blow hard: half of them will exceed sixty kilometres per hour, one in twenty will exceed the hundred kilometres per hour.

That, then, is the chinook. You now know enough about it to sound complacently knowledgeable here in the West and to bore your friends back east. And you only need to experience one to know why we have made it our talisman. No wonder more than fifty commercial enterprises have gratefully included the term in their titles!

The Stampede:
The Stampede History

"The city and the Stampede grew up together here on the prairies in the late 1880s; they struggled together and flourished together."

By Elaine Dixson

You can see everything from the ridge of Scotchman's Hill (nick-named for the fact that the view is free as well as complete). You can see the fairgrounds, the racetrack, the grandstand, the barns and the exhibition buildings.

You can see the buildings of downtown Calgary: the centres of commerce and industry, the columns of glass and steel and concrete that push upward like the bars on sales graphs. Looking westward from the ridge, the buildings on the Stampede grounds and the buildings in the city's core meet and blend, and it seems very natural that they should. That simple observation says a lot about the histories of both the city and the Stampede. They grew up together here on the prairies in the late 1800s; they struggled together and flourished together.

It's true that the first rodeo to be called "The Stampede" was held in 1912, but Calgary had had an annual exhibition for nearly twenty-five years by then. The Calgary Agricultural Society was established in 1884, just a few short years after Calgary began to emerge. Society members felt that Calgary's population of some twenty-five hundred people could support a fair and that it would be an opportunity for the farmers and ranchers in the district to show the excellent quality of the grain and cattle they were raising. The exhibition was not held in 1885, the year of the Riel Rebellion, but came back in style in 1886. That year it was

61

held in a downtown building, and a total of about nine hundred dollars in prize money was awarded for the best of everything from cattle and horses to grain and vegetables to cooking and ladies' handicrafts.

The fair was very popular over the next few years, for it was more than an opportunity for farmers and ranchers to show the products of their labours. It was an opportunity for everyone in the district to socialize. By 1889 the exhibition needed larger facilities and bought ninety-four acres of land from the federal government (at $2.50 per acre) in Victoria Park, the present site of Stampede Park. The Agricultural Society promptly mortgaged the land and built new buildings and barns. The depressed economic conditions in the 1890s hurt the exhibition, though; they defaulted on their mortgage, and one R. B. Bennett, the lawyer who held the mortgage, threatened foreclosure. In an agreement between the exhibition and Calgary's city council, the city paid the mortgage in exchange for title to the property which would then be leased back to the exhibition for one dollar a year. To this day, the Calgary Exhibition and Stampede pays one dollar per year to the city for the use of the grounds.

By the time the exhibition had been operating for some twenty years, Calgarians were solidly behind the effort. In 1908 the exhibition hosted the Dominion Exhibition, which qualified it for federal grant money and raised it to national prominence. In these years, too, the entertainment aspects of the fair were developed: organizers realized they needed to offer something to the ten thousand urban residents of Calgary, while still maintaining the agricultural flavour.

Then along came a travelling "Wild West" show from the United States, a show patterned after those of Bill Cody. A vaudeville entertainer and trick roper with the 1911 show named Guy Weadick took a look around town and thought it was ready for rodeo. He was something of an organizer and promoter, and he was aware that the traditional cowboy ways were fast disappearing. Rodeo was a way of preserving them in an entertaining form. All he needed was money.

Weadick returned the following year and began to promote his idea. He went first to the exhibition, but the exhibition board didn't want any part of it. The idea looked like a loser to them, and in those days, they could not have tolerated a financial loss. The exhibition finally agreed to provide the facilities but made clear it was assuming no responsibility for the rodeo. Undaunted, Weadick began to look around for investors and found them in four prominent Albertans: George Lane and Patrick Burns, both millionaire cattlemen; A. E. Cross, a brewer; and A. J. MacLean, a rancher and provincial secretary for Alberta. Each put up $25,000 to promote the rodeo.

In the weeks before the great event, excitement was building to a feverish pitch: Calgary was expecting great things, and Weadick was promising them. The *Eye Opener* was full of anticipatory items concerning the Stampede.

Calgary's frontier celebration is to be officially known as "The Stampede." People who have attended those miserable bucking contests with which Calgary has been afflicted from time to time of late years must get it out of their noddles the idea that the big celebration in September is going to be anything like that. This affair is to be one of educational value and will be an accurate and elaborate visual representation of the evolution of the West. The parade will be an immense one, . . . which will be held on each of the four days, and will be extremely striking in its magnitude and panoramic effect. The moving picture man will be on hand to catch the scene for exhibition abroad.

For the information of the Mexican cowpunchers within our gates, we beg to state that there is a Chili Con Carne restaurant to be found in the Allan Block, just behind the Post Office. And where chili con carne is found, so shall hot tamales be also.

Calgary's first "Stampede" was held 2–5 September 1912 and, in spite of the rain which dampened everything but the spirits of the thirty thousand people who attended, it was a great success. Weadick got the Duke and Duchess of Connaught and the governor-general to attend, brought in Indians and had both American and Mexican competitors in the rodeo. His show was everything he had promised. But it just managed to break even. And with World War I looming on the horizon, Weadick's investors were reluctant to put up funds again, so the exhibition continued, but the rodeo did not.

After the war was over, however, Weadick came back and convinced them to hold the "Victory Stampede" in 1919. It was only moderately successful. A merger between the exhibition and Weadick's rodeo enterprise seemed inevitable and finally took place when the exhibition needed something more to support its own production. And so, in 1923, the Calgary Exhibition and Stampede was born, and it has been an annual extravaganza ever since. In 1923 as well, Weadick introduced the chuckwagon races, the thrilling event that forever set Calgary's "Stampede" apart from any other rodeo.

If you sit on the ridge of Scotchman's Hill when the Stampede is on, you can see the tens of thousands of people milling around the Stampede grounds. They stream through the lanes of the midway, they cluster around exhibits. You can see the sun flashing on the twirling rides. You can hear the sirens, the hawkers on the loudspeakers, the thundering horses and wagons in the chuckwagon races, the cheers of the grandstand crowds and the beating of the drums from the Indian Village.

If you close your eyes, you can go back in time and stop at any year. The sights and sounds are much the same. The extraordinary thing about the Stampede is that it has remained faithful to the original intentions of Guy Weadick and the Agricultural Society.

Since 1923, there have always been a parade and a rodeo. There have always been the chuckwagon races, the exhibition of animals and handicrafts and an entertainment program in the grandstand. The Indians have always played an integral part, and there has always been the attempt to provide something of interest to almost everyone.

Of course, the content or arrangement of some of the features of the Stampede has changed, because people change. Technology keeps finding new ways to test the nerves (and stomachs) of midway patrons. Rodeo schools now teach the rangeland skills that were dying out even as Weadick organized the first rodeo. In the chuckwagon races thoroughbred horses are used in place of the original quarterhorses and heavy horses, and the canvas-covered wagons are quite different from the farm wagons that were hauled around the track during the first few years. The course is longer now, and the winner is the first one to cross the finish line with all his outriders close by, not the first one to produce smoke from his stove. (Since the competitors had been using coal oil, gasoline or wood chips to do so, it became obvious that some rules were needed!)

The story of the Stampede is remarkable if for no other reason than that its success has been the result of the dedication of many people. The city of Calgary and its citizens have stood steadfastly behind the enterprise, and they have been rewarded for their loyalty: the Stampede has brought fame to the city and has been credited with attracting business here, simply because it has made Calgary more than a dot on the map. As well, the profits of the Stampede are turned back into the organization and are used for capital improvements. Nearly one thousand volunteers work year-round to put on the show, and there are fewer than two hundred paid permanent staff with the Stampede. It has always been this way, and it makes the Stampede one of the few attractions of its kind in the world that has never depended on the taxpayer's purse.

The Stampede has maintained its following through the toughest times. Even through the thirties, when the twenty-five cent admission price might have bought eggs or milk, when the prize money for the rodeo events slipped, the Stampede persevered.

If you leave Scotchman's Hill and walk through the grounds during the Stampede, you'll find that sophisticated, modern Calgary nearly disappears from view—for as long as you're at the Stampede, you're in Cowtown again. It's an image the Stampede would like to perpetuate, yet it is an image that the city beyond the pallisade gates tries to bury beneath the glass and steel.

Perhaps the Stampede's greatest value is that, over the years, it has caused millions of people to be touched by the West as it was and to see and do things that will stay with them for the rest of their lives.

The Stampede:

The Stampede Breakfast

"Much like the Stampede itself, the Stampede breakfast, another peculiarly Calgary phenomenon, is a state of mind."

By Gillian Steward

Much like the Stampede itself, the Stampede breakfast, another peculiarly Calgary phenomenon, is a state of mind. It doesn't seem to matter whether the breakfast is held in a rancher's field in the foothills, in the parking lot of a suburban shopping centre or in the venerable Palliser Hotel. It doesn't even seem to matter whether the orange juice is spiked with vodka or served neat. For some strange reason all kinds of people—bankers, lawyers, housewives, geologists, politicians, teachers and construction workers— will get out of bed as early as six o'clock in the morning to join hordes of other people eating pancakes and bacon simply because it's Stampede Week and this is one of its most important rituals.

The breakfast tradition goes back to the days on the cattle ranges when the chuckwagon was the cowboys' mobile kitchen. Up at the crack of dawn so they could work with the cattle for as many daylight hours as possible, the cowboys would gather at the chuckwagon for a hearty, if not heavy, meal of pancakes, beans and coffee. Nowadays, of course, most people start their day in the privacy of their own home with a bowl of cereal and a glass of juice. And maybe that's why Calgarians are devoted to their annual Stampede breakfast: it's a way of starting the day not only reinforced by good food (and sometimes good spirits), but with music, dancing and good company. And during Stampede Week there's no question that some sort of extraordinary reinforcement is needed to face the continuous round of barbecues, parties and bar-hopping.

In the days since its humble beginnings, the chuckwagon breakfast has been modified and elaborated to suit all kinds of tastes and pocketbooks. Not only that, it has so proliferated that it's hard to go through Stampede Week without stumbling into at least one Stampede breakfast. Many of the shopping malls, both downtown and in the suburbs, sponsor free breakfasts along with western bands and square dancers.

One of the most famous is the one put on by **The Bay** at the corner of 1st Street and 7th Avenue S.W. Held every morning (except Sundays) during Stampede, it's a good way to start the day because there are always rousing bands, including the famous fiddler Roy Warhurst, to get you in the mood. And right after breakfast the Stampede downtown attractions—such as marching bands, Indian parades and square dancers—show up to begin their daily rounds.

Another traditional—and free—breakfast is the one held on the first Saturday of Stampede from 7:00 A.M. to 10:00 A.M. at the **Chinook Shopping Centre** in the south end of the city. Sponsored by CFCN Television and Radio, Woodward's department stores and the Chinook Centre merchants, the breakfast has been held for over twenty years and attracts more than thirty thousand people. There's a two-hour stage show, music and dancing as well as pancakes (sixty thousand of them), sausages, bacon and coffee for everyone. And, according to Mac Lindsay of CFCN, the breakfast is so well organized that no one has to wait more than twenty minutes for his or her breakfast.

Every morning during Stampede Week, the same chuckwagons that race nightly at the grandstand are out and about the city, serving impromptu breakfasts. The wagons show up at various locations throughout downtown and the suburban shopping centres. Stampede volunteers dish out the mandatory pancakes and bacon, which are supplied by the Stampede itself.

Besides the free breakfasts, there are dozens of private ones for which tickets can be purchased or invitations carefully garnered. One of the rowdiest—and the one for which tickets go the fastest—is undoubtedly that held by the **Ad and Sales Club**, aptly named the "Whoop-Up" breakfast. By 7:00 A.M. the first arrivals straggle into the Palliser Hotel for the traditional Stampede fare and a potent punch, the recipe for which is a secret apparently known by only two people. Before it's over at 11:00 A.M., more than 650 people will have danced to the music of the country and western bands as well as entertainers brought in from other hotels and nightclubs.

For those who like to hobnob with the rich and famous, the best bet is the **Hays** breakfast, founded by the late Senator Harry Hays and now well past its twenty-fifth year. This is a by-invitation-only affair, but the guest list features over two thousand names, many of them well-known Calgarians and VIPs in town for the Stampede. It's held on the first Sunday of Stampede near the Hays' residence overlooking the Glenmore Reservoir. Besides the traditional menu of pancakes, scrambled eggs, sausage and bacon, the Hays breakfast features a secret concoction known as "sillabub," guaranteed to make your hair stand on end after only one snort. Whether it's the heady company, the exhilarating view, the food or the sillabub, the Hays breakfast has become Calgary's equivalent of the Queen's garden party. Invitations are keenly sought and much cherished.

But perhaps the most enjoyable Stampede breakfasts, and the ones that offer the most in old-fashioned western hospitality, are those held in the country. The **Priddis Community Association** puts on such a breakfast the first Sunday of Stampede that attracts local farmers and ranchers, and Sarcee Indians from the nearby reserve as well as people from the city. Designed as a family affair, the breakfast features the traditional pancakes and bacon, and although no liquor is served, everyone seems to get high on the sunshine, fresh air and mountain views. Entertainment is provided by country and western bands, square dancers and Sarcee drummers and dancers. Priddis is about thirty-five kilometres southwest of Calgary and tickets can be obtained from members of the Community Association.

Listing all the breakfasts would be impossible since they range from the very private, to the corporate (some companies hold them for employees and their families in the parking lot or out on the front sidewalk), to the very public. But there's no doubt that the Stampede breakfast is to the Stampede what turkey dinner is to Christmas. And most Calgarians can't imagine Stampede without at least one crack-of-dawn rip-roaring breakfast to start the day.

The Stampede:
Dressing
Western

"Most tourists make the mistake of wearing the working gear of cowboys. It looks silly."

By Tim Christison

Calgarians and real cowboys can spot a tourist in western clothes a mile away.

Most tourists make the mistake of wearing the working gear of cowboys. It looks silly. If you know the reason for the gear, you'll avoid it—the same way the cowboy does when he comes to town.

For example, the underslung-heel **cowboy boot** (the one that looks as though the heel has been attacked and driven under the instep). This heel has a function, but it has nothing to do with walking. It is designed to keep the cowboy's foot from slipping out of the stirrups and is excellent for the purpose. Try walking in it, though, and you'll soon feel like riding: anything to get off your feet! Look, instead, for a boot with a walking heel. You won't even have to sacrifice looks for comfort, since this lower, squarer heel is found in combination with the natty, characteristic pointed toe of the riding boot.

All good cowboys boots are leather—anything from elephant to ostrich to lizard, though usually cowhide for workaday purposes. Buy whatever leather appeals to you since, when they dress up, working cowboys, rodeo cowboys, entertainers and ranch owners all wear boots made from one of the more exotic leathers. Since you'll want to protect the leather from rain or snow, you'll be happy to know there are even specially shaped rubbers to fit over cowboy boots.

When you have decided on the type of boot you want—colour, leather and heel—then be prepared to spend an hour being fitted. The feel of the boot may be strange if you are accustomed to wearing slip-on shoes or even a good oxford. The snug covering of leather over the ankle, originally designed to ward off snake bites and protect the rider's ankle in bush country, takes some breaking in—of the wearer. The steel shank in good cowboy boots accounts for some of the stiffness of the boot. You'll need to walk around in the salesroom to get the feel of the heel height, the leather sleeve over the ankle and the way the boot top hits the leg. Boots that will have pant legs tucked into them should be roomier than if you intend the boots for under your jeans. (Cowboys wear them both ways.)

Be prepared to pay from $75 upward for good boots. Tony Lama, Larry Mahan, Fry and any exotic leather start around $125 and keep going right past $600. Once you have a good fit in a pair of cowboy boots, you don't want to take them off. Boots are comfortable and practical. That's why you'll see lots of businessmen in Calgary wearing cowboy boots—it's not affectation, it's comfort.

An item you'll see, but probably won't buy, is **chaps** (pronounced "shaps"). They look like scooped-out, low-slung, leather overalls and are worn over trousers to protect the rider's legs from scrapes with bushes and thorny scrubs. Vertical fringes down the outside seam are common on chaps and not just for show. They provide a "spillway" for the rain, thus drawing it away from the leg and helping to keep the cowboy a little bit drier. Rodeo cowboys wear chaps, too—in their case, for protection from scrapes against the side of the chute as the bull or horse does his level best to throw the cowboy before the contest even officially starts.

Next, belts—specifically, **belt buckles**. A belt is a belt, but the variety to be found in these buckles is something to behold. They come every way you can imagine—huge, engraved or carved, in all sorts of shapes, and fashioned from brass-tone material, real brass, pewter, silver or even gold. Since championship buckles are awarded at rodeos (even *truck*-driving rodeos!) and special buckles are given to rodeo managers, the one being worn by a working cowboy will often commemorate some special event and be an object of great pride to its owner. There is plenty of variety in the buckles carried by stores as well. Just take care that the one you choose doesn't give you a jab in the gut when you sit. Avoid ones with bottle-openers on the back if you have any surplus flesh around the middle—"Ouch!" is not a cowboy yell.

Now for the **cowboy shirt**. Like the belt buckle, it is an inducement to work off those extra pounds because it is close-fitting and relentlessly takes on the exact shape of the body underneath. The classic design has long sleeves (which may be rolled up) and V-yokes front and back. Entertainers pick flashy satins and the like; working cowboys pick cotton (or, these days, a cotton blend) in dark colours or denim or a plaid that won't show the dirt.

The shirts have snap fastenings, not buttons. What started as a practical solution to the nuisance of losing buttons has evolved (only in Stampede Week, mind) into a test of the wearer's sex appeal: bar-hoppers love to boast about how many women have ripped open their shirts at a single enthusiastic yank.

But back to real life . . . Dressier shirts may have fringe on the yoke, pearl-covered snaps and come in brighter colours. Entertainers wear what are called "Nashville shirts," eye-jarring visions of embroidery, Day-Glo satin and sequins. If you'd like to stop short of Nashville but still step out like a real dude, a cowboy dressed to be noticed, buy the triangles of silver or gold designed to cover the tips of your collar. Save this shirt for a wedding or party, though, don't wear it for a casual stroll down the street.

Since shirts are usually worn slightly open (just *one* button), **ties** are not really part of the look even though rodeos used to give away bolo ties (the ones with slides) the way they hand out belt buckles today. As a friend of mine sniffed, "Real cowboys don't wear ties. Not many fake cowboys do, either."

Now for the ultimate Calgary symbol—**the cowboy hat**. Actually, the symbol is the white Stetson (Stetson being the manufacturer's name, not a style). Back in the good old days, a cowboy's hat was more likely to be creamy-coloured or slightly darker, since most cowboy hats were made of beaver felt. These hats were much more practical than the white ones popularized at the 1948 Grey Cup Game by then-mayor Don Mackay, but it's the white hat that has caught Canada's fancy.

If we wanted to pick a cowboy hat that originated with the men of the range, perhaps we should adopt the Guy Weadick hat (which was given some publicity a few years ago by the Stampede Board). Weadick, a city-born cowboy, affected a high-crowned beige hat.

(An aside: the hard truth is, if you want to know how *not* to dress, take a look at old pictures of Weadick. He wore a bandana around his neck. Its purpose is to keep dust out of the mouth while driving cattle or to act as a sweatband under a wide-brimmed hat. It is therefore working gear and not genteel enough for street wear. Weadick also wore spurs. A rodeo cowboy wears spurs to get a good ride from a bronco but never uses them on a horse he values.)

Cowboy hats come in several variations on the basic theme and range from the tall-crowned Guy Weadick hat to one more similar to a farmer's sunhat. No rules here, except to find what is flattering to you. There are low crowns, high crowns, pencil-creased crowns, square-creased or Bull-dogger style or a crown without a crease so you can steam in your own. High crowns are popular because they are flattering to most faces and give some body height as well.

Flat brims without an edging are more popular than brims with a contrast piping. The colour or fabric of a hat is primarily based on personal preference, but always remember that western cowboys, ranchers and the like, want to look good but hate ostentation.

Prices for hats, even straw hats, start around thirty dollars. A smart-looking, well-built hat costs sixty to seventy dollars, and entertainers often pay two to three hundred dollars.

Now that you own a hat, you must still pass two more tests. One is the way in which you put the hat down (apart from on your head, that is) and the other is how many feathers or other ornaments (such as beaded or braided leather bands, pins) you put on the hat.

A person who values a western hat will rest it on its crown. That's right: turn it upside down. The crown can take the weight but the brim can't and will lose its shape. Cowboys steam their hats to conform either to the most flattering shape (for their best hat) or to the most useful shape to shadow the face or allow the rain to run off (for their work hats).

Bands on hats are usually plain and blend in with the original hat. Cowboys like to show their own sense of style, too, so you find fancy bands for hats. There are silver and gold ones that clip around the hat, but most decorative bands are made of fabric or feathers. Separate long feathers are stuck individually into the band. Restrain yourself—the more feathers in your band the more you will look like a tourist. One or two is the limit for good taste. Entertainers wear long billowing feathers but working cowboys are more conservative.

Fit is important in hats as well as boots. The fit will be snug. The inside band of the hat will probably be leather and will stretch to fit your head comfortably. The hat sits low on the forehead—quite disastrous to a woman's bangs but flattering for a bald-headed man. Many cowboys show the signs of constantly wearing a hat—thin spots in their hair where the hat sits.

A white cowboy hat can be cleaned by sprinkling it with dry oats or cornmeal and then applying a light dusting of baby powder.

Frontier suits are a favourite of some Calgary businessmen and Alberta ranchers. The slim cut of the trousers with side-slashed pockets and narrow legs passes slightly over a middle-aged spread. The jackets are the traditional, narrow blazer/riding-jacket style, again with slanted pockets. These suits are not designed for wandering the Stampede grounds but rather to command attention at board meetings and other formal occasions.

Some Fast, Final Tips:
Buy boots with a walking heel and snug fit.
Buy a hat that fits snugly, worn low on the forehead.
Wear a feather if it appeals to you.
Find a buckle that is attractive but doesn't hurt.

If you want to find the real stuff when it comes to western clothing, shop where the cowboys and ranchers shop. As a bonus, you'll be able to see how *they* dress.

Western Outfitters (128 – 8th Avenue S.E.) is on the mall in downtown Calgary. The walls are hung with framed pictures of their customers, which include all four types of cowboy—rodeo, working, entertainer and sometimes.

Look for the wooden horse outside **Grand Saddlery and Western Wear**, also downtown (210 - 8th Avenue S.W.). There is a suburban outlet as well, in Marlborough Mall in the northeast.

Riley and McCormick has several outlets both downtown and in suburban malls. Downtown the store is across from The Bay at 7th Avenue and 1st Street S.W. Check the phone book for the other six locations. This company outfits both urban cowboys and the working types.

If you want to be outfitted like an entertainer or movie version of a cowboy, try **Wild as the West** in Mount Royal Village at 8th Street and 16th Avenue S.W.

Only buy clothes on the Stampede grounds if you don't mind paying a premium.

Note that I have not even mentioned jeans. Cowboys wear good old traditional heavy denim jeans. What about designer jeans? Well, as a ranching friend told me, "A real cowboy don't wear *nobody's* brand."

PART TWO:
Places to Go and Things to Do

The Arts

The Glenbow Museum

"To ask for big money, a museum first has to do big things. And this the Glenbow has begun to do. It has become very good at the Great Canadian Tightrope Act—excellence on a shoestring."

By Louise Bresky

The only street-side clue to one of Canada's unique cultural treats is a large sign reading "Museum." This is a little like hanging the word "Restaurant" outside Maxim's in Paris— it's accurate, but it doesn't begin to suggest the quality and variety inside.

At least the sign lets you know where commerce ends and culture begins. Without it, the eight-story Glenbow-Alberta Institute would blend seamlessly into the Four Seasons Hotel and the Calgary Convention Centre.

The multipurpose block, finished in 1976, is a true, impersonal hunk of Calgary Modern. Yet in the part labelled "Museum," Governor-General Edward Schreyer opened the 1981 Treasures of Ancient Nigeria show on its only Canadian stop. In its art gallery, Calgarians peered, not without some bafflement, at the only North American showing of Four Modern Masters and flocked to see a major exhibition of the works of Pablo Picasso.

The modest Glenbow façade tells you less about the remarkable institution within than it does about the man who made it all possible. The late Eric L. Harvie, Q.C. liked a low profile. An Ontario native who made millions in the Alberta oil boom of 1947, Harvie was a quiet millionaire with a passion for history who, on his travels, collected anything that spoke of the past: art, armour, artifacts from all parts of the world, but particularly from Western Canada.

In 1954, Harvie set up the private Glenbow Foundation to sort, analyze, catalogue and display his treasures with the overriding dream "to preserve in permanent form the history of Western Canada and to maintain a record of its living history." Yet Harvie had amassed an astonishing hoard of things which went far beyond that regional interest: paintings, books, historical documents, coins, statues, weapons and objets d'art which included Chinese ivories, antique European porcelain, Haida totem poles and replicas of the Crown Jewels.

In 1967, having never stopped collecting, Harvie turned over his Glenbow collection, which had an insured value of $5 million, to the provincial government. A proviso of the mind-boggling gift was that an independent corporation be established ("as a memorial to Centennial Year") to administer on behalf of the people of Alberta the collection, its buildings and properties. Harvie also persuaded the Alberta government to preserve its sixty-year-old downtown Provincial Court House as a temporary home for the collection.

In his history of Canadian museums, *Beyond Four Walls*, Calgary's Archie Key (former director of the Canadian Museums Association) tells us that the Harvie treasure trove was at this point "an over-sized *cabinet de curiosités*," comprising an art collection of over fourteen thousand items by more than one thousand artists, a twenty-thousand volume library and general collections ranging through archaeology, archival material, earth sciences, ethnography, fine art, and military, natural and pioneer history.

At first, many Calgarians tended to shrug off the gift as "Harvie's attic," especially when they saw it in such cramped quarters. The sandstone court house, a charming but somewhat musty relic itself, displayed the armour and weapons (from neolithic times to the present), the ethnological potpourri, the Crown Jewels and the Western Canadiana, including displays telling the history of the RCMP and prairie pioneer life. Meanwhile the art collection, dominated by nineteenth century landscapes (some of which were more historic than artistic), was exhibited in an improvised gallery in a former car parts warehouse. The archival material was made accessible in the converted Memorial branch library, but tons of mysterious miscellany simply lay on hold in the dark.

Yet even then, in make-do quarters, the collection and its philosophy began to change, to develop a public purpose.

Curators began to refine it and enrich it and dream up ways of sharing it with its new owners. Some truckloads of items, such as barn doors and old wagon parts, were weeded out ("deaccessioned" is the word) as being not of museum quality. Changing and increasingly artful displays offered a sharper, more unified version of history. The gems among the early Western Canadian paintings were restored and linked to both history and the evolution of art. The art department struggled out from under the shadow of history to exhibit new paintings as well as old and hung touring shows of contemporary Canadian and American art, including works by Calgary artists. Slowly, the "one-man" label was fading, yet only when the Glenbow moved to its present home did the ordinary Calgarian begin to feel a proprietary interest.

The new $8 million Glenbow—an enormous Glenbow which can finally house most of its Harvie heritage and new acquisitions under one roof—opened in September 1976. The space is impressive: 250,000 square feet, including 100,000 square feet of exhibition space. There are library facilities, a 370-seat lecture hall, Class-A security and climate control, space to store paintings and objects not on display so that researchers can view them and, on the second floor, the largest temporary art exhibition space in Canada. A shimmering burst of brushed aluminum and acrylic by sculptor-writer James Houston rises three storys from the lobby. Called "Aurora Borealis," it seems to symbolize both the glitter and the soaring goals of the new Glenbow. The institute is now far removed from one man's attic, yet it owes much to one man's passion for the past, his curiosity, his global interest.

September 1976 should be the end to this Cinderella story, with nothing left to recite but a happily-ever-after list of Glenbow triumphs. But this is where the hard part begins. The big time has brought big expenses and big responsibilities. A higher profile forces higher standards. The expectations of a growing public are shaped by the great old museums of Europe and the United States. Harvie's gift had to be more than maintained, it had to be interpreted for the community in vital new ways. There were conflicting theories on how to do it and who would pay.

In 1979, as the expanded museum began to settle into its roomy new home, a new Harvie legacy rocked the Glenbow.

His Devonian Foundation presented the institute with an estimated $20 million worth of paintings, sculpture and ethnographic specimens. The range of the new collections was true to the collector: it included three thousand rare books, sixty-three thousand birds, mammals and butterflies, forty-nine hundred original North American illustrations, thirteen hundred pieces of pre-Columbian archaeology and thirty-five horse-drawn vehicles. The gift, probably the most important single contribution to Canadian museum resources in the nation's history, increased the Glenbow's collection by seventy percent and its operational headaches by two hundred percent. The Devonian offered $2 million to the Glenbow, provided the new collections would be made accessible to the public through displays—a small fraction of the ultimate cost of expansion and operation necessitated by the gift. The province agreed to bear the major burden of this escalating sum, and, ever since, the Glenbow Board and administrators have been grappling with the challenge of meeting the terms of the bequest. The job, slowed by the shrinking dollar-value of museum funds in a non-expansionist but inflationary economy, is likely to take years.

It's not surprising that, in the year of the great gift, the Glenbow decided to clarify its major goals: "To provide in Alberta, western Canada's principal museum, international in scope and stature, with a pre-eminent concern with the art, history and development of the western plains and surrounding areas, with a significant but secondary emphasis on the north-west portion of North America." The full story of the West is to be presented "in an international context of human history, art and culture" through exhibits both at the museum and elsewhere, through books, films, television and educational programs for all ages. This typically Calgarian goal has spurred a running debate inside and outside the Glenbow on how to keep the western plains "pre-eminent" in an "international" context. Meanwhile, from that first day in its new home, the Glenbow's money problems went from minor to major.

In retrospect, Duncan Cameron, who took over as director of the Glenbow-Alberta Institute in 1977, sees those first months "after the enthusiasms and flourishes of the September 1976 opening" as a low ebb. And, as he recalls with administrative understatement in his March 1981 annual report: "The tide did not turn quickly."

But it did turn. In 1977 the province bit the bullet and agreed to fund the Glenbow at a high level for four years to help it reach its objectives. In 1982, for instance, the Glenbow operated on a $6.5 million budget, with nearly half paid by the province, plus $900,000 in imputed rent. The city of Calgary supplies more than a million dollars in maintenance and utility services, plus a 1982 fine arts grant of $30,000. Federal government grants, which have doubled in three years, exceed $300,000. Endowment income and private and corporate donations make up the rest.

Some observers still consider the Glenbow underfunded compared to the country's other major museums, but in 1977 the government's participation made long-range planning possible at last. Cameron repaired staff gaps, shored up weak departments and began to upgrade public programs— lectures, exhibitions, music and services throughout the province. He had trained at the Royal Ontario Museum, served as chief of planning of the Ontario Science Centre and in the early seventies was head of the Brooklyn Museum in New York City—all well-endowed institutions with clearly defined cultural and community roles. At the Glenbow, Cameron administered an institution still trying to find its role in a community unused to supporting and savouring the facilities of a top quality museum.

This has changed: attendance almost doubled between 1980 and 1981 (passing the quarter-million mark for the first time) and private and corporate donations are up, too, enabling the museum to boost its ridiculously small acquisition budget to $300,000. That's a long way from the $1.5 million the Glenbow feels it needs, but it is a sign the museum has begun to make its mark.

To ask for big money, a museum first has to do big things. And this the Glenbow has begun to do. It has become very good at the Great Canadian Tightrope Act—excellence on a shoestring. "The Treasures of Ancient Nigeria—a Legacy of 2,000 Years" dazzled just about everyone. It came to the Glenbow in the spring of 1981, accompanied by a series of lectures by renowned experts. Reflecting five major cultures, the show combined esthetic beauty with such an eloquent reflection of man's life cycle, his environmental struggles and his faith that, in the words of critic Nancy Tousley, "it sent the breath of life across the centuries." There was no doubt that this was one vital answer to the problem of prairie pre-eminence in an international context. The show's presence here (its only Canadian venue) plus its exquisite display by the museum gave the Glenbow a certain world stature. Calgarians who boast about being on the international map through oil or the Olympics found this kind of cultural importance heady indeed. Art fanciers, a more specialized breed, relished the Glenbow's next coup: an unusual 1982 show of European surrealists René Magritte, Giorgio de Chirico, Max Ernst and Joan Miró, mounted to tour outside the United States by New York's Museum of Modern Art. Once again, Calgary was the show's only Canadian call.

Such are the splashy activities, the events that mobilize most of the museum staff for months. In between, there is a constant round of changing shows covering art, history and ethnology, compiled either from the Glenbow's permanent collection or on tour from major institutions. And museum watchers note a high level of curatorial care and imaginative display these days—everyone is stretching to meet those high expectations. There are concerts every Sunday in the second floor gallery, film showings at noon and a procession of distinguished lecturers. There are photo-archives and a library of rare historical books and documents; there is a book publishing arm, specializing in regional history; there are accessible resident experts, such as writer and historian Hugh Dempsey and art curator Jeremy Adamson; there is an education and extension department; there are caravans that bring artifacts and lecturers out to schools and Alberta communities; there are docents ready to give you a guided tour.

Drop in and you'll find the Glenbow's Western Canadian essence on the third floor in a series of vivid displays that describe the development of Western Canada, starting with the fur trade, through the explorations of the 1800s, the missionaries, the North West Mounted Police and land settlement. The heritage of the native peoples of North America, particularly those of the Canadian plains and west coast, comes alive through a stunning array of artifacts. In the second floor art gallery, there is a changing panorama of contemporary painting and sculpture reflecting all styles and regions, alongside gems from the Glenbow's permanent collection of thirty-five hundred oils, three thousand sculptures and twenty thousand works on paper. New temporary exhibitions keep coming: old Japanese prints, for example,

Amish quilts, a $30,000 moose-hide Métis coat, Andy Warhol's Marilyn Monroe, Emily Carr's British Columbia, a pioneer photographer's Riel Rebellion.... And a Henry Moore sculpture, Victorian valentines, eighteenth-century African gold weights and cartoons on Western alienation.

In short, this underfunded, overstuffed, endlessly outreaching institute answers with class the same kaleidoscopic curiosity that first animated Eric L. Harvie.

There's a word for it, actually . . . "Museum."

The Insiders'
GLENBOW MUSEUM

The **First Floor** is dominated by the information desk, museum shop and bookstore and your first glimpse of the four-story chandelier, Aurora Borealis, which provides an arresting focal point for the spiraling staircase. The lecture theatre is also on this floor, plus some huge education rooms where herds of school children hear all about everything.

The **Second Floor** is given over to temporary exhibits, an eclectic lot that runs the gamut from argillite to gold weights to photographs to sculpture. These shows are handsomely mounted and — witness the pacesetting Treasures of Ancient Nigeria — have earned the Glenbow an international reputation.

Permanent exhibits start on the **Third Floor**. Emphasis here is on the history of Western Canada, with particularly striking sections on the Riel Rebellion, homesteading life during the Roaring Twenties and Dirty Thirties, petroleum industry exploration and the native peoples of the region.

The **Fourth Floor** has all the military items, everything from samurai suits of armour to European handguns and swords. There is also a mineralogy section . . . and replicas of the Crown Jewels.

The historical library and archives on the **Sixth Floor** are open to the public, but otherwise floors five through eight are devoted to the behind-the-scenes activities that make the public floors possible.

The museum has no cafeteria of its own, but it adjoins the Convention Centre and Four Seasons Hotel facilities, and you can go in and out all day on one admission ticket.

Art Galleries

"17th Avenue is *the* high-density commercial art district, a good place for art fans new to Calgary to begin and a touchstone for us resident art-watchers . . . ."

By Danna Leaman

The 17th Avenue Hub

There is no mistaking the hub of the Calgary art scene. It is lodged as firmly between 7th and 8th streets on 17th Avenue S.W. as are the art hubs of Toronto, Vancouver and Montreal, respectively, in Yorkville, on Granville and on Sherbrooke. At least . . . it is for the present. The rate of redevelopment (the going euphemism for building-bashing) in Calgary being no myth, rumour suggests that there will one day be another "village-style" shopping complex on that stretch of 17th Avenue instead, replacing some of Calgary's oldest buildings (as venerable as 1910) and most established galleries, not to mention the best bagel shop west of Winnipeg.

But for the present, the 800 block of 17th Avenue is *the* high-density commercial art district, a good place for art fans new to Calgary to begin and a touchstone for those of us resident art-watchers who like to maintain a casual sense of visual art in Calgary. At last count, there were thirteen galleries within easy walking distance from one parking spot: five print galleries, six galleries showing original art and one photography gallery. But density alone does not make a hub. (The cappuccino and chocolate chip cookies at Bagels and Buns are an indisputable draw.) Among the galleries in this cluster that show original art, you will find a broad range of different styles, both in the art they show and in the galleries themselves. There is a strong cross section of

Canadian art, much of it by our own regional artists.

The regional artists represented in these galleries include the early painters who died before their work gained the appreciation it enjoys today—impressionists such as W. L. Stevenson and Maxwell Bates and realists such as Nicholas de Grandmaison. There are also artists whose work is perhaps known as well beyond the prairies as here at home—painters of landscapes such as Illingworth Kerr and Dorothy Knowles; a younger generation of prairie impressionists such as Barbara Ballachey and David More; and an increasing number of abstract painters, printmakers and sculptors such as Alexandra Haeseker, Derek Besant and Anne Marie Schmidt-Esler.

Canadian Art Galleries (811 - 17th Avenue S.W.) is the "basic black" of this cluster of galleries—no nonsense, no frills. Nothing at Canadian will distract your attention from the art, including the staff (they're not ignoring you, just leaving you alone). Canadian is one of Calgary's oldest galleries, but its style is fashionably modern and its specialty is contemporary work by painters of the western provinces.

Where Canadian is cool and austere, **Masters Gallery** (815 - 17th Avenue S.W.) has the traditional warmth—and some of the stuffiness—of the old-world gallery. The specialty, as the name suggests, is reliable blue-chip art by Canadian master painters in general and the Group of Seven and their contemporaries in particular. These are found in the office-cum-private salon behind the main gallery, and this arrangement sometimes creates an off-limits aura. But Masters' upstairs gallery is remarkably full of strong landscape and figurative paintings by younger Canadian artists, many of them local.

It is sometimes easy to forget that **Mira Godard Gallery** (854 - 16th Avenue S.W.) is not a public gallery: the favoured work is the sort of bold, contemporary painting that seems too large and ambitious for most private spaces. The staff is never rushed, never distracted, and, like everything else about the gallery, invariably tasteful. The recent arrival of this gallery in Calgary—a western branch of a long-established Toronto gallery—has been a pleasant surprise to Calgarians weary of patronizing easterners who think it their mission to rescue the West from its cowpoke backwardness. There is the expected (and welcome) access to eastern artists, both known and unknown, but there is also a commitment to a growing number of local artists who are therefore getting more national exposure than they might otherwise have.

The avant-garde category of gallery, where we the bourgeoisie are shocked out of our mundane hypocrisies, is firmly filled by **Gallery Moos** (802 – 16th Avenue S.W.). This gallery is also connected to an established Toronto gallery, and it shows a lot of work by well-known national and international artists. The specialties are abstract paintings, drawings and sculpture, but Gallery Moos, too, has begun to show an intriguing range of work by local artists. Best of all, this is the one gallery in town where the staff will happily engage in debate over the nature and utility of "aht."

Agghazy Gallery (519 – 17th Avenue S.W.) is a little beyond easy walking distance from the main gallery cluster, but it is the archetype of the family-style, meat-and-potatoes gallery. The work shown here is nearly all representational, realistic and mostly landscape. There is a good mix of painters from all regions of Canada and absolutely no sense of snobbery. If galleries intimidate you, give Agghazy a try.

Photography-as-art is a fairly fresh concept in Calgary, and the **Centre Eye** (1717 – 7th Street S.W.), located in the one-time ballroom of the Anderson Apartment Building, is a new gallery dedicated entirely to photographs. Since it is a member-run, nonprofit gallery, the work may not often be for sale, but at least (and at last) it's coming out of the darkroom.

Downtown Galleries

The only other place in Calgary where you can visit more than one gallery at a time without driving is downtown. Distance makes the downtown galleries much more difficult to tour as a group, but they do provide some interesting alternatives, both in style and location, to the 17th Avenue hub.

If you've been wondering where the *real* western art is—the grain elevators, the wheat fields, the bucking broncos— **Gainsborough Galleries** (805 – 8th Avenue S.W.) is where you'll find it. This gallery deals unabashedly in straight western realism, although it is also a frequent first gallery for young local artists working in traditional (but not always western) styles.

Kensington Fine Art Gallery (513 - 8th Avenue S.W., downstairs) used to be a lot like Agghazy in style but has recently begun to favour photography over the traditional paintings and is regularly exhibiting collections of photographs by local and international photographers.

In the glass jungle of office buildings, **Gold Design Gallery** (335 - 4th Avenue S.W.) has created self-contained variety by covering a lot of styles simultaneously. This gallery combines something of the elegance of Mira Godard, the range of Masters and the contemporary western-province emphasis of Canadian—and even keeps a classy selection of bucking bronco bronzes.

Around the block from Gold Design, **Canadiana House** (509 - 2nd Street S.W.) is a very traditional gallery that deals almost exclusively in secure investment art—often landscapes—by well-known Canadian artists, some of whom are local, most of whom are deceased.

On the Stephen Avenue Mall, near the Glenbow Museum and above a pinball arcade, are two of the most whimsically wonderful galleries in Calgary. Since exhibition is more important to them than sales, both take the avant-garde style beyond the limit of Gallery Moos. The **James Ulrich Gallery** (118 - 8th Avenue S.E., second floor) is a long, narrow space between pastel pink walls where the art is installed rather than hung. The work displayed here is often that of members of the city's art faculties and other local artists working in bulky and nontraditional media. Above the James Ulrich Gallery is the **Off Centre Centre** (118 - 8th Avenue S.E., third floor), a nonprofit, artist-run gallery that exists by the slim grace of public funding. The work shown here—usually by members of the centre—is even more bizarre and sometimes extends into audio, video and performance art.

Art in Public Places

"Public art is—well, it's like the pickle with the sandwich."

By Elaine Dixson

Public art is—well, it's like the pickle with the sandwich. When it's there, it's often consumed rather absent-mindedly. When it isn't, that unnameable "something" is missing.

Public art dresses up many of Calgary's parks and buildings, and we'd miss it if it suddenly disappeared. It may be a mural or a sculpture, a carving or a painting. It might be in bronze or steel, ceramic or glass, porcelain or wood or even cork. The variety in form, medium and technique is as limitless as the artists' imaginations.

See how many of these pieces you know and recognize from your own travels in the city, and remember that there are a great many more than are listed here. Keep your eyes open for the rest—and enjoy the pickles, please!

The Lions — Centre Street Bridge

James Thomson created the four lions who have kept vigil over the Centre Street Bridge since 1916. Thomson had a sculptured lion on his own porch, and an alderman saw it and thought something similar would be just the thing for the bridge. The concrete lions on Centre Street are modelled after the bronze lions at the base of the Nelson Column in Trafalgar Square, London.

Prince's Island Park

Look for Calgarian Katie Ohe's "Cracked-Pot Fountains."

Ohe's fascination with the shapes of cracked or split pottery inspired her to include cracks in the shapes for these fountains, and so they were named.

A bust of Polish astronomer Copernicus was placed in Prince's Island Park in 1975 by the Polish Community of Calgary, honouring Calgary's centennial year and the five-hundredth anniversary of Copernicus' birth.

You can also see Peter Smith's welded metal sculpture "Bird in Flight," and Enzo Di Palma's metal sculpture trilogy "Prairie Progression."

Sadko and Kabuki — 205 - 5th Avenue S.W.
(Bow Valley Square)

Sorel Etrog's provocative sculpture looks like a group of giant screws and bolts . . . *humanized* screws and bolts, as a bemused passerby once commented. Add to this reaction the work's title—Japanese Sadko ballet dancer (bright red part) and Japanese Kabuki dancer (hard yellow part)—and feel the sculptor's fascination with the interdependence of tool and hand.

Cork Mural — Alberta Wheat Pool Building lobby, 505 - 2nd Street S.W.

Bob Oldrich carved into this mural everything he could think of that symbolized Alberta: the sun, the grain fields, mountains, oil derricks, wheat sheaves and elevators. The unique mural is carved in cork and covers the entire panel. It's every inch Alberta!

The Calgary Zoo

Thanks to John Kanerva, visitors to the zoo can stroll through the domain of the brontosaurus and other prehistoric monsters. A total of fifty-six concrete and wire models are on display, perhaps the most accurate and complete in the world.

The whimsical images of an elephant and giraffe greet you at the entrance to the Large Mammal House, while imaginative plant life adorns the Conservatory-Aviary. Bob Oldrich created the designs for both, and a construction crew reproduced them in concrete.

Look closely in the Conservatory-Aviary for the one-twelfth life-sized bronze entitled "Fisherman," by well-known Alberta artist Cornelius Martens.

Brotherhood of Man — 515 Macleod Trail S.

The group of ten aluminum figures which stands in front of the Calgary Board of Education Building was originally part of the United Kingdom pavilion at Expo '67 in Montreal. The statues were sold to a company that had recently completed two construction projects in Calgary. The company, in a gesture of good will, then presented the figures to the citizens of Calgary.

The Gargoyles — Terrace Gardens, Convention Centre

Lovers of the grotesque, the humourous and the satirical— these are for you! Commissioned by the Southam family, the gargoyles satirize the newspaper business and once graced the old Herald Building. There were sixty gargoyles originally; forty were destroyed during renovations in 1966, causing a public outcry. The remaining twenty were preserved and are now on display in the Terrace Gardens.

The Stephen Avenue Mall — 8th Avenue, between 1st Street S.E. and 3rd Street S.W.

Relax on a bench in the park at 1st Street S.E. with a brightly painted mural as the backdrop. The mural covers the exposed eastern wall of Western Outfitters and is a colourful alternative to brick and mortar.

Or, join in "The Conversation," two cast-bronze businessmen by Bill McElcheran who are talking things over. They can be found near 1st Street S.W. on the mall.

"Inuit Man" by Karoo Ashevak and "Bird of Spring" by Etungat are "heroics," or enlargements, of smaller works.

Aurora Borealis — Foyer, Glenbow Museum

The workmen wore white jeweller's gloves to attach the thousand-plus acrylic prisms to the core of James Houston's four-story creation. It is a focal point at each of the exhibition floors; each set of stairs circles the sculpture which comes alive with subtle light and sound each half hour. The program replicates the drama of the northern lights.

Devonian Gardens

Above street level in the green sanctuary of the Devonian Gardens, some sixteen sculptured and cast works are on view. These anonymous pieces include two fountains, "Maiden and Four Toads" in bronze (circa 1920) and "Boy and

Swan" in lead (circa 1870). Another work, "Garden Seat" (circa 1860), is just that—a cast-iron garden seat in which four connecting seats each represent one of the seasons.

Central Park — 12th Avenue S.W. between 3rd and 4th Streets

The Boer War Memorial was a tribute to the contribution made by the Lord Strathcona Horse in the South African battle. It was acclaimed at the time of its dedication in 1914 as being one of the finest equestrian statues in the world.

At the 3rd Street end of the park stands the World War I Memorial, a gift to the citizens of Calgary from the Colonel Macleod Chapter IODE.

John J. Bowlen Building — 620 - 7th Avenue S.W.

The mural by Ronald Spickett in the lobby of the Bowlen Building measures forty-four feet by eleven and a half feet and depicts life in Alberta using human resources as the theme. Alberta's history, cultural heritage and technological developments are portrayed in the work, done in plastic paint and then varnished to make the mural washable.

Century Gardens — 8th Avenue and 8th Street S.W.

Just a few blocks past the mall on 8th Avenue is a park named Century Gardens, the location of another of Calgary's striking sculptures. "The Alberta Family" by Stanley Bleifeld depicts a contemporary family at play. A graceful, fluid piece!

The Planetarium — 701 - 11th Street S.W.

The Planetarium has several works of art on its premises, two of which are particularly distinctive. Victor Thompson produced ten portraits of famous astronomers by painting with metal oxide on opalescent glass which he then fired in a kiln. The portraits are three feet in diameter and are recessed in the outside wall of the planetarium dome.

Near the main lobby, three finely crafted carved wooden plaques done by Nels Weismose depict astronomers Tycho Brahe, Ole Roemer and Galilei Galileo. Danish-born Weismose came to Calgary and established a fine furniture store which featured hand-crafted pieces. A woodcarver all his life, he spent hundreds of hours on his projects, some of which can be seen elsewhere in Calgary.

Bookstores

"Cities do mature—that's the next phase—and bookhounds develop. That's what's happening now in Calgary . . . ."

By George Parry

I have a rubber band theory about the development of bookstores in Calgary in the last twenty years. In the early sixties, we had two bookstores, owned one each by Evelyn DeMille and Carmen Moore—and in retrospect, they're still considered two of the more nicely run stores in Canada. Apart from that . . . corner stores had a few books, so did the university bookstore and Eaton's and The Bay. That was all.

When I was starting to pay attention to the scene in the mid-sixties, the building boom was starting, *cranus uranus* started appearing—and so did the chain stores, on a rubber band right behind the cranes. It was a Canada-wide phenomenon: W. H. Smith came over from England and hit Toronto first; Classic Bookshops was already strong in Montreal and Coles in Toronto. And then they moved west through Winnipeg, Calgary, Edmonton and Vancouver.

David Fallis and I both opened stores at about the same time—my store, Laughing Rooster, in late 1969 and his, David Fallis Books, in early 1970. That was really something, two more independently owned and operated bookstores, bringing the total to four. It's not that books weren't available—Carmen Moore and Evelyn DeMille were already running two of the more decent bookstores in Canada right here—but we wanted to push back the frontiers a bit. I stressed more political things and books about Indians that got away from the "Noble Savage" approach, while David

Fallis really concentrated on his psychology section. Another store opened up about the same time in east Calgary, but it went bankrupt (government statistics say bookstores are in the top three for bankruptcies).

The chains really boomed in the seventies. By the end of the decade, there were still only a few more independent stores than there had been at the beginning—but there was a total of thirty bookstores in the city. To me, this means there can be a boom, and a big population growth, but the number of real bookhounds doesn't increase at the same rate.

But cities do mature—that's the next phase—and bookhounds develop. That's what's happening now in Calgary, and in just the last few years several more independent bookstores have opened up. If I look around now, I see a selection of books that is as good here as in Edmonton or in the Duthie shops in Vancouver and, in some fields, as good as anything in Canada.

Let's start with an area of real strength—Canadian books, especially Western Canadian ones. Go to **Sandpiper Books** (1414 – 8th Street S.W.), owned by Bertha Hansen and Kerry Longpré, for the newest coffee-table books, bestsellers and a really solid background in established Canadian authors, in both hardcover and paperback. If you want something a bit more historical, go to the **Glenbow Bookstore** (in the Glenbow Museum, 9th Avenue S.W.). Carol Smith, who runs it, worked a good fifteen years in Hamilton and really helped Indian people from the Six Nations Reserve to find the books and historical materials they were after. Anything she doesn't know, she can find out by calling upstairs to Hugh Dempsey, chief curator, in the museum proper.

If you want to search for an out-of-print Canadian book, go the Glenbow Archives for help; if you want to buy it, order it through Robert Stamp's **Heritage Books** (call 243-8232 for an appointment). Stamp also publishes a monthly catalogue of rare and out-of-print Canadiana.

If you're looking for a really international range of fiction, poetry and politics, you can visit back and forth between two stores that seem to fit together like two pieces of a jigsaw puzzle, each filling in the other's gap—**City Limits** (503 – 22nd Avenue S.W.) and **Books-N-Books** (738A – 17th Avenue S.W.). City Limits is a little more political, a little more into alternate-energy fields; Books-N-Books a little stronger in film and drama and maybe some bestsellers.

There's a good choice in children's books. The proprietor of City Limits reads voraciously in the field and carries a lot, so that's a good place to try. Sandpiper has a really strong children's section. And you should certainly visit **Treehouse Books** (Lake Bonavista Shopping Centre) because it is devoted entirely to children's books and is a very fine store.

Close by Treehouse, while we're talking about that part of town, is **Mark My Words** (Willow Park Village), which may well have British and continental fiction titles that you can't find anywhere else in the city. Another good store to know about is **Self Connection** (Northmount Drive and 19th Street N.W.) because it has the city's best selection of self-help books, right across the whole range of areas and concerns. The owner, Rosella Mahoney, also has good professional contacts for special problems.

If you're in the oil patch, or want business books in general, your first stop should be **DeMille Technical Books**—Evelyn DeMille is back in business with a downtown location (918 - 6th Avenue S.W.). If you want a slightly more intellectual or academic approach, go to the **University of Calgary Bookstore**.

Then there are the secondhand bookstores. I think the first bookstore I was ever in in Calgary was **Bob's Books**—he has a last name, but it doesn't matter, he's Bob's Books. He has a really interesting, eclectic selection, and his present location (1026 - 16th Avenue N.W.) reminds you of one of the older bookstores in Berkeley or New York. Go just a little farther north and east to **Golden West Book Store** (2614A - 4th Street N.W.), which maybe has a little bigger selection of magazines and Canadiana than does Bob's Books. **The Calgary Book Store** (1314 - 1st Street S.W.) has very nice subject areas and carries absolutely everything. One day I found twenty different books on Indian subjects there, four or five of them out-of-print.

The interesting thing now is that, as the rubber band snaps around these days, sales in the independent bookstores aren't down that much. Those stores are going to survive. Bookhounds are always in the minority—but they're faithful customers.

Theatre

"Unlike other Canadian cities, Calgary was slow to subsidize the performing arts and very slow to build them a home. Now this catch-up-quick town surpasses most in per capita arts grants and has finally committed itself to a civic culture palace."

By Louise Bresky

If home is where the heart is, Calgary professional theatre has no problems—it's all heart. But in terms of a place to call their own, the city's two major professional companies are still poised between yesterday's sod hut and tomorrow's culture palace.

This is truth, not poetry. **Theatre Calgary** (TC), the city's senior company (though only founded in 1968!), has worked all these seasons in a converted diesel warehouse; **Alberta Theatre Projects** (ATP), which combines commercial shows with a major commitment to Canadian plays, has performed since its 1972 birth in a seventy-year-old, 160-seat log "opera house" in Heritage Park. (A 1980-81 construction project raised the seating to two hundred.)

Like other Canadian cities, Calgary built its theatre tradition on fireside theatricals, little theatre groups and gymnasium drama festivals. Unlike other Canadian cities, it was slow to subsidize the performing arts and very slow to build them a home. Now, this catch-up-quick town surpasses most in per capita arts grants ($1.37 in 1982) and, with massive provincial—as well as federal and corporate—help, has finally committed itself to a civic culture palace. The $74-million-plus Centre for the Performing Arts, scheduled to open in late 1984, has permanent homes in it for both Theatre Calgary and Alberta Theatre Projects.

Meanwhile, **Lunchbox Theatre**, the oldest and healthiest of Canada's surviving noon-hour companies (the other is

Toronto's Solar Stage) has found a rare, rent-free home in a downtown skyscraper; **Areté**, a Calgary-based, nationally touring professional mime troupe, has found a residence, if not a home, as "professional company in residence" at Mount Royal College; **Loose Moose**, an amateur company with plans to go professional, has settled into a former agrimart on the edge of town; and the city's many amateur and pro-am theatre groups continue a desperate chase for space.

Back at the warehouse and the cabin, both Theatre Calgary and Alberta Theatre Projects face an interesting question: will a plush new home blur their distinctive and hard-won images? Each has been shaped by the very challenge of poor facilities, by the need to prove themselves in a practical town. There's nothing like living on the edge to keep those creative juices running. Will success spoil our theatres? It will be a luxury to ask the question . . . tomorrow. At this point, having watched both companies from day one, I find them growing tougher, not softer. The artistic integrity is there, along with a fiscal integrity that has enabled both companies to pull themselves out of debt and salt away surpluses for their big move.

Presiding over Theatre Calgary's rented warehouse (once the home of the now-defunct Allied Arts Centre and now owned by a developer who plans an office tower on the site) is artistic director Rick McNair. A rangy, rumpled Nova Scotian who taught school and coached basketball in Ontario before plunging late into theatre, McNair supervises a flawed but cosy 490-seat theatre and four companies: the mainstage, seven-play series; Midnight Theatre, a five-play, avant-garde package targeted at young adults; and Stage-coach Theatre, two touring troupes which cover small-town Alberta with plays for schools and community, many of which McNair writes himself. All four are going great guns. In his first year at the helm, McNair and his astute business manager Marcia Lane wrote off an inherited deficit and began to push attendance to a record ninety-two percent for the 1981–82 season. He also did what doubters didn't believe possible: he broke TC out of the safe-hit syndrome with plays of excitement and scope, and he gambled on Canadian plays. It paid off. So did his dynamic you-saw-it-here-first policy toward three high-powered Calgary playwrights now getting international notice: John Murrell, Sharon Pollock and W. O. Mitchell. Mitchell's Faustian curling comedy, *The Black Bonspiel of Wullie Macgrimmon*, got a smash production and will likely become a Canadian classic. McNair directed a stunning 1981 revival of Pollock's award-winning *Blood Relations* and, for the 1982 world premiere of Murrell's *Farther West*, nabbed as director that controversial genius and former artistic head of Stratford, Robin Phillips. The fascinating if uneven play got a stunning production, graced by several performers who had worked with Phillips at Stratford, including leading lady Martha Henry. For a change, theatre agents, producers and critics were flying from east to west, and Theatre Calgary had stepped firmly into the leadership role of a senior regional theatre.

The 1982–83 season is a good example of the various theatres' evolving directions and interests. TC lined up a strong year. In addition to the world premiere of Pollack's comedy about rum-running across the U.S.-Canadian border during Prohibition (*Whisky Six*), it included: the North American premiere of *Stage Struck*, a West End suspense comedy; the Canadian premiere of *Mass Appeal*, a Broadway hit about the conflict between a Catholic priest and a young seminarian; Eugene O'Neill's rarely performed drama, *A Moon for the Misbegotten*; Alan Stratton's farce about Mackenzie King, *Rexy!*; and *Let's Get a Divorce*, a nineteenth-century French farce just made for our time.

Up at Alberta Theatre Projects' little log house, artistic director Douglas Riske and administrative director Lucille Wagner declared 1982–83 "a season for celebration of the human spirit." The season could equally be called a celebration of their own extraordinary first decade as a theatre company.

Riske is a native Calgarian who studied theatre at the University of Alberta, the Banff School of Fine Arts and in London, England before coming home to head the Allied Arts Centre Children's Theatre. When the centre folded, Riske and his wife, playwright Paddy Campbell, launched Alberta Theatre Projects as a professional troupe to dramatize local history for school children on contract to the Board of Education. They got permission to use the Canmore Opera House, a tiny log hall moved to Heritage Park from its original mountain-town home, while the park was closed for the winter. The history plays, like Campbell's bright revue stylizing Southern Alberta history in songs and skits, were so popular that ATP began showing them to adults in the evenings.

Over the years, the company added a three-play adult season of Canadian plays to its school productions and began a playwright-in-residence program to encourage local dramatists. Both John Murrell and Sharon Pollock received crucial support in that position: ATP premiered Murrell's *Power and the Blood* and Pollock's *Generations*. Riske's mandate was to produce Canadian plays but, like the wine, not before their time. While Lucille Wagner firmly moved the company from red to black, Riske sneaked a few "foreign" non sequiturs into the increasingly popular adult series, like the wacky musical *Dames at Sea*. Musicals go well in the intimate opera house, despite the postage stamp stage. With composer Bill Skolnik, Campbell wrote *Hoarse Muse* about maverick pioneer editor Bob Edwards; Riske grabbed John Gray's *Billy Bishop Goes to War* before New York did; but ATP's greatest coup was undoubtedly *Tomfoolery*.

Wagner got Canadian rights to this London revue compiled by producer Cameron Mackintosh from the satirical songs of Tom Lehrer; Doug Riske directed the North American premiere, with staging assistance from Geoff Ferris, of the original production. *Tomfoolery*, the classiest show anywhere in Calgary that year, then went on a four-month national tour—a first for ATP. The tour didn't make money but it did gain Riske and Wagner both a reputation and an education. And *Tomfoolery* showed me that a small company can have strong regional roots and still reach out for international excellence.

ATP's 1982–83 season shows that this is indeed their objective: *A Lesson from Aloes*, an apartheid drama by South African Athol Fugard; *Servant of Two Masters*, by eighteenth-century Italian playwright Carlo Goldoni, adapted by Canadian Tom Cone; *Dreaming and Dueling*, by Vancouverite John Lazarus; *Duet for One*, a new English drama about a handicapped violinist and her psychiatrist; *Step/Dance*, a play about Maritime fishing life by Nova Scotian Tom Gallant; and *Bedroom Farce*, a nonthink piece by Alan Ayckbourn.

If a log cabin seems an unlikely place to launch a professional theatre, would you believe a skyscraper? When Lunchbox Theatre first opened its doors in 1975 in the heart of the downtown business district, it was hailed more as an alternative to the daily dash-and-gulp than as an artistic event. At least the plays changed more often than Eaton's windows and the actors were funnier than the boss.

But thanks to the shrewd artistic direction of founder Bartley Bard, a California-born graduate of the University of Texas and Canada's National Theatre School, the noontime novelty developed both staying power and cultural clout. As the office towers around it grew, so did Lunchbox. Hammerson Canada Inc., developers of the four-tower Bow Valley Square, even drew a rent-free space for Lunchbox right into its building plans. Thanks to that rare form of corporate enlightenment, Lunchbox has expanded from one large, temporary office and a hundred folding chairs, through a tiny lobby-level former print shop to its just-refurbished two-hundred-seat mezzanine home between the second and third Bow Valley towers. By the end of the 1981–82 season, Bard had presented seventy plays, a lively blend of condensed classics, contemporary comedy and musical revues, dotted with Canadiana. Attendance hit a high at eighty percent.

Bard attributes his success to three things: "Location, location and location." He is too modest. Sure, it's great to be in the heart of the fastest growing city on the continent, but the real Lunchbox secret is a mixture of quality, variety, energy and surprise. With his wife Margaret, a gifted comic actress and director, Bard has ransacked the English-speaking world for good short plays. And he has come up with some gems: Canadian premieres of Lanford Wilson's Pulitzer Prize-winning *Talley's Folly*, for instance, and the biting anti-Catholic comedy, *Sister Mary Ignatius Explains It All to You* (a 1981 sell-out). Michel Tremblay's scorching vision of God and the devil in *Damnée Manon, Sacrée Sandra* caused a few conservative Calgarians to choke on their pickles, but many more to cheer. The Bards haunt favourite off- and off-off Broadway theatres, hoping to pounce on promising new plays, like James McClure's raunchy *Lone Star* and *Private Wars*. Margaret Bard, after a summer working under Alan Ayckbourn in England, returned with a handful of one-acts by that comic master along with a polished directing technique. Joi Beckett, Lunchbox executive assistant, has adapted Shakespeare and resurrected Carmilla the Vampire. Shaw, Stoppard, Noel Coward, Edith Piaf, Flanders and Swann, Sherlock Holmes and even the wartime musicals of 20th Century Fox have had their merry turn. Even the flops, like *Charlie the Chicken*, have a certain flair, and Bard takes them with an if-you-don't-like-tuna-try-chicken-salad shrug. But flops are not in the majority and Lunchbox is clearly thriving on its self-styled diet of "ham on wry." The line of loyalists with lumpy brown bags starts forming at 11:45 A.M. Bartley Bard is the chap in horn-rimmed glasses making sure everyone gets a seat.

Areté Mime, keeps one foot in Calgary and the other on the road. The road extends around the world: Areté, one of Canada's four professional mime companies, has logged more touring miles than any other theatre group in Canada. Since they formed the troupe in 1976, Randy Birch, Kevin McKendrick and Don Spino have performed to three hundred thousand persons of all ages on four continents, from toney French mime festivals to the Calgary Stampede.

When the Areté trio comes home—to rest, to create new sketches, to teach master classes at Mount Royal College— their Calgary shows are in the don't-miss category. They trained together in classic mime at the Canadian Mime School at Niagara-on-the-Lake but are proud of incorporating all aspects of traditional mime into their repertoire: clowns, masks, dance, acrobatics, *comedia dell'arte*. They are young, energetic, lyrical, farcical and downright funny. As they grow, you can see them extending the definition of theatrical art.

If that definition isn't broad enough, try amateur theatre, university theatre, fringe theatre—the town is teeming with stage alternatives, including that gastro-cultural phenomenon known as dinner theatre.

But the first thing a real fan should do is check out the warehouse and the log cabin. Then, when Theatre Calgary and Alberta Theatre Projects start to light up the new culture palace, you can say you knew them when.

Classical Music

"No one ever came to Calgary for the music."

By Eric Dawson

No one ever came to Calgary for the music. For the Stampede, possibly; for the mountains, certainly. But who would think to find themselves sharing a passion for the music of the great composers with thousands of others similarly inclined in the very heart of cowboy country? It happens every day: in a cab, waiting for the bus, standing in the evitable lineups for a seat in a favourite restaurant, someone will bemoan the lack of things to do in Calgary and be surprised when a stranger apprises them of the wealth of musical activity that crowds the concert and recital halls almost year-round.

There has always been some musical culture in the city. Its relative isolation from the international centres of musical life has never denied it this one aspect of the good life. In the days of the great touring artists, the Grand Theatre in the centre of town (at 1st Street and 6th Avenue S.W.) played host to some of the finest instrumentalists of this century. Memories are short, and no one would now think to mount a plaque on the walls of the Grand—these days divided into two cinemas specializing largely in soft-core porn and kung-fu movies—stating that "Artur Rubinstein played here."

He did, though, and the city has seen any number of his peers pass through. Calgary has feted Rostropovich and the younger Oistrakh, Menuhin and the all-conquering Guarneri Quartet. The story that the agent for that grandest of grand opera divas Leontyne Price once laughed when he was asked if he planned to bring his star to Calgary is probably apocryphal. The money is here, as is the cheering stamping crowd that makes every artist's sweat worthwhile. What could possibly keep them away?

You wonder. The fact is, though, that many of the best artists of the last decade haven't played Calgary's pre-Arts Centre trio of halls—the Jubilee Auditorium, the University Theatre (at the University of Calgary) and the Leacock Theatre (at Mount Royal College). Audiences want to see and hear artists they recognize from recordings. But they don't appear on the roster of the Southern Alberta Opera Association, Calgary's resident troupe, and, with a handful of exceptions, they have not recently been featured with the Calgary Philharmonic Orchestra. With chamber musicians, however, the situation is different: Calgary regularly hears the best. Indeed, competition between Pro Musica and the Chamber Music Society of Calgary is so fierce that one almost expects fist fights to break out every spring when it comes time to see which group will play host to the Beaux Arts Trio the following season. But the grand old ladies of the symphony and opera have no competition, and it is endlessly surprising to see how many young up-and-coming artists and aging never-weres these organizations promote with shameless abandon.

The problem with the Philharmonic for the better part of a decade has been politics. The board disposed of British conductor Maurice Handford in the mid-seventies because he became a nuisance: he insisted on more and better musicians and expected the board to raise money to that end. When he resigned in a gruff move to make his point more strongly, the board happily accepted his withdrawal and with indecent haste began searching for someone more accommodating. In 1977 they thought they had found him in Arpad Joo, a young Hungarian émigré who was then leading The Knoxville [Tennessee] Symphony. Finding him less malleable than they had originally assumed, the top members of the board fired and later rehired him in 1980 in a curious cloak-and-dagger escapade for which the board has earned an international infamy exceeded only by the board of the Stratford Festival. It did nothing for music in Calgary, but it *was* entertainment.

The battles have been so lengthy and so well publicized

that the casual onlooker could be forgiven for thinking that the board preferred infighting to promoting the artistic standards of the orchestra. Every five years or so, Calgary seems due for another round of watching lawyers and oilmen insult each other in the name of art. The whiff of scandal on the French model seems irresistible to them. That it does enormous damage to the orchestra morale each time and makes the business of finding a new conductor when the time comes increasingly difficult (who would work for such employers?) has never deterred the ladies and gentlemen of the board from their mud-slinging rounds.

While the locals brawl, the outside world has occasionally made its views of the Philharmonic known, not generally to the greater glory of the city or its musicians. Conductor Franz-Paul Decker, who led the orchestra on an interim basis between the close of the Handford fracas and the arrival of Joo, never concealed his opinion that the CPO was a decidedly second-rate ensemble. Having said that, he at least worked harder than anyone else to raise the orchestra's standard. But when William Littler of the *Toronto Star* examined the Philharmonic in the middle of Decker's term, he found it still sadly wanting. Rating the ten best Canadian orchestras, Littler placed the Calgary Philharmonic ninth, just ahead of the London, Ontario Symphony.

The humiliation! If Littler returned today, however, he would have to alter his list. Joo made a considerable number of changes in the orchestra personnel in his years as principal conductor and enforced a higher overall performance level. Anyone walking into a Philharmonic concert for the first time today could be guaranteed creditable performances of the nineteenth-century classics. It is not always exciting work, however, which is why the orchestra cannot fill all the seats for the main concerts in the Jubilee Auditorium. But until management realizes this, and does something about it, the CPO will continue to mount ever more florid ad campaigns and still play to half houses.

Oddly enough, the conservatism that occasionally makes an evening with CPO an elaborate way of inducing tedium has made its still-dowdier cousin, the Southern Alberta Opera Association, a box-office hit. Now mounting three grand operas each season and one operetta, the SAOA has survived sopranos towing law suits, attacks from the press and its own lack of imagination to become financially one of the healthiest opera companies in Canada. It is frankly terrified of German opera, shy of star performers and has a sharp distrust (you would guess, after sitting through a production or two) of tenors who can actually sing. Only in Calgary, or in some very obscure Italian town, would you expect to hear the likes of Eugenio Fernandi in a leading role twenty years after his sudden rise and equally rapid fall from favour in the major opera houses. Only in Calgary would a soprano with no voice be allowed to speak her way through an opera because she would not give up her part. Firing her, so the argument went, might have landed the SAOA in yet another court battle such as ensued when they fired a Donna Anna before the opening of *Don Giovanni* the year before.

Through it all, the audience has been quiet and attentive. No one in Calgary ever boos, which is a shame. When the romantic lead in Puccini's *La Bohème* turns out to be shorter than some of the on-stage furniture, looks ready for the singers' retirement home and sings, as musicians say of colleagues who don't come up to snuff, like a pig, he still receives a polite response. No one has ever publicly complained that while Edmonton hears Joan Sutherland, Marilyn Horne and Beverly Sills, Calgary is treated to a horde of Canadian singers that only the CBC could love and Italian has-beens. Were it not for the eternal vigour of the great operas, the best of which are proof against bad singing, there would be reason for despair.

So far, the record seems rather dim. The Philharmonic you attend out of duty unless, like one prominent composer who insists on anonymity, you announce that you have done your duty and are taking a year off. You go to the opera because it is there, hoping that at least once you will be able to rush out into the night after a performance truly excited by what you have seen.

But when you come to talk about individuals rather than organizations, about the intimacy of chamber music and about solo artists rather than music on the grand scale, the picture changes. The riches that have accrued alongside the province's oil wealth have included the wealth that only a collection of significant talent can guarantee. From all parts of the world they have come, composers from the United States, pianists from the Soviet Union and New Zealand, violinists from such diverse locales as Prague and the American South.

They come and go with startling rapidity, following the call of opportunity elsewhere. But each makes his or her mark while here. Joo's record as the conductor of the Philharmonic is mixed, but as a pianist and, briefly, as a chamber music series leader, he gave performances that had the rare quality capable of making an audience leap to its feet at the end of a program cheering. His concertmaster, Cenek Vrba, quite apart from his work with the symphony, proved to be a fine musician in the chamber repertoire, forming a partnership with pianist Marilyn Engle that earned them both national plaudits for their work in classical and contemporary music. Gloria Saarinen has earned a special place in the development of musical life in the city, not only as a solo and chamber artist but as an entrepreneur. While others whine, she has worked tirelessly to bring more and better musicians into the city's concert halls. When there was next to no music, she helped establish the Carillon series. When that seemed insufficient, she set up the Astral series as well (both of them under the aegis of the Chamber Music Society of Calgary). She was a driving force behind the Chinook Piano Festival and Competition, which started in 1982, and she has plans for a full spring music festival to be set in motion before the decade is out. The festival will showcase local, international-calibre musicians and offer the full range of vocal and instrumental fields—opera, chamber music and symphony concerts.

Saarinen's enterprise, and the work of countless others, has ensured that while living thousands of miles from a major artistic centre, Calgarians can still hear some of the best. When I warily moved to Calgary in the mid-seventies, I expected the worst. Instead, I can share with every other musically inclined Calgarian the talents of the likes of the Borodin String Quartet, Steven Staryk, Canadian baritone Allan Monk and others of the same rank. With more than 160 concerts to choose from each season, there is music enough, and of a quality ranging from acceptable to beyond peer, for everyone.

Popular Music

"Calgary's taste lies somewhere between its country and western roots and the raunch of rock and roll."

By Paul Hepher

What's that sound?

It's the musical sound of money, fuelled by Calgary's oil boom and a rapidly growing city's appetite for live music. So far the boom has produced no superstars, though there are the famous like Ian Tyson, the nearly famous like Diamond Joe White and the successful like jazzman Eric Friedenberg.

Then there are the musicians who work each week in this city's taverns, lounges and restaurants. They mirror trends, styles and songs started elsewhere and brought here by the radio airwaves, and for them music has become as much taking care of business as it is an individual expression. They will likely never be famous but they, too, shape the Calgary music scene.

Cut off geographically and politically from Eastern Canada, Calgary music has developed in its own haphazard fashion. It has been strongly shaped by two apparently irrelevant factors: the city's economic climate and the provincial government's efforts to fit liquor legislation to a rapidly changing population.

In thirty short years Calgary has gone from a cattle-based economy to an oil-based one. Its population has more than tripled in that time and now Calgary's taste lies somewhere between its country and western roots and the raunch of rock and roll. The largest generation in history—the baby boom children—are now filling Calgary clubs and bars.

Raised on rock and roll and prosperity, they are quick to spend on entertainment, and they are the largest consumers of recorded and live music.

The annual peak for consumption comes each year at the Calgary Stampede, the ten-day party that is also the jackpot for local musicians. Bands start work at 8:00 A.M. at Stampede breakfasts, hustle off to noon-hour or afternoon stints at barbecues and shopping mall square dances and then settle into an evening of providing dance music for a horde of fun-seeking Stampeders in lounges, taverns and restaurants.

For the duration, country music is king and Stampede Week is Calgary at its best and worst. Hundreds of patrons line up for hours to pay inflated prices at huge downtown cabarets, and bands play from noon until 2:00 A.M., churning out a stream of country and rock favourites.

In such an atmosphere—where familiarity counts for more than originality—it is hardly surprising that Calgary has produced no superstars. Yet Calgary has become a comfortable and profitable home for musicians who aim to give the folks what they want. Many find a niche, usually a circuit of clubs where they are popular, and stay in it until fashion or other circumstances forces them to change. (This makes naming names a risky proposition, but here are a few examples that may still apply by the time you read this. Try **Kensington's Delicafé** for folk music; **Lucifer's** and the **Beacon Motor Inn** for rock; **Pardon My Garden** for soft rock; and the **Horned Toad Lounge** in the Delta Bow Valley Inn for jazz.)

But audience taste is only one factor. The current state of the provincial government's liquor laws has a great deal to do with what kind of music is offered where. The government, you see, decides where liquor can be served, when it can be served and the permissible size of any club, lounge or tavern. These rulings, in turn, go a long way toward determining what type of entertainment will be heard.

The smaller an establishment, the fewer musicians it will hire. So small lounges usually feature singles, duos and trios playing anything from country to blues to middle-of-the-road pop, while taverns are now the home of rock and roll. However, there are a number of larger lounges in the downtown area which function as nightclubs (although they are licensed as lounges) and feature full bands. As the number of lounges grows so does the trend toward specialization in music, not to mention decor.

But wherever you go, you will be constantly reminded of the commercial nature of Calgary's live music scene.

The challenge facing local musicians is a formidable one. If they wish to support themselves through music, they must deal with the ever-present reality of keeping the customer satisfied. On the other hand, if they wish to pursue recording careers and chase their personal brass rings, they must show originality. Some (like the country-rock band **Earthshine** or country singer **Danny Mack**) have tried to resolve this dilemma by outflanking it. They play for pay when they can and present a commercial face to the public. On tape and record they try to promote their original songs.

Recording is the way out of a lifetime of club work and, though it is a long-shot bet, many are making it. At least they now have somewhere to record: the opening in the last few years of Smooth Rock Studios and Thunder Road Studios has brought world-class recording facilities to town. So far, though, recording is still a matter of hopes and promises, not breakthroughs. Calgary has yet to outgrow its national reputation as a cowtown, and Calgary bands have yet to come up with an identifiable sound.

Perhaps the closest thing to a Calgary sound is the short-grass music of country singer **Diamond Joe White**, whose two albums combine elements of country, folk and rock. The albums have brought success in Western Canada, but their impact has been obscured by the urban cowboy explosion. Still, White's shortgrass music captures the prairie style without losing the lyricism more common to folk music.

Folk music deserves some emphasis. It is Calgary folksingers who are leading the way in originality, perhaps because their milieu is less directly affected by commercial pressures. Calgary is home to a number of folk clubs (such as the **Calgary Folk Club** and the **Nickleodeon Folk Club**) that have fostered folk and acoustic music by promoting regular concerts every two or three weeks during the winter season. These clubs have kept acoustic music alive in the city and have provided a stage for locals who wish to play music without making the full-time commitment. In addition, the folk clubs now provide an inexpensive and congenial alternative to bars and lounges.

There is another, and growing, alternative—the party circuit. Businesses, athletic clubs and all sorts of social organizations are now hiring frankly commercial groups to play at their social gatherings. The resulting scene is organized, professional and most profitable for the bands involved. Indeed, many musicians who have spent ten or twenty years in the rock and roll world now find the party-band circuit to their liking. They've put aside their dreams of fame and have settled instead for a good-time atmosphere and a brand of money they hadn't seen before.

In truth, Calgary rock and rollers should be considered an endangered species. Hundreds, perhaps thousands, of groups have come and gone since the early sixties, victims of the grind of trying to make a living in a crowded, competitive setting. Those who have tried to pursue recording careers have found themselves at a disadvantage compared to eastern Canadian groups or those from the more supportive Vancouver scene. The few that have tried to crack the Canadian record market have run into insurmountable financial problems.

Still, there is no shortage of rock music in Calgary and local groups (like **The Unusuals**) are busier than ever as they, too, live the dual life of club performer and aspiring recording artist.

As Calgary grows larger and its media grow more aware of its homegrown music, the ground is being prepared for the sprouting of local starts. Calgary clubs and restaurants have provided a financial base for Calgary musicians and a place for them to learn their trade. But the enormous difficulty in rising above the club level has stymied and stifled the great majority, and Calgary has yet to produce a star who will define the sound of Calgary music.

The mainstream still leads back into the local pond—yet it is most likely that mainstream country, rock or country rock will give Calgary its first national hit. It's been a long, long time since **The Stampeders** conquered Toronto (remember "Sweet City Woman"?) but Calgary recording studios are full of musicians aiming to duplicate that success.

Movie Houses for Movie Buffs

"In the province with Canada's highest per capita movie attendance, the time was right: film rep was a hit from the first night."

By Louise Bresky

Film buffs have a happy home-away-from-home at the **Plaza**—a cosy, four-hundred-seat theatre at 1133 Kensington Road N.W., which houses Calgary's first (and only) repertory cinema.

Plaza Rep was founded in 1977 by Flemming Nielsen and Don Carroll, two movie nuts who discovered thousands of others just as nutty. It offers a rich diet of golden oldies, cult favourites, director retrospectives, festival art and foreign classics—as many as nine different movies a week, two shows every night with midnighters Fridays and Saturdays.

The theatre itself is an antique jewel of the colourful Louise Crossing district near the Bow River. It is a former livery stable-turned-automobile garage which served as a commercial movie house for forty years before being purchased by Mike Brar to show Chinese and Hindi films on weekends. Nielsen and Carroll, TV production partners, subleased it for an office and, finding the theatre free Tuesday through Friday, decided to take a wild flyer into art and nostalgia. In the province with Canada's highest per capita movie attendance, the time was right. Film rep was a hit from the first night, when fans flocked to see *The Maltese Falcon* and Humphrey Bogart became the Plaza's patron saint.

Now Nielsen, who runs Plaza Rep assisted by theatre manager Glenn Fletcher, hustles to meet the eclectic tastes of a growing public, including twenty-five hundred members who for ten dollars a year enjoy special discounts and members-only showings of rare films.

Cinemascope, Nielsen's newsy film-fan quarterly, tempts the addict with a précis of every film, plus meaty articles on everything from Bergman and Fassbinder to Hitchcock and cult horror. *Casablanca*, which plays the Plaza two or three times a year, remains the runaway favourite (followed by two of Peter Sellers' best, *The Party* and *Dr. Strangelove*), but Nielsen is forever ready to premiere foreign prize-winners or to stage film "events" like the 1982 Good Friday showing of Louis Malle's six-hour documentary, *Phantom India*. Buffs can even buy an art-deco T-shirt reminding you to "Catch a flick at the Plaza."

Filling further film gaps for the insatiable cinemaniac is the twenty-five-year-old **Calgary Film Society**, which offers both a classic and a main international series.

The **University of Calgary**, through various academic and continuing education departments, presents several "movies to think by" discussion series.

The **Planetarium's Pleiades Theatre** has won sell-out audiences for its continuing Sunday afternoon Family Film Classics series, featuring such grand old goodies as *Little Women*, *Wuthering Heights*, *I Remember Mama* and *How Green Was My Valley*.

Documentary film buffs gather Tuesday noons and Sunday evenings at 7:30 at the **National Film Board Theatre** in the Federal Building for showings drawn from the renowned NFB collection. The **Glenbow Museum** also schedules regular noon film showings, with an emphasis on both art and Western Canadiana.

The Outdoors

Urban Walks

"'A walk through Inglewood will quickly dispel the notion that there was nothing in Calgary before 1950,' says Robert Stamp."

By Gillian Steward

Calgary is not as much a walker's city as some places, but if you look beyond the obvious and listen to some of the people who have spent time exploring Calgary on foot, you'll find some revealing, not to mention pleasurable, strolls to be taken. One of the reasons Calgarians go out on foot with some trepidation is the constant construction upheaval that leaves streets blocked off and sidewalks ripped up. And despite the introduction of the Light Rapid Transit (LRT), which has seen thousands of people leave their cars at home and opt for the train, Calgary is still a city where the car is king. While the one-way streets and expansive thoroughfares may have facilitated the use of the car, they don't always make it easy for pedestrians to get around. Downtown, many pedestrians have been taken off the streets altogether by the Plus-15 system, a network of enclosed, above ground bridges that connect parking lots, office buildings, shopping centres, indoor parks and restaurants. The system is still the source of controversy as some critics believe street level would be more interesting if there were more retail stores and pedestrians. But there's no question that in the winter the popularity of Plus-15 soars because pedestrians don't have to brave subzero temperatures to get from one building to another.

Still, while walking may be difficult in some parts of the city, other parts are designed specifically with walkers in mind. The **Stephen Avenue Mall** (still popularly known as the 8th Avenue Mall), for example, is completely closed off to vehicular traffic and stretches for five blocks right through the centre of the downtown core. Another area designed with pedestrians in mind is the city's **river pathway system**. It is by far the most popular spot for Calgarians who like to take a daily constitutional. The pathways wend their way through parks (see "Park Profiles" by Peggy Weddell for a detailed account), exclusive residential areas, historic sites and some of Calgary's quainter, aging districts, so it's not difficult to get all the flavours that are Calgary on a river pathway walk.

Art consultant Joanne Brook's favourite river walk is along **the south side of the Bow near Point McKay** in the city's northwest. One of the most interesting aspects of this walk is that it is just around the corner from the glistening glass and steel towers of downtown yet, heading east from **Edworthy Park**, the trees are thick and the wildlife abundant (sometimes a deer or two can be seen since they follow the river in from the foothills). The steep slopes also contain one of the few Douglas fir stands in southern Alberta. It's a fairly rough climb, but worth it. Further along, closer to the river, you'll come to **Lowrey Gardens**, about four kilometres from the city centre. The word "Gardens" is used loosely here, because the flowers are wildflowers that grow whenever and wherever they want—crocuses and buffalo beans in the spring; daisies and Indian Paintbrush later in the summer; Saskatoon berries and rose hips in the fall for the picking. Sometimes it's hard to believe that fragile wild flowers could exist so near the hard, sophisticated edges of downtown. But it also reminds Calgarians just how quickly their city has changed from a big prairie town to a vibrant city.

If you're more of a city slicker and don't fancy arduous wilderness walks, the river pathway still has something for you. Pick up **the path along the Elbow at Stanley Park** in the city's southwest and follow it west until you get to **Sandy Beach** (about a forty-five-minute walk): you'll be touring some of Calgary's most exclusive neighbourhoods. Here the river wends its way through the gracious lawns and expansive patios of some of Calgary's most prestigious properties. And although you won't be able to walk beside the river for a good part of the way, you can walk beside it in the park and look across to the private gardens that roll down to the river's edge. (If you *really* want a good riverside view of those properties, take Calgary's favourite aquatic version of an urban walk: grab an inner tube, inflatable mattress or rubber dinghy and float down the Elbow from just below the Glenmore Reservoir to just above the Stampede grounds.)

The path hugs the river for about four blocks beyond Stanley Park (on Elbow Drive it even ducks down under the bridge). At this point, continue along **Riverdale Avenue**. Unlike much of Calgary, the streets and houses here have a more settled, permanent look. Some of them are very large and have been extensively renovated, but others are small and quite charming. The farther down Riverdale you go, the more you begin to feel as though you are in a little-known and travelled pocket of Calgary, one that has become a true retreat for the people who live here. At the end of Riverdale the land becomes wild again for a short distance and then breaks into Sandy Beach, a small picnic and fishing area. Although the steep, grassy banks on the river's edge may make you feel as though you've come to the end of Calgary altogether, right on top of the bluffs on the east side of the river is **Britannia**, which in the fifties was Calgary's newest and most prestigious suburb. It is still a prestigious neighbourhood (Jack Gallagher of Dome Petroleum lives there) but is no longer a suburb and is firmly ensconced in the inner city.

Another river walk will take you through one of Calgary's oldest neighbourhoods—**Inglewood**, located on the south side of the Bow River just a few blocks from the city centre (and a stone's throw from **Fort Calgary**). The properties here aren't as grand as some of those in the previous tour, but they make up for it with quaint architecture and historical significance. The Victorian gingerbread and expansive porches on many of the houses on or near the river attest to the fact that these are some of Calgary's original homes. **St. Monica's Church** and the sandstone **Alexandra Centre** are also evidence that this was an important neighbourhood in Calgary's early days. One of the most outstanding houses is that owned by alderman and architect Jack Long on New Street. It was built by the first commanding officer of the North West Mounted Police in Calgary and is now a historic site. Not surprisingly, the river area in Inglewood is one of the favourite walks of Calgary historian and author Robert Stamp. "A walk through Inglewood will quickly dispel the idea that there was nothing in Calgary before 1950," he says.

Another favourite of Stamp's and other Calgary history

buffs is the **Stephen Avenue Mall** walking tour, starting at the corner of the Macleod Trail and 8th Avenue. Named after Lord George Mount Stephen, the first president of the CPR, the mall is like an open history book that stretches back one hundred years. Since this has always been Calgary's most prestigious shopping and commercial street, the buildings lining the mall include some of the city's best architecture. The decaying, old building right on the corner is the Burns Building. While it may look as through it is about to be demolished, it is actually awaiting renovation. Built by cattle baron Pat Burns in 1913, the Burns Building is a fine example of the Edwardian commercial style then popular in Western Canada. The mosaic tile floor, brass fittings, curving marble stairs and column facings made Burns' ground floor meat market and mezzanine for managers one of Calgary's most elegant commercial interiors.

On the end of the same block is the Calgary Public Building, which was built by the federal government in 1930. As is typical of government architecture of the time, it was designed by a Department of Public Works architect in Ottawa and combined modern structural methods with oversized and chunky classical ornamentation, such as the elaborate Ionic order entrance. Since the building is so theatrical, it is indeed fitting that it will provide the lobby and administration space for the Calgary Centre for the Performing Arts, which is being constructed right next door.

Right across the street from the Public Building is the Dominion Bank Building, built in 1911. Although banks always like to look imposing and stable, this three-story terra-cotta building, designed by Winnipeg architect G. W. Northwood, displays some of the most elaborate classical ornamentation to be seen on the mall. The bank's exuberant beaux arts style introduced a new architectural sophistication to Calgary, a marked contrast to the earlier sandstone buildings. Farther along the mall the buildings are smaller and narrower and somewhat friendlier. The Doll Block (116 – 8th Avenue S.E.) was named after L. H. Doll who opened a jewellery story there in 1907. Although its lower floors have been radically altered over the years, its third-story leaded-glass bay window, surrounded by two round arches and scalloping, is delightful.

The Bay at the corner of 1st Street S.W. and 8th Avenue is a Calgary landmark and the busiest corner in the city. Built in 1913 (and expanded in 1929 and 1957), its design was inspired by Selfridge's department store in London, England, and resembles other Bay stores in Vancouver and Victoria. The unique arcade, which adds such a note of graciousness to downtown Calgary, was built during the expansion of 1929.

Another building on the mall that uses the graceful style and feel of terra-cotta is the Hollinsworth Building (301 – 8th Avenue S.W.) built in 1914. The building's architects, Brown and Vallance of Montreal, had strong architectural links with Paris, London and the United States, and the international influence shows. The terra-cotta is wrapped carefully around the building's northeast corner, drawing attention to its main entrance. The pressed metal panels between the windows lend height and a feeling of trim elegance to this noble building. It is presently being renovated and will become part of the Bankers Hall complex soon to be constructed next to it.

Calgary's Heritage Planner, Penina Coopersmith, recommends the Stephen Avenue Mall tour for anyone interested in delving into Calgary's roots. But, as a keen observer of cities in general, Coopersmith also recommends a couple of other walks in Calgary, walks that can put you in touch with the Calgary of today. One of the most interesting places to walk, says Coopersmith, is **17th Avenue** between 4th Street and 14th Street S.W. "It's a very visual part of the city. The shop displays are always changing, there are lots of art galleries, new buildings, old buildings and always lots of people." Architect and writer Stephanie White emphatically agrees: "It's an occupational hazard for a designer to be a real sucker for style, whether it be high-tech or English country house, and the most stylish part of the city right now that fits into a reasonable walk is 17th Avenue S.W." The stores along this popular strolling area range from antiques to delicatessens to hand-crafted furniture outlets, and they are all small, often owner-operated. Some of them are also quite pricey. But if it's just people-watching you're after, 17th Avenue S.W. has plenty of space for that, too. There are lots of restaurants, coffee shops, pizza parlours and bakeries. You'll even pass Western Canada High School, which White affectionately (really) dubs, "a good example of Early Depression school architecture."

Louise Crossing is another area of Calgary that's great for sightseeing and people-watching. Located on the north side of the 10th Street bridge, this commercial arena is full of tiny shops, old bookstores, small cafés and cosy houses. It is also the home of the Plaza theatre, which features old and foreign movies and never seems to be without a lineup that wends its way out onto the sidewalk. Louise Crossing has a small village feel to it and fits comfortably into the larger community of Hillhurst-Sunnyside. The whole area is a lively mixture of entrepreneurs, university students, old hippies and trendy townhouse. Like Inglewood, it's one of Calgary's oldest communities. But as a walk through either its residential or commercial streets will attest, there's still lots of life in this old lady, too.

Park Profiles

"There is even a provincial park within Calgary city limits . . . ."

By Peggy Weddell

Colonel James McLeod named Calgary after another Calgary on the Isle of Mull, commenting that the Gaelic word means "clear running water." There is now some learned linguistic dispute about whether or not this is the most accurate translation, but none at all about the aptness of his choice: in 1875, when this city was still a fort, the most dominant feature of the immediate landscape was the Bow and Elbow rivers, running swiftly with cold, crystal clear water and joining right at the point where the fort was built.

The fort is still there (uncovered and given proper commemoration as a centennial project some years back) and the most dominant feature of Calgary today is still those two famous rivers.

Not surprisingly, most of Calgary's park areas can be found along the riverbanks. Calgary's riverbank pathway system is a maze of trails for walking or biking that connects park to park. Thanks to this network, you can explore both sides of the Bow and Elbow and all around the Glenmore Reservoir. (See "Urban Walks" by Gillian Steward for examples of how the city and the pathways interact.)

The river park closest to the city centre is **Prince's Island**, which sits right in the middle of the Bow River and can be reached from 4th Street S.W. or Memorial Drive N.W. It's a great place to escape the concrete jungle, if only for an hour. Stop at a cafeteria on your way and pick up a lunch to go or buy a hot dog and soft drink at the park's snack bar. If you feel the need for exercise, there's a Trim Track (a Swedish system of jogging paths and exercise stations) in the park. If you are more concerned about rest and relaxation or just sunbathing, there are landscaped gardens as well as secluded spots in the midst of wild brush and trees.

Prince's Island is also an excellent starting point for a trek along the river pathways. On the north side of the Bow, the pathway extends about ten kilometres west to the Silver Springs subdivision. Six kilometres into the walk, you'll come to **Shouldice Park** which features extensive athletic fields as well as picnic facilities. Further along is **Bowness Park** which is an excellent place to spend an entire day. You can rent boats and paddle around the quiet lagoon. There are barbecue pits, picnic shelters and a snack bar.

There is also a large and imaginative playground and amusement park. Because Bowness Park is a fairly lengthy walk from the downtown core, you might want to get there by car or city transit.

If you start out from downtown on the south side of the Bow River heading west, you'll be travelling a more secluded route. **Lowrey Gardens**, about four kilometres from the city centre, is a completely natural area full of colourful birds and wild riverbank plants and flowers. Fishermen are often lucky at this spot and catch a wily trout in the swift-moving waters of the Bow.

Above and beyond Lowrey Gardens is **Shaganappi Slopes** where you can find the intriguing Douglas Fir Trail. It's a fairly rough trek that climbs and winds its way among one of the few remaining Douglas fir stands in southern Alberta.

At the west end of the trail is **Edworthy Park**, a natural riverbank area bequeathed to the city by the Edworthy family. The park is divided by the Canadian Pacific tracks— which somehow add to rather than detract from its atmosphere. As you wave to the conductor when the "Canadian" roars past, all your childhood excitement about trains is suddenly revived. There are numerous picnic tables and shelters in this park, attracting large groups of picnickers by day and campfire songsters at night. The children's area (protecting them from the tracks by a tall fence) has all kinds of contraptions for climbing and crawling, slipping and sliding.

When you've had enough of monkeying around the

parks . . . head east from Prince's Island Park to **St. George's Island**, the home of the **Calgary Zoo**, and see some *real* monkeys in action (along with a great many other exotic and local animals). The zoo offers picnic facilities, an indoor garden (great for the rotten days) and thousands of brilliant flowers (in the summer) stretching to every corner of the grounds. The Conservatory has flowers all year round and the Christmas show is especially beautiful. Indeed, winter is as good a time to visit the zoo as summer — the zoo has wisely made a point of seeking out varieties of species that are well adapted to our tough winter climate.

East of the zoo is the **Pearce Estate**, a partially landscaped park which is another excellent fishing spot as well. The **Sam Livingstone Fish Hatchery** is also here, and staff members are usually more than willing to take a few minutes to give a tour.

Still heading east, the **Inglewood Bird Sanctuary** (pedestrians only) is a riverbank haven for native and migratory birds. Lecture tours are available. Plan to make this one a spring or fall tour when the birds are on the move.

While the Bow River is swift, deep and dangerous, the Elbow is a lazy, meandering stream that wanders through the city's older residential districts on the south side. Its river pathway begins at historic Fort Calgary, extends all the way to the **Glenmore Reservoir** and follows a twenty-kilometre loop around the man-made lake. There are many delightful parks along the way.

First is **Stampede Park**, which is forever bustling with activity. Year-round events include the harness and thoroughbred racing, big-time wrestling matches, agriculture shows, flea markets and exhibitions of all kinds. And of course there are the "Ten days that shake the West," when the riverbanks become the temporary home of several Indian tribes, annual special guests of the Calgary Stampede.

Next is **Lindsay Park** with its brand new olympic aquatic centre; farther along is **Woods Park**, a quiet, groomed, contemplative kind of place.

As the river jogs west, we come to **Stanley Park**, one of the larger city parks, complete with an outdoor swimming pool, beach area (yes, people do wade and frolic in the river) and tennis courts.

Glenmore Park and Reservoir is the city's largest parkland area, and the Elbow River pathway stretches all the way around the reservoir. Along the way you'll see sailboats, canoes and the big SS *Moyie* paddle steamer as it lumbers across the lake with another load of tourists and visitors to **Heritage Park**.

You could easily spend an entire day delving into Alberta's history at Heritage Park, located within Glenmore Park. The reconstructed pioneer village contains many original pre-1914 structures from around the province. These include the Canmore Opera House, the Wainwright Hotel and the Munson Bank of Montreal. On the lake's west side is **Weaselhead Flats**, Calgary's largest natural park. This area, bordered by the Sarcee Indian reservation, has a fantastic view of the Rocky Mountains to the west. This is a favourite biking and cross-country skiing spot but has no picnic sites or shelters.

There is even a provincial park within Calgary city limits—the twenty-eight-hundred-acre **Fish Creek Park** on the southeastern outskirts of the city. It features numerous walking and hiking trails, a man-made lake and picnic facilities. This was once the real working ranch of Senator Patrick Burns, one of the "Big Four" founders of the Calgary Exhibition and Stampede. The park is open year-round and offers interpretive tours and activities daily. The visitor centre even has film presentations.

Confederation Park, located in the northwest section of the city, is one of the few parks not found near a river (but it has Nose Creek . . .). This is a large, landscaped park which includes picnic sites, tennis courts and a public golf course. The Christmas light display at Confederation Park has become a special yearly tradition ever since the park was dedicated to Canada's centennial.

Don't miss Calgary's *indoor* park! The **Devonian Gardens**, in Toronto Dominion Square downtown, is a two and a half-acre glassed-in park, landscaped with more than fifteen thousand trees and plants. In addition, you'll find a skating rink (pool in the summer) and an amphitheatre which has on-going free concerts and happenings, all sponsored by the city.

Calgary honours the soldiers of World Wars I and II with the Cenotaph in **Central Park** across from the Colonel Belcher Hospital on 12th Avenue S.W. Every blade of grass seems to receive individual attention in this horticultural haven. Lots of flowers.

Possibly Calgary's most beautiful park is the **Burns Memorial Gardens** (named after the aforementioned senator) along 10th Street N.W. These gardens are very British, with orderly formal rows of plants, flowers and rockery. How appropriate that **Riley Park** (immediately south) should feature tranquil cricket matches all summer long!

Organized Sports

"Calgarians really are sports and recreation crazy.
Winter and summer, we watch and we participate."

By Alister Thomas

Happily for the sports-mad, Calgary is finally growing out
of its "Stampeders . . . period" image. Baseball and hockey—
not to mention the upcoming 1988 Winter Olympics—have
joined football to make Calgary a place to watch sports of all
kinds. There's a boom in amateur sports as well. The people
at Sport Alberta (which exists to promote and develop
amateur sports in the province) point to the zooming
popularity of soccer, softball and hockey in particular when
they talk about the strain on our sports facilities, but, as they
well know, *everything* is popular these days—badminton,
lawn bowling, orienteering, ringette, soaring, table tennis,
horseshoe pitching and yoga. And more.

In other words, the myth is reality: Calgarians really are
sports and recreation crazy. Winter and summer, we watch
and we participate.

Winter

One sport conspicuously absent from the list of attractions is
professional soccer. Well, Vancouver entrepreneur Nelson
Skalbania would be the first to point out, with some pique in
his voice, that we can't blame *him*. He did, after all,
bequeath Calgary not one, but two, professional sports
teams—all in the misguided hope of making money. In 1980,
he brought us an NHL franchise, the Flames, from Atlanta,
Georgia. He followed that up in 1981 with the Boomers of

the North American Soccer League.

The Flames cost Skalbania $16 million (U.S.) and the only place he had to house them was the Stampede Corral, which seats 6,492 and stands another 1,400. With numbers like that, the seat price had to be high. Fortunately, with numbers like that, management can convincingly argue that every seat in the building is a good one. Patrons bought the argument, and the seats—at twenty-one dollars each. (The seats remained unchanged, but the price jumped to twenty-five dollars for the 1982–83 season.)

After the first year of operation in Calgary, Skalbania decided to sell the team to six Calgary businessmen (Doc Seaman, B. J. Seaman, Ralph Scurfield, Harley Hotchkiss, Norman Green and Normie Kwong). Though the Flames finished their first year on ice here on a high note by being the last Canadian team to be eliminated in the playoffs (by the Minnesota North Stars in the semifinals), they plummeted in the 1981–82 season and lost to the Vancouver Canucks in the first round. They also, along the way, managed to lose $2 million. The 17,400-seat capacity of their new home, the Olympic Saddledome, can turn them into money-makers but it can't guarantee any improvement in their dismal playoff record. In seven of their first eight postseason activities, they never got past the preliminary round.

(Oh well—at least the Flames are in the same division as the Edmonton Oilers. That means we get to watch the magic of Wayne Gretzky more often than other hockey zealots.)

Uninspired as it is, the Flames' record looks good next to the Boomers'—the Flames are still here, after all. Skalbania lost $1.5 million in one year on the soccer club, thanks to the double-whammy of fan apathy and pricey player acquisitions. The club, for example, had to pay striker Franz Gerber's European team $150,000 just for the right to acquire him, and then his multi-thousand-dollar contract had to be paid as well.

In the end, however, it was an act of God that terminated the Boomers' stay in Calgary. The team couldn't play on home turf during its 1981 playoff series against Fort Lauderdale because the Billy Graham Crusade had been booked into McMahon Stadium long before the Boomers could know they would be in the playoffs. It was the final blow: the Boomers lost the series . . . and their home in the city of Calgary.

Where Billy Graham was bad news for the Boomers, Calgary's host role for the 1988 Winter Olympics is nothing but good news for the Flames. By summer 1982, despite construction strikes and controversy over its name, the 17,400-seat $84-million-plus coliseum, the Olympic Saddledome, was rising from the ground, aiming for its target completion date of spring 1983. Since it is also the new home of the Canadian Olympic hockey team, it is designed for both an NHL-sized ice surface and, when needed, the larger Olympic dimensions. How? Easy, once you think of it: the first two rows of seats can be removed and the boards moved back whenever the larger ice surface is required.

The Saddledome's ice surface is just as suitable for international figure-skating meets, which means the competitors at last have Calgary on their list of stops—stars the likes of Brian Pockar (a hometown boy, three-time Canadian champion and, in 1982, number three in the world).

The 1988 Olympic Games are bringing other new facilities to the Calgary area as well. They, like the events they will house, will be outside the city. Cross-country skiing and the biathalon will take place near Bragg Creek, a half-hour drive from Calgary; ski jumping, bobsledding and slalom and downhill skiing will be held in mountain locations. A new ski resort is to be built for the skiing events, which means—once the two-week Olympics are over—another recreational ski area for local skiers. The general Olympic legacy will be world-class facilities that will allow future Olympic teams (and anybody else) to practise here at home, instead of going overseas.

It's not as if we have no recreational ski areas now, of course: the rest of Canada comes here to ski Lake Louise (the site of a World Cup Downhill race in 1983), Sunshine Village and Mount Norquay, all situated in Banff National Park. There are other ski resorts closer to Calgary, including Fortress Mountain in Kananaskis Country, Paskapoo on the Calgary city limits, and a brand new hill in Bragg Creek. The hill, eleven years in the making, has an elevation of 1,529 metres with a 195-metre vertical drop. No, it doesn't rival the mountain resorts, but it is on a par with, say, Collingwood in southern Ontario.

Let us at least mention that the winter sport of suitcase racing began here in Calgary. In April 1980, the Samsonite people invited media types to Fortress Mountain, issued them open suitcases and crash helmets, and sent them spinning down the mountain. Then they did it all over again in 1981, at Paskapoo. Calgary's six best racers that year (yes! I was one of them!) flew to Toronto for national championships—and exposure on CTV's *Wide World of Sports*. The excitement was obviously too much for someone because the event was not held in 1982. However, there are encouraging rumours about 1983 . . . .

One other winter sport that attracts a lot of attention is curling. There are bonspiels throughout the season, and some of Canada's best men and women curlers are from Calgary.

Summer

Contrary to popular myth, Calgary is not perpetual winter— even if, over the years, snow has been recorded every month of the year. We also have summer. Therefore, we also have summer sports, ranging from the tried-and-true to some pretty exotic (or unexpected) newcomers.

Let's start with the tried-and-true. In contrast to the newly arrived Flames, already-gone Boomers and not-yet baseball team (of which more anon), we have the long-established football Stampeders. There is an economic contrast as well: the Stamps, like other members of the western conference of the CFL (but unlike teams in the eastern conference), are community-owned and cannot show a profit. However, they usually show a surplus of points at the end of their games. Still, despite their generally winning ways, the Stamps have to contend with the four-time Grey Cup winners, the Edmonton Eskimos. Occasionally, the Stamps come up big and actually beat their northern rivals, but when it comes to life and death situations the Eskimos prevail. In the period 1946–1981, the Eskimos have won the coveted forty-eight dollar Grey Cup eight times, and the Stamps only twice (1948 and 1971). However, as head coach Jack Gotta has been known to say, "This is a rebounding year," and here in Next Year Country, patient Stampeder fans keep waiting.

Where soccer failed, the promoters of triple-A baseball hope their sport will succeed. At the moment, Calgary pro baseball consists of "The Baby Expos"—Calgary Expos, for purists—the Pioneer League child of parent Montreal. If all goes well, however, Calgary's Foothills Park (with its $800,000 facelift, including five thousand more seats) may soon be the site of the next best thing to the majors, triple-A ball. That could mean that Calgary would compete against the Edmonton Trappers, Vancouver Canadians, Spokane Indians, Portland Beavers and the Tacoma A's in the northern division.

Rodeo seems synonymous with Calgary, yet fans (and riders) had to suffer through an acrimonious dispute with management that kept professional cowboys away from the Calgary Stampede for three years. The two sides finally came to terms in 1982, which means that once again the chuckwagon, saddle broncs, bareback riding, bull riding and steer wrestling events are the best to be found anywhere in the world.

Other horses, other events: the Stampede grounds also house Calgary's racetrack. Each year sees more patrons and more money wagered. What economic slowdown? What recession? In 1982, 4,529 people flocked to the opening day of harness racing and wagered $567,174—up $50,000 from the 1981 start. Harness racing brackets the thoroughbred season, by the way, running from April to August and again from November to January, while the thoroughbreds run from August to November.

Other thoroughbreds can be found at Spruce Meadows, a horse-lover's dream just south of the city. It is owned by Ron Southern, president of Atco Ltd., who built it to help his daughters learn how to ride. Along the way it has grown into a facility appropriate for world-class meets, and so Spruce Meadows now hosts The National (North American competition) each June: the Junior Horse Show (for riders under eighteen) each July; and The Masters (show-jumping) each September with competing teams from France, Germany, The Netherlands, the United States, Great Britain and Canada. It is not unusual to have fifteen thousand spectators a day at the four-day Masters event.

We don't only watch events in summer, we participate as well. Once again, the common refrain is lack of facilities. Take golfing, for example. There are exactly nineteen courses within the city limits (that's public *and* private), so, as a result, courses within a forty-five-minute drive of town—Turner Valley, High River, Carstairs and Canmore—have all expanded to eighteen holes. In this instance, the grass is definitely greener on the other side.

You may not want to be that energetic. You may just want

something pretty to look at on a warm summer day. If so, wander down to the Glenmore Reservoir and gaze at the beautifully coloured sailboats, or go to Chestermere Lake and marvel at the windsurfers, or make your way to Riley Park and watch some cricket (two pitches, two games simultaneously, Saturdays and Sundays, all season long). Then again, you may feel like watching a brutal, physical contact game. Take heart, there is a busy rugby season under way at Kingsland Athletic Park!

A few relatively exotic sports have taken a grip on the city: hot-air ballooning, hang-gliding, parachuting and building homemade aircraft (Calgary is second only to Los Angeles in the number of plane builders in North America). What have they in common? Flying. Our generally good weather, sunshine (in fact, Calgary leads Canada in the number of sunny days per year), wide open spaces, good winds and the frontier's love of a challenge all combine to make flying by any method a delightful pastime both for those who do and for those who would rather just watch, thanks.

All right, you expected wind-related sports. Did you expect to learn that Calgary can host prestigious sailing competitions? Despite the arid prairie all around, we have the Glenmore Reservoir (in the city) and Chestermere Lake (just east of Calgary), both of them just big enough to attract top-notch sailors. They attract championship meets as well. The 1981 North American Tasar Championships were held at Chestermere, and Calgary is to host the third Western Canada Summer Games, starting 31 July 1983 and going into August.

The Summer Games, which will draw about twenty-four hundred athletes from the four western provinces and two territories for twenty-three Olympic events, guarantee even more improvements in local sports facilities. A new multi-million-dollar aquatic centre and fieldhouse near Stampede Park will handle swimming, diving, gymnastics and basketball; the $1.4 million boathouse at Glenmore Reservoir will be headquarters for canoeing, rowing and sailing; the Calgary Velodrome will be site for the cycling events (its high-banked speedway, built in 1975, is one of only five in Canada); and improvements at Foothills Park allow for soccer and track and field events.

Where to Run

"The Douglas Fir Trail is a great conditioner, an undespoiled jewel of wilderness in the midst of suburbia, and it hurts like hell."

By C. D. Evans, Q.C.

Long distance runners are lonely because they are boring. Calgary is full of both bores and runners. I belong to both groups, I am well equipped to comment upon the running locales of Calgary and the local hazards, both natural and unnatural, to be expected when in full flight.

For the long distance runner, there are no parks of any decent size in Cowtown, and few parks of any distinction. Most of them are at the terminus of, or merely traversed during, a good run. The one exception (again from the selfish point of view of the runner) is **Prince's Island**, a quasi-acceptable archipelago dead north on 4th Street S.W., off the coast of the Eau Claire condo-ed development for the with-it [sic] types. What distinguishes the island is a definite red shale track, 0.9 miles in circumference (I absolutely refuse to go metric); two water fountains and toilet facilities (sometimes); regular—almost devoted—city maintenance, sometimes even to the point of clearing the track in the winter; and a merciful tendency on the part of frequenting proles to congregate and cluster in their simian tribes on the centre lawns. The track, therefore, is relatively free of detritus.

Since a mile loop is no challenge to a serious runner, Prince's Island attracts certain of the lower-class "jogger" species, especially at high noon on our rare temperate days. It is a great place to meet, however, as a starting point for a long run or to do strides and intervals.

From Prince's Island, on both the south and north sides of the Bow River, one can run the riverbank on the same red shale pathways almost the year-round, in both west and east directions. On the north side heading west, one can follow the riverbank trails past **Edworthy Park** all the way to the Shouldice Bridge in Bowness, and from thence link right up to the famous "B and G" (of which more anon). Heading east, one can attain the zoo (or, in spring thaw, ooz) and provide an exhausted lunch for one of its captive carnivores.

The runner is warned that the north-side path deteriorates from time to time to a wide asphalt trail, thus providing an opportunity for the dread bicyclists to run over one at great speeds. Calgary cyclists are notorious for failing to warn of an approach, passing on the side you least expect, and being generally rude and boorish. It is great fun for them to knock down a runner. It is even greater fun for a runner to knock a cyclist from his steed and throw him and it into the river.

The south banks of the Bow are more primitive and concomitantly more private. The south river trails can become impassable in a severe winter. Over nine or so months of the year, however, heading west from Prince's Island on the south side, one can run all the way to Edworthy Park, spending the last stretch of a mile or so on a unique ankle-wrenching tie track courtesy of the CPR. The runner can instead leave the red shale at the 24th Street overpass (Crowchild Trail) and then literally leave Calgary as well via a little-known and little-used path of punishment called the Douglas Fir Trail. This trail transports and trans-figures the athlete on a river of pain that goes up, down, and swoops and plunges and grinds up steep steppes and across rickety bridges, all the way to Edworthy (south side), across the southern promontory of that park (toilet, fountain) to a steep climb up a utility clearing, and down, back to Edworthy, joyous collapse, and the unpleasant prospect of doing the Douglas Fir back to Crowchild.

The Douglas Fir is a great conditioner, an undespoiled jewel of wildness in the midst of suburbia, and it hurts like hell.

Downtown to Edworthy and return is about ten miles. Note again that you can avoid the Douglas Fir and do the whole thing on the flat along the river.

East from Prince's Island on the south side of the Bow, you can go hard all the way to the **Inglewood Bird Sanctuary**, and now beyond it on a trail that is being constantly extended to meet—eventually—Fish Creek Park (so they say). In the meantime, the voyage to the present end of that trail, including a mile turn about the Sanctuary isthmus itself, is a good thirteen miles. Oh, exquisite pain.

The Bird Sanctuary trail, from New Street to the south of quaintly decayed 9th Avenue S.E., is a runner's delight. Few bicycles can invade this haunt, as there are treacherous stands of gravel and crumbly shale that will put many a speed rider to an early cropper. The Sanctuary itself is truly a holy place. One crosses a wooden footbridge over a lagoon shared by trout, muskrat, wildfowl and purple pollution from the stink plant up-river. On the lawn of a brick mansion overlooking the lagoon, rabbits and ducks literally frolic together: the bunnies think they are ducks and vice versa. Canada geese march about in imperious squadrons, hissing and—yes—running at the ankles for a nasty nip. Those tough birds have a great sense of territory.

The Sanctuary has a wood-chip path, ideal for a hike or lope. It is the highlight of any run, coming at the spiritual and physical turnaround. It abounds with wild birds of all species, rabbits and a perennial deer family—plus one dread interloper indigenous to these hallowed precincts, the Calgary birdwatcher (*Boobus Calgarianis*), armed cap-à-pie with hip waders, rain gear, field glasses, city guides to nature, cameras and all mod cons. The cries of the woodlark are frequently interrupted by the exchange of useless information among these earnest granola-gropers, as they argue vociferously over whether they are viewing a red-breasted mudwallower or a flute-snooted sandpiper. Exciting stuff.

Given all this splendour, how thoughtful of the federal transport mavens to designate the main jet run into Calgary airport right over the startled feathered heads of the real winged creatures. Only in Calgary.

On the way east toward New Street, just past the boring Fort Calgary reconstruction (an invention of perfervid local revisionists), one comes upon the historic (not really) confluence of the Bow and the Elbow rivers. This is the Morton's Fork of the runner, to match his Morton's foot, as he can here decide to eschew the Sanctuary in favour of the fork up the Elbow and thus skirt the grounds of the overrated Calgary Stoopede, the Largest Open Air Insane Asylum in the World. But if the runner perseveres past the racetrack and the LRT station, he can follow the Elbow River to **Stanley Park** (which is always polluted by barbecue parties, tennis players and thousands of horrible children), swing through posh riverbank development to Sandy Beach Park (with neither beach nor sand in evidence) and up a nasty hill to 14A Street and plunge along the narrow strip of Ravine Park to the verboten precincts of Mount Royal. There the runner is halted and turned back, as the rich have erected toll booths to stop the invasion of common folk.

Time now for the aforementioned **B and G** ("Blood and Guts")—a delightful, fairly gruelling run west to Bowness Park from the University of Calgary. In the old days, when you and I were young, Maggie, no hand of man defiled the challenging dirt trails that crisscrossed the northwest Calgary cliffs overlooking the Bow as it streams in from the mountains. Then a lunatic with a macadamizing machine wrought havoc, widening the trails, paving them, and inviting bikers, strolling families with large uncontrolled dogs, mothers with prams, and all manner of opprobrious interlopers to this once-pristine hinterland.

One can still stick to the old trails for the run. The neophyte should be at the parking lot west of the University of Calgary residences just before 10:00 A.M. on Saturdays and Sundays. The Calgary Roadrunners will take you in tow for the round trip to Bowness Park (thirteen miles or so). At 85th Avenue, just on the edge of the park, the masochist can put a few more miles in the bank by taking the Ghost Dam road which gives the sensation of running on the far side of the moon. In the winter, the Roadrunners leave from the same spot at the same time, but take a convoluted route through dreary northern suburbs. One has to keep up, or one is left to wander in circles like the Lost Tribe and, eventually, to perish of the cold and exposure. Spring clean-up funeral rites are held yearly for stragglers.

A favourite place for a long hard session of fartlek is the **Glenmore Reservoir**. Start at the vulgar wooden "H" at the west end of Heritage (82nd) Avenue S.W., the entrance to Heritage Park (sort of a latter-day poor man's Valhalla, where the spirits of the dead brave pioneers are taken by Calgary's version of the Valkyrie, the goody-two-shoes Young Canadians of the Calgary Stoopede). Follow the trail around the reservoir and mercifully away from the bogus fort and choochoo train, which leads you past the Yacht Club into the thickly wooded Weaselhead Flats, then up a stinky hill to Glenmore Park and about the park for three or more miles. Turn around and go back the same way: sixteen to seventeen miles total, perhaps, and a tough distance workout for each Saturday.

Glenmore and the Weaz are overrun around high noon on warm days with every type of running hazard, natural and unnatural: shin splints and other self-inflicted wounds, falling into the reservoir, packs of dogs or children, speeding bicycle riders who swoop on and by without warning, rabid Brownies, the full catastrophe. Parental guidance is advised.

My final recommendation hops us back to the north side of Prince's Island, to Memorial Drive (presumably the movie set for *Death Race 2000*), and the Calgary Curling Club. The only reason for mentioning this last edifice of the plebes is the long pull behind it up to **Crescent Road**, which is great hill training. On the way up, one can run ten times up and down a wicked set of wooden stairs, if one is mad enough. Running Crescent Road in the winter gives you a view of the downtown core that is almost breathtaking. It looks, in a winter setting, evocative of Camelot without hormones, which is better than it looks from any other angle. In the summer, on a clear day, from the vantage point of Crescent Road, one can look up the winding sparkling Bow to the very Mountains of the Earth. Ohhh and ahhh.

I have alluded to the unnatural hazards of bicycle riders and perambulating matrons. Be on the alert, also, for the following:

- Dopes running with cassette players on or about their conks. That which was once blissfully empty, like the belfry of the sunken cathedral, is now filled with hysterical sound. Characteristically erratic behaviour is noted in these people. They often run into runners, poles, parked cars and themselves.

- Proles and scroats: Cowtown abounds in Cro-Magnon bipeds of revolting aspect, mouthing monkey-gabble. They are quick to harass runners, crying "Left, ri, lef', ri." And "Faster, faster," from slack, cigarette-filled mouths. Subtlety is wasted on these creatures. I have found "Shut up, fatty!" to the women with their hair in curlers, or a choice obscenity to the males to be the most effective control. They can never move fast enough to catch a runner, and one can insult them with impunity.

- "Running families:" No more horrible and off-putting sight in God's ordered universe may be visited upon the runner. If you encounter one of these, do mankind a favour and do them dirt. Oh, the horror, the horror.

There are a number of track clubs in Calgary, full of hysterical, competitive and neurotic teenagers driven to excesses of achievement. They turn up at a lot of races and take a lot of honours, but stay clear of grizzled old distance runners.

The largest running club is the **Calgary Roadrunners** (clever name, that), which has been going since 1066 and tends to dominate the local running scene. One is welcome to join for a modest membership fee; it has a newsletter, and in its ranks are a lot of experienced and decent members full of information about races, shoes and injuries. As well as peopling the Saturday and Sunday runs already mentioned, the club has a fanatical subgroup that meets at an early hour on Saturdays and runs about two hundred miles in two hours. Their dead are left by the side of the road.

However, the most famous and exclusive running club in Calgary is the Plastic Ono Track, founded by Bill Bizzlewarple, President for Life. POT's once flourishing membership of twenty-five to thirty top runners has been cut down to seven pulpy-hooved nags, including one senior (a linguist), one hermit (Canmore branch), the terrible Groarke triplet clones who look like identical Long John Silvers, a master (me), Tully Bascom from *The Mouse That Roared*, and a female person of pulchritudinous aspect. POT world headquarters is upstairs over the Grand Theatre, for those who are interested. A few ancient Roadrunners are allowed to speak to POT members on high feast days and after the Calgary Marathon only.

The reader now knows all there is to know of running in Calgary. Be of good cheer: after ten miles, one can almost forget one is here.

Water, Rock and Concrete Sports

"Some of the sports we enjoy most are slightly unusual . . . ."

By Cayt McGuire

Calgary is the place to get involved with, stay involved with, sports. Acquire a skill, refine a skill, but don't just sit back and watch—not here, not in the city where participaction is a way of life instead of a slogan brought to you by Nanny Ottawa. Some of the ones we enjoy most are slightly unusual—but they take maximum advantage of the geography both in and around our city.

Bouldering (and Buildering)

Until the mid-sixties when John Gill, a professor of mathematics at the University of Colorado, perfected the one-arm, one-finger pull-up, bouldering was not really considered a sport at all; it was just a means of practising for the real mountain ascent. Today's avid boulderers refer to it as an art form requiring more skill, discipline and creativity than Alpine climbing. Calgary enthusiasts can enjoy the sport on any number of erratics (rocks left behind by glaciers) in the immediate area.

Okotoks Rock, sitting in a field south and west of Okotoks, has free access since the government claimed it as a historic site. From Simons Valley Drive northwest of the city, there is access to **Split Rock** (just below the old Circle 8 Speedway); **Crater Rock** is about a mile farther north again.

There are sandstone bluffs at **Bearspaw Dam** that are almost eighteen metres high, base to top. Ropes are recommended here, for a route this high requires the commitment of an Alpine climb.

But not all climbs are out there in the wild. Some are indoors—there is a climbing wall in the basement of the Physical Education building at the **University of Calgary** with routes to challenge the best of climbers. Technically, only those with student cards should use the facilities . . . but it is not unknown for other members of the local climbing community to go up there and strut their stuff. (If playing fast-and-loose with regulations isn't your style, you can always go climb on the outside wall of the building instead.)

There's also a climbing wall at **Mount Royal College**, but they like you to use lots of equipment and rope off. The staff will also insist on checking out your climbing ability before they let you on the wall.

If you're staying downtown and have no access to transportation, you might like to try the urban equivalent of bouldering—buildering. At the base of the Calgary Tower is a stacked stone wall that's good for edge work. You'll find a friction climb between the towers of Bow Valley Square, and the park behind the courthouse has a number of mantels. In the alley between 5th and 6th avenues S.W., from 6th to 8th streets, are a couple of office buildings with crack climbs and an off-width chimney.

The best time of day to go buildering is in the early evening or on a Sunday afternoon when the downtown core is devoid of foot traffic. During busier hours, you may attract a crowd, and the local police are not likely to approve. If a police officer does happen upon you during a quiet time he will probably only ask what on earth you're doing. Give him a polite answer and he will leave you alone to continue. Security guards are another story: they're extremely territorial (as they are paid to be) and will order you off their wall if they see you. Your only option in this instance is to move quietly on to the next building on your route.

If the thought of going bouldering, or buildering, appeals to you but you don't have appropriate boots, the **Calgary Hostel Shop** will rent you a pair from their outlet at 1414 Kensington Road N.W. between 9:30 A.M. and 5:00 P.M. on weekdays. You can buy the rest of the equipment there as well, or from **Mountain Equipment Co-op** (131 – 12th Avenue S.E.).

144

Paddling

The Calgary area has a number of lakes and rivers suited to any type of paddling that might interest you. There's lots of room for flatwater on **Ghost Lake**, recreational on the **Red Deer River** toward Drumheller, and whitewater on the **Bow River** between Ghost Dam and Cochrane. Travel Alberta puts out an Alberta canoeing map showing routes on different rivers, but if you want more extensive information, pick up the whole set of **Alberta River Guides and Maps**. They'll tell you everything from stopping points and what kind of fish swim the area to how deep and cold the rivers run. This set of waterproof books and maps is available from the Queen's Printer in room 601 of the John J. Bowlen Building (630 – 7th Avenue S.W.).

Canoes for recreational use can be rented from **R.W.H. Recreational** (723 – 53rd Avenue S.W.) and the rental fee includes life-jackets, paddles, and sponges for the edges of the canoe so you can tie it directly to the roof of your car, plus a little friendly advice from Bob Herron on the area you're planning to paddle in. If you have a large group of canoeists, Bob can also rent you a trailer that carries four to six canoes at once. There are other places to try as well: **Sports Chek** (37th Avenue and 37th Street S.W.); **Prairie n' Peak** (223 – 10th Street N.W.); **Ideal Rentals** (202 – 17th Avenue S.W.); and **Econo Rent** (2323 – 32nd Avenue N.E.).

Local paddling clubs include the **Bearspaw Canoe Club** (289-9781), the **Bow Waters Canoe Club** (235-3818), the **Calgary Canoe Club** (242-3388) and the **Calgary Whitewater Club** (233-8713). The people at any one of these clubs will be happy to let you know if they have any planned outings going on that you might be able to join.

If kayaking interests you, but you've never even held a paddle before, Al and Marian Scheaffer operate a school made especially for you. From June through September they provide weekend students with equipment, food and a campsite. You will have the opportunity to try out, not just the sport of kayaking, but different kinds of equipment as well—a good idea before you invest in your own. To find out more information and make a reservation, call Al or Marian at 678-4102 in Canmore or 638-2490 in Sundre.

If you're already an accomplished paddler of kayaks or decked canoes, you might want to get in touch with the **Alberta Whitewater Association**. The purpose of the AWA is to administer competitions and courses that develop paddlers progressively from beginners to leaders in kayaking and canoeing on, of course, whitewater. The AWA man to talk to in Calgary is Jeff Grutz at 283-7499. He'll be able to tell you of any clinics worth attending or competitions to watch in the near future. He'll also be able to put you in touch with other paddlers who get together informally for paddling practice.

Rafting

Calgary's proximity to the mountains affords our city a number of close, outdoor amenities, not the least of which is fast-flowing rivers for exciting whitewater rafting. Just west of the city, you can launch a raft at the **Ghost Dam** and ride the rapids down to Cochrane, a distance of about ten kilometres.

The **Red Deer River**, west of Sundre, is fast and deep. There's not too much danger of rocks but there are often great holes that a raft can get caught in, causing it to go round and round until it flips over. To avoid such hazards, use a raft with a motor or at least a tiller. When rafting unknown whitewater, take the time to walk the bank along the rapids before you run them. Pick a course, memorize it, and then follow it.

If you're after something a bit easier going, get on the same river east of Red Deer. By this time, the river has stretched out over the prairies, widened, and settled into a regular, smooth flow. No surprises, except the scenery. As the Red Deer River flows into the Drumheller area, the landscape quickly changes from lush farmland to arid desert. Giant Hoodoos loom up from the river's edge as it winds its way between them. You're now in **Dinosaur Park**, taking in a view that motorists have to walk miles to see, leaving their cars at the entrance to the park.

To rent a raft, talk to Bob Herron at **R.W.H. Recreational** (723 – 53rd Avenue S.W.). He has rafts to accommodate two to eight people with or without motor and tiller. The raft rental fee includes paddles and life-jackets.

Don't forget that right here in town we have the gentle little **Elbow River**. Rent a two-man raft for the day, launch it below Glenmore Dam and spend the afternoon soaking up the rays as you drift lazily down to Stampede Park.

If professionally organized river trips are more your style, there's **Kootenay River Runners** in the Jasper and Panorama areas. For schedules and reservations, call them at (604) 347-9210 in Edgewater, British Columbia. They supply transportation arrangements, life-jackets, rain gear and waterproof bags for your personal gear for an afternoon, a day or overnight. The meals they serve, including mid-morning coffee and pastries followed by a deli-style lunch, have earned them the reputation of wilderness gourmets.

Windsurfing

Want to try the latest rage in water sports? It's windsurfing. During the summer months **The Windsurfing Shop** (135 – 16th Avenue N.W.) offers lessons on **Chestermere Lake**, just east of the city. They use a graduated method of teaching not unlike GLM in skiing. You will start with a ground school in rigging, and then you'll learn the basics on a board simulator—a windsurfer mounted to a pivot on dry land. This way you have the instructor right beside you for coaching, and you don't get nearly as tired as you would if you were actually falling into the water every time you made a mistake. From the simulator you move to a small stable board on the water, with one instructor to every three students. All this happens in one afternoon and by the end you should have a good head start in handling your own board.

If you don't plan to buy a windsurfer but do want to pursue your interest and rent boards, The Windsurfing Shop recommends you take another afternoon of lessons. They'll use the time to coach you on the use of a big board so that, when renting, you won't have to waste time getting used to the larger size and reduced stability of the rental equipment.

A second shop co-operates with Windsurfing in offering these lessons—**The Sail and Surf Centre** (1321 – 1st Street S.W.). It, too, has equipment, clothing, information and boundless enthusiasm to offer.

Once you know what you're doing with a windsurfer, it's obviously time to go out and sail the local lakes. In spite of Calgary's location at the edge of a flat and fairly dry prairie, there are a surprising number of lakes within just a few hours' drive of the downtown core.

The closest is Chestermere Lake, which is just beyond the city limits going east on Highway 1. If you drive west past Cochrane on the 1A for about forty minutes, you'll come upon Ghost Dam which holds back (what else?) **Ghost Lake**.

With the unpredictable winds swirling down from and between the surrounding foothills, the Ghost is one of the more challenging lakes for windsurfers and sailors alike.

North of Calgary are **Gull Lake** and **Sylvan Lake**, both near Red Deer. These lakes are ideal for the beginner as they cover large areas of sandy shoal where the water is only waist deep. Not having to tread water every time you fall from your board can save a lot of energy for the actual sailing once you get the hang of it.

East of town are **McGreggor Lake** and **Eagle Lake** near Strathmore. These, being man-made lakes on the flat prairie, are not particularly protected by trees or hills. However uninspired this sounds for the family picnic, it's a perfect situation for windsurfers. The wind is strong and steady, since it sweeps across those vast prairies without any interruption by irregular land forms.

If you've seen much of the city you will have noticed that Glenmore Dam plays host to all manner of sailors and paddlers on warm summer days. Calgary residents get their drinking water from that reservoir and swimming has always been forbidden. Unfortunately, windsurfers fall in the water a lot, thereby presenting the same sanitation threat as swimmers, so they are not allowed to sail on the dam.

More information on local lakes is available from any **Tourist Information Stop** or from the **Travel Alberta** office on the fifth floor of 999 – 8th Street S.W.

Alpine Skiing

"It's expensive, it's exhilarating and it is definitely the thing to talk about in the office on Monday morning."

By Peggy Weddell

To love Calgary in the winter means, for the most part, to love skiing. It's expensive, it's exhilarating and it is definitely the thing to talk about in the office on Monday morning. There is no other city in Canada with as many world-class ski resorts right at its doorstep and, although all are nestled among the vertebrae of the spiny Rocky Mountains, each has a personality and flavour all its own.

The legendary **Mount Norquay** is perhaps the most thrilling of the park areas. Just getting there is part of the thrill. Rising above the town of Banff, it is reached by a five-kilometre road that winds up the mountain—no wonder skiers frequently take advantage of the various viewpoints along the way to stop and enjoy or photograph the beautiful scenery.

Mount Norquay has the lowest lift capacity of the Banff areas, but what it lacks in lifts it makes up for in stature. Two particularly famous ski runs should not be missed by any skier worth his slats: **Lone Pine** and the **North American**. The Lone Pine, a challenging expert slope, is ranked among the top ten in North America for its length and steepness. Because of these slopes you will find a higher ratio of expert skiers at Mount Norquay than at the other resorts. You will also find an older crowd (especially for the spring skiing) who have remained loyal to Banff's original ski area.

These expert runs are complemented by twelve more runs on Norquay's lower reaches. Since they are shorter and gentler, they are well suited to beginner and intermediate skiers.

On weekends and holidays a shuttle-bus service allows skiers to continue down the North American to the **Widow Maker** route (or via the easier **Prune Picker** run) right to the **Timberline Hotel** on the valley floor.

The Bavarian-style dining room in the Timberline welcomes skiers and is a great spot to stop for a relaxing lunch before heading back up to the lifts via the bus. The lounge is another good place for a refreshing mid-ski break or après-ski.

Skiers and spectators alike can watch the experts negotiating their way down the famed Lone Pine mogul field during one of the many regularly scheduled world-class (Freestyle and Alpine) competitions throughout the year.

One of the most romantic spots in Banff for a glass of wine and lunch is the **Cliff House** at the top of the Norquay Chair. From a sensational vantage-point overlooking **Mount Rundle** and the **Bow Valley**, skiers can dine in style.

Sunshine Village, a twenty-minute drive west of Banff, gets more snow than any of the other areas. Belying its name, the area's average annual snowfall is an amazing 1012 centimetres (400 inches). Sunshine therefore enjoys the longest season of all the resorts, stretching well into the spring—when it really *is* sunny every day.

Until the new gondola opened, Sunshine attracted a younger crowd and all the school kids (it seemed), as they were usually patient enough to endure the long waits and dreary bus rides up the winding road. Sunshine's image changed dramatically with the introduction of a gondola that whisks skiers of every age into the village. It can handle eighteen hundred people an hour, and the twenty-minute ride gives everyone a chance to sit back in roomy comfort and enjoy the scenery along the way.

With a 180-bed hotel right on the mountain, a huge day lodge, and several eating and drinking establishments, Sunshine is the only complete resort in the parks in terms of on-hill facilities (that is, the only place where you can jump out of bed, have breakfast and ski to the lifts). Sunshine's location, right at tree line along the Continental Divide, offers sheltered runs on the lower slopes and wide open treeless skiing in the bowls and on the upper reaches. A ski week spent at Sunshine will seemingly put you thousands of miles away from the city hassles because it truly is a world of its own.

If Banff is a feast for skiers, then **Lake Louise** is the gourmet smorgasbord. Headlining itself as Canada's largest ski area, Lake Louise does have runs of every description and level of challenge. The snow-laden **Boomerang** runs on the back of the Summit are a haven for the powder-hound while the meticulously groomed **Wiwaxy** run on Whitehorn attracts skiers looking for the perfect pitch and conditions on which to carve a turn.

The area is immense—almost seventeen square miles encompassing three distinct mountain faces. Getting around the area in one day is an accomplishment. A total of eight lifts and three day lodges interlink over thirty designated runs (plus unmarked tree skiing).

Almost everyone (with good reason) likes Lake Louise so it is also the most crowded resort. Remember this when planning your holiday weekend skiing, and decide whether, for you, the magnificent runs are worth the lineups at the lifts.

Part of Lake Louise's appeal is its beautiful setting across from the famous **Château Lake Louise**, framed by the emerald clear lake and glacier. At an altitude of 1645 metres, the ski slopes offer a wonderful view of **Mount Temple**, **Mount Fairview** and **Silvertip Mountain**.

Although the resort lacks on-hill accommodation, it does have three licensed day lodges, a licensed restaurant and a cocktail lounge, and you'll find several excellent lodges and motels in the town of Lake Louise just on the other side of the highway.

Travelling farther north, you come to the unsung heroine of the Canadian Rockies—**Jasper's Marmot Basin**. (There are still more skiers from Edmonton at Marmot than from Calgary, but increasingly we too are discovering the area's attractions.) Marmot's "basin" practically vacuums the snow from the atmosphere, piling it deeper and deeper in the upper bowls and providing plenty of untracked deep-powder skiing.

For years, Marmot has been offering early season ski-improvement weeks, and although you have to be prepared for some of the earliest weeks to be cancelled due to lack of snow, they are a real bargain and most of the time the snow conditions are good.

With the exception of the **Knob Chair** there is an easy run from every lift as well as a more difficult one. This feature makes Marmot a super family area, because it means all the members can ski the same lift. The seasonal snowfall at

Marmot ranges from six to ten metres and, because there are fewer skiers, the snow stays around longer. The lifts are limited (three chairs and two T-bars), but the runs make up for it: they are long and varied, and congestion is rare.

The closest mountain skiing you'll find is in **Kananaskis Country**, closer even than Banff. This is where **Fortress Mountain** makes its stand. Formerly known as Snowridge Mountain, Fortress is this area's newest ski resort, and it boasts the same superb snow conditions found in Banff and Jasper. Fortress is popular with the student crowd and because of its proximity to Calgary (an hour and a half drive) attracts many day skiers midweek. Wind can be a problem at Fortress, and it is best to check the weather before heading out. Most days, though, the sky is clear, the sun shines and the snow is great. If you want to double-check before heading out—to this or any other area—just turn on the radio or TV. Stations give full ski reports all season long.

Cross-Country Skiing

"A sneaky trick for discovering seldom travelled ski trails is to stop by a cycle shop and talk to a bored salesperson."

By Cayt McGuire

Calgary's winters are so unpredictable that you can never really tell if you're going to be able to cross-country ski from one day to the next. As a rule, our snow is of the cold, angular crystalline variety requiring the use of hard polar or blue purchase wax and no binder. Of course the rule does not apply under chinook conditions—but once that warm dry wind starts to blow, the snow won't stay long enough to worry about skiing on it anyway.

There are a number of flat cross-country touring routes in the city. One of the best is around the Weaselhead at the top of **Glenmore Reservoir**. If you leave your car at the 37th Street entrance to Glenmore Park, you can strap on your skis right away and head west along the shore. You'll cross a footbridge where the Elbow flows into the reservoir and then continue on a well-marked trail in a complete circle back to your car, a trip of about four hours. For wide open spaces, **River Park** runs for two miles across and back again, covering a couple of gentle hills. It's reasonable to ski down the **Elbow River** if you're sure there's been a long cold freeze before you go. The Elbow River is shallow from below the dam to Stanley Park so even if you were to fall through, the water would be, at the most, waist deep.

A sneaky trick for discovering seldom travelled ski trails is to stop by a cycle shop and talk to a bored salesperson. He (or she) should be able to give you all sorts of information on local bike paths which, when covered with snow, often convert to acceptable cross-country ski routes.

Within a half-hour drive of the city, in the **Bragg Creek** area, are a number of trails through treed parkland. For more information on out-of-town trails, stop by the **Mountain Equipment Co-op** (131 – 12th Avenue S.E.). The Co-op has an extensive library of guide books, a place to sit down and read before you buy, and a number of keen skiers on staff who will be more than happy to share the knowledge of their experiences with you.

If you're interested in the hairy mountain-slope brand of cross-country, where telemark turns are your only means of control, Calgary offers excellent access to the Rockies. The downhill resorts of **Sunshine** and **Lake Louise** have, in recent years, begun to recognize the needs of the cross-country skier with clearly marked trails in areas away from the downhillers.

At **Sunshine Village**, you can take the gondola from the parking lot or ski up to the resort on a five-mile switchback trail that used to serve the buses before the gondola was installed. Once at the village, it's just a short trek over the top of Strawberry to a huge mountain bowl at an altitude of about nine thousand feet. The bowl is only accessible to cross-country skiers because the snow is so deep that the only way to get out of it is on snowshoes or cross-country skis.

In winter, transportation to the downhill resorts is just a matter of phoning up the Greyhound or Brewster bus lines and inquiring about their schedules. There's also a train that will take you to the town of Banff every Friday afternoon. For information on skiing conditions, just turn on your favourite radio (or TV) station. Ski reports used to concentrate exclusively on downhill conditions, but the cross-country boom of the past decade ensures that, these days, there are good reports on trail conditions as well.

Accommodation will be no problem—especially if you are prudent enough to reserve ahead—since Calgary and Banff offer as wide a selection of hotels, motels and cabins as you could possibly wish. You might also like to check out the **Youth Hostels**. There are eleven hostels between Canmore and Jasper, each with a number of ski trails leading almost from their doorsteps. It's a good idea to make reservations if you're travelling in a large group or at least let them know you're coming, as each hostel is closed one night a week.

Information on Alberta hostels and the facilities that each provides (running water, electric lighting) as well as their schedules of operation is available from the **Hostel Shop** (1414 Kensington Road N.W.). The Hostel Shop also rents cross-country equipment at very reasonable rates.

There are some other shops to know about if you want to rent or buy equipment, or just talk cross-country. Among them: **Valley Ridge Ski Hut** (in Valley Ridge Park, west of Calgary on Highway 1), **Russell Sporting Goods** (1001 – 1st Street S.W.), and **Prairie n' Peak** (223 – 10th Street N.W.).

The Central Y

"The fact is, the health club of the Central Y is the quintessential economic and political barometer of Calgary."

By C. D. Evans, Q.C.

Scratch the average Calgary Captain of Industry, and you will find a latent jock, screaming to get out at noon to join the other striving blobs of cholesterol as they heave their sweaty selves about the perimeter of the back-to-back gyms at the Central YMCA.

The noon gun brings out these corporate jolly rotters, dodging vehicular and pedestrian traffic as they sprint purposefully for "the club." Eminent and prominent though many of them are—yea, even attaining the very ranks of generalissimos—the Y is the place they want to be. The regulars eschew the more fashionable sybaritic fitness palaces; not for them the plastic posh of the Petroleum Club or the dank mouldy recesses of the Ranchmen's. These regulars of the Y are oilmen, lawyers, accountants, Whigs and Tories, engineers, architects, businessmen: in sum, Men of Affairs frequent the YMCA health club over the lunch hour.

It is not just the obligatory ritual of the Daily Sweat that drives them thither; the camaraderie of the jockstrap set wears thin under close scrutiny. If an otherwise rational man wants to punish his enfeebling body with dreaded exercise, he does not necessarily need the cramped quarters of the club.

Their perfervidly faithful attendance is therefore grounded in some metaphysic more substantial than the roar of the running shoes or the smell of the crowd, all pervasive though these may be.

The fact is, the health club of the Central Y is the quintessential economic and political barometer of Calgary. While the other aforementioned lairs of the cognoscenti yield little but the conventional wisdom, with encounters therein resulting in little but an exchange of mutual ignorances, the health club is a veritable common market of information, ideas and opinion.

Following the obligatory swim, grunts and jerks, stationary bike, rounds of the gym, fairy dancing, or what have you, the Fellowship of the Jacuzzi Tub Ring foregather in, first, the steam room and, second, the spartan lounge. In these holy places, over a single lunch hour, one can be privy to the current state of the realty market, the wellhead price, the latest Supreme Court of Canada decision (analyzed critically), the most recent outrages and excesses of the federal bureaucracy, the prospects of this or that politician or party, and the views of small business and self-employed professionals upon any contemporary topic.

Generally speaking, those knowledgeable men know each other mainly through their common interest in a minimal level of fitness. Motivated initially by the alarming spread of the corporate avoirdupois, the convenience of the location and the entirely reasonable membership fees, new members quickly determine that this clean, well-lighted place is one of the last bastions of freedom of speech and expression in the western world.

One may speak English and not be assailed with Bi-and-Bi; one may weigh oneself in pounds rather than the meaningless K's; one may excoriate the Feds or the Infernal Revenue with impunity. No one at the Y would ever rat on a fellow member. Honour prevails and is paramount.

Therefore, the members feel free to hold forth without fear or favour, and they surely do. The steam room is the closest thing extant, I suspect, to the original Scandinavian parliament: debate is restrained and considered. The man who has the floor is heard out. All are canvassed for their views. Those who wish to remain silent may do so, without same being an admission against interest. Denouement, if not consensus, is achieved during the final stages of the male toilette.

The participants then break into study groups in the cafeteria and exchange views on the fine points of the day's topics over their frugal and unpleasantly healthy cottage cheese and fruit compotes, or yoghurt and cheese-on-brown.

That is why the lads come back time after time, day after day: there is a great deal more than the smelly fellowship of the locker room. These are decent chaps and earnest fellows: they believe in the family unit and a fair day's wage for a fair day's work. Most of them have a touching faith in the democratic process. None of them purports to be privy to the recondite secrets of the universe. In the twenty-odd years that I have frequented the hallowed precincts of the Central Y, I have learned one great truth above all others: clad only in towels, all men are equal.

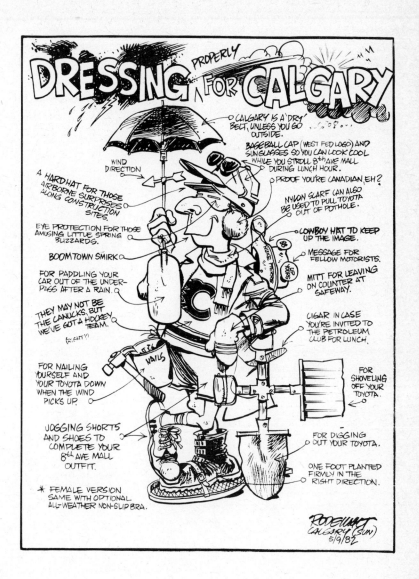

Getting Away

Banff

"It's so easy to pick out the Calgarians in their baseball caps and grubby T-shirts, their Hollywood mufflers rumbling like thunder, a foil to the natty, dapper, cheerful crowd of Japanese visitors."

By Jon Whyte

Some days—long weekends in particular—I wish a whirl-wind would pick Calgary up, false-front skyscrapers, cowboy consciousness and all, and move it a hundred or so miles east. Putting it just a little farther away from Banff the Beautiful, so Banff wouldn't be quite so accessible to Calgarians and a visit here would be more special for them. Then they wouldn't take Banff quite so much for granted. Calgarians would cherish Banff the way Edmontonians revere Jasper. It's so easy to pick out the Calgarians in their baseball caps and grubby T-shirts, their Hollywood mufflers rumbling like thunder, a foil to the natty, dapper, cheerful crowd of Japanese visitors. Calgarians notoriously take their misconceptions for granted. (After all, how could you ever learn more about your own background?) A Calgarian will say "Norky" (instead of "Nor-kway") for Norquay, "Sheffren" (instead of "Ke-fren") for Chephren, "Pay-toe" (instead of "Pee-toe") for Peyto, and believe he's skiing Mount Brewster when he's skiing Lookout Peak at Sunshine, and Mount Brewster is twenty-five kilometres away.

Increasingly, Calgarians regard Banff as the place where the gas barbecue sits on weekends; increasingly, condo-questing urbanites look for weekend digs in the mountains, frustrating my hometown's efforts to stay small, compact, dignified, small-townishly pleasant. If Calgary were three-and-a-bit hours away, rather than an hour and a half, the party crowd would choose some blithe largish slough as the site for its bashes, and Calgarians would realize they are essentially the prairie people we mountain folk know them to be.

My uncle used to say, when Calgary was the last of the false-front towns and a mere fifty thousand strong, that he was grateful for the existence of the Stoney Indian Reserve at Morley, for it would provide a buffer and barrier to the growth of Calgary. Calgary might grow to the top of the Scott Lake Hill, but the reserve would make such a large hiatus the city would grow no further west. Now that the city's pushing a million, our gratitude to Treaty #7 can know no limits, even if Calgary can. I doubt the torquing can stop, as much as I'm sure Calgary will never be wafted "over the rainbow."

But, inasmuch as Banff and Calgary lie uneasily in bed beside each other (Banff afraid that the experience will turn into a rape as the Olympics and its associated foofaraw draw nigh), other things can be said. Calgary has provided Banff a year-round economy, skiing in the winter so augmenting business that Bom Ami rarely opaques shop and café windows as it frequently did in the forties. The stronger base means services—restaurants in particular, lodgings in general—are better than ever. The increasing use of the backcountry of Banff National Park means more users will defend the mountain wilderness against the schemes of zealous park planners (who, as recently as 1969, proposed cutting the park into a pizza by a network of roads). Many of those recreational hikers are Calgarians, and that's important: Banff's conservationists are noisy, but lack the numbers the Calgarians can muster. And Calgarians have improved: these days they rarely bring their own teabags to plunk into a thermos they've brazenly filled with hot water from a restaurant urn . . . .

But the best thing to say about Calgarians is that they are such a wonderfully swaggering bunch of know-it-alls, they leave the quiet places of Banff's environs alone.

I should perhaps isolate three different Banffs. There's the one we all have a love-hate relationship with, the two blocks of **Banff Avenue** that cluster T-shirt shops, novelty and souvenir shops, hotels and restaurants, dactyl by digit beside some quite wonderful stores. Those twenty-five acres are bane and boon, and so well concentrate the smarmy hordes that most of the rest of the town is left a quiet, serene place, rarely visited by the four or so million annual visitors.

The next Banff in the hierarchy is that quiet, serene place, the greater town. It has three wonderful public museums, a beautiful riverside, a cemetery that contains more works of art than many public galleries in Western Canada, some wonderful architecture and a splendid choice of untrammeled parklike woodsy walks. On a day when the first Banff is aswarm and the person in a rush must slalom his way through the crowd, it's possible to walk from the bridge to Bow Falls on either side of the Bow River and see no more than a dozen to twenty other people at the most. *This* Banff has a publicly accessible cave that is rich in historical redolence. It has a diminutive mountain that anyone can walk up. It has the classiest hotel in Western Canada (Banff Springs), the lobbies of which alone are thrilling. The dappling of artworks about the town is so profuse—though tucked into the cornices of bridges, over the lintels of businesses and in the stained glass windows of the older churches—that on occasion I take friends out for a tour and we need half a day to see them all. (Such stained glass! You've never seen such combinations of postcard scenery and biblical themes. Happily, church doors are usually open.)

The richness of the second Banff, spruce forest, aspen copse, **Luxton Museum**, **Peter Whyte Gallery**, **Banff Springs** lobby, Charlie Beil's packhorse on the Mount Royal, the Douglas firs on **Tunnel** beside the timber pine viewpoint of **Bow Falls**, has kept me engaged for better than thirty years. And so few see it.

The third Banff is the **National Park**, a paradise of valleys, lakes, mountains, glaciers, meadows, streams and rivers that the usual visitor sees from automobile or tour bus. I do not begrudge his seeing **Bow Lake** and the **Mistaya River Valley** from a position of luxury, knowing his time is limited, but it is a veneer view, removed from experience by the glass he sees it through. Banff's immensity at this scale is unfathomable, or at least so great that most of us who dedicate our weekends and days off to seeking out its remoteness have long lists of places still to reach.

But the experience is not all so remote or gruelling that the visitor should deny himself the possibility of the reward. Canyons beside the road can beckon him to almost-solitudes in a few hundred metres, and lovely little lakes, albeit lacking alpine character, are often no more than three-quarters of an hour from the parking lots. Each visitor should feel what it's like to walk through duff-floored forest, the sharp scent of pine reminding him his nose can work, and glimpse a lake or waterfall through a screen of branches. The more exalted pleasures of trekking through a mountain pass or ascending a mountain summit are rarer, but they're at hand in Tunnel outside Banff or **Saddle Col** and **Mount Fairview** above Lake Louise.

It seems so elementally correct for a visitor to debark from his vehicle and walk a while beside a stream or to a nearby tarn that I had to remind myself it's the principal reason most visitors come to Banff in the first place—even if the seductions of Banff Avenue lure them from their intentions.

The prime Banff is wilderness—and not those hurly-burly blocks of "Main Street." In the summer months—when northern latitude, daylight saving and Banff's location on the western edge of the time zone conspire to keep the evening light enough to walk a mile or two after dinner—every visitor should take advantage of these happy circumstances, go for a walk, draw in deeply a visceral reminder of the universe and sleep justly in his bed that evening. Even the tour bus schedules leave the evenings free enough for such honest activity.

The risks are minimal, and the rewards are supreme. I hear the wary asking about bears. Sure, they exist, but in a couple of thousand miles on mountain trails I've never had the good luck to see a grizzly or a cougar, and visitors are reminded herewith that the Trans-Canada Highway is much more likely to maim or murder them than is a hungry bruin, yet the statistics don't keep them off the highways or the main street.

There is a fourth Banff. It's the Banff that exists intimately and privately for each of us, the sort of place we come to know from the artists and writers who have lived here. It's the attitude toward the land we find in Belmore Browne, Carl Rungius, Peter and Catharine Whyte, and Walter J. Phillips, the painters who've lived here, and in the writings of Earle Birney and Jasper's Howard O'Hagan, the authors of the Canadian Rockies. It's a place where we realize again our meaning in the natural world. You need not even search out the works of art to find yourself profoundly wondering about the mystery and majesty of mountains. It may require deeper thought than in the wilderness of cities, but if you ponder geological time and the harmony of weather, life and landscape, you'll find a fourth Banff to take home with you as privately rich as you would wish, and be the wealthier for it.

The popular slogan, "Take nothing but pictures, leave nothing but footprints," does its job well; it suggests the ethic we must all abide by in the park. But I would suggest that we take home realizations: they may not be quite so easy to insert in the carousel as trophies of a vacation, but their value is greater.

Who would ever have expected a vacation could have such a morally redeeming excuse for getting away from it all?

The Insiders'
BANFF HOTELS

Calgarians love Banff. Just about everybody you meet has his or her own list of places to stay, places to eat and ways to have more fun and encounter few lineups. Here is the insiders' short-list, culled from some of Calgary's more devoted Banff enthusiasts.

WHERE TO STAY
- **Banff Park Lodge:** "Height of luxury, even Peter Lougheed stays there. It has an excellent dining room; warm, informal lounge with a fireplace; indoor pool; and rooms on the east side have a river view."
- **Banff Springs Hotel:** "Very grand, and at night you can go looking for the ghosts—I myself have seen the skull in the painting in the Rob Roy Room. Or hunt for the lost room—from the outdoor pool you can see the window, but nobody can find the door." And if the natural hot springs further up Sulphur Mountain aren't enough for you, try the hotel's Jacuzzis (some in private rooms, one by the indoor pool).
- **Mount Royal Hotel:** "Cheap, clean, on the main drag [Banff Avenue], good beer and close to the action. What more do you want if you're skiing?"
- **Rimrock Hotel:** "Up on Sulphur Mountain, with a fantastic view of the Bow River Valley—Cascade, Tunnel and Rundle mountains. Close to the hot springs and to the Sulphur Mountain gondola, which goes year-round up to a very nice tea house. Or you can walk up on a wide switch-back trail. This, incidentally, was the

favourite necking spot for local teenagers in the forties and fifties. I should know."

• **The Stockade:** "Just outside the park gates on Highway 1 at the Harvie Heights turn-off. Cosy little cabins, several with fireplaces, all with kitchens. There's also a main lodge. Really quaint."

• **Tunnel Mountain Lodges:** "On Tunnel Mountain, each with its own kitchen, queen-size bed in the master bedroom, open fireplace, and there's a convenience store across the way. You get a view of the entire Bow River Valley. It's a mile to town, but the view is worth it."

WHERE TO EAT

• **Le Beaujolais:** "Continental food, quiet surroundings . . . just a great finale to a relaxing trip to the Upper Hot Spring."

• **Café La Ronde:** "A French restaurant that has great open-face sandwiches at lunch and good food in general, but the big thing is the live jazz and amazing array of deserts, so this is a place people go in the evening to hang out."

• **Grizzly Bar:** "For fondu-lovers . . . meat, cheese and chocolate-dipped fruit."

• **The Caboose:** "Still the town's railway station, but part of it is now a restaurant. You get huge portions of steak and other meats. Try the house dressing when you visit the salad bar — it's a family secret."

• **The Silver City:** "Visit the lounge side for a good time — excellent music, everything from jazz to country to rock and roll. And a great, big, long, bar."

• Outside the park: not a restaurant name, but a geographical reference — visit nearby **Canmore**. Those who know recommend **The Fireside**, "for good steak and seafood;" **The Rose and Crown**, with "English beer, dart games, English curries and a roast of the day;" and **The Village Green**, "great soups, build-your-own sandwiches, home-cooked food and terrific pastries."

TIPS
Park Gates

• "Avoid them any time after 9:00 A.M. Though there's a lull in early June and another, usually, in late September. Oh, all right, seriously, weekdays aren't bad — except for Stampede Week — but avoid weekends, long weekends especially."

• "Buy a year pass, then you can zip by in the outside lane. And what a bargain! It's cheap and it's good for a whole year in every national park in the country."

Crowd Control

• "Visit the park in spring

and fall. It's beautiful then and there are fewer tourists."

• "Stay outside the park, there are lots of motels and cabins near the park gates."

• "If you're camping, avoid Tunnel Mountain campground and head for **Two Jack Lake** instead. It's prettier, and you have a better chance of getting in since it's a little further off the beaten track."

• "Try canoeing or bicycling to the **Vermillion Lakes**. You can rent the equipment in Banff. Biking is a good idea because roads can be really congested and there are bike trails all the way."

Common Sense

• "Always have a sweater handy. The mountains can be cold. And if you're visiting in winter, make sure you're appropriately dressed for a walk or for cross-country skiing. If you're not sure what's appropriate, *ask*!"

• "That's real wildlife out there, not Walt Disney characters. So enjoy the glimpses you catch, but leave the animals alone! Let them be wild animals, and keep your popcorn to yourself."

• "Bears? Yeah, bears are having quite a people problem. So read the pamphlet you receive at the park gates, believe it and act on it. You and the bears will be much happier."

• "After all this good-citizen advice, shouldn't we also say: *Enjoy*? These mountains are, literally, one of the most beautiful sights—and sites—in the world. How lucky we are!"

The Banff Centre

"In 1979, when Dr. Leighton announced plans to turn the centre into a year-round arts conservatory, he predicted an immediate impact on the community. He was right."

By Louise Bresky

For many years, Calgarians were known as people who couldn't ski down mountains and go to concerts at the same time.

No one could figure out whether this was a mental block or a physical one, until the visionaries at the Banff Centre recognized it as a simple problem in logistics.

While busy building the centre into a world-class professional arts school, administrators incidentally discovered something basic about skiers that applied to other high-country addicts anywhere, anytime: they don't live by boards alone. Far from being a bunch of yodelling Philistines, they would love to hear fine music—if only the concert hall were at the foot of the ski slope. The same cultural visionaries knew that many of the world's great musicians would be thrilled to perform amidst snowy peaks—if only the mountain goats would pay to listen.

Since everyone who survives in the West becomes skilled at practical compromise, the fifty-year-old arts school on Banff's Tunnel Mountain offered a splendid solution: they would turn the summer school into a year-round conservatory of the arts, starting with music. Illustrious teacher-performers could make winter music with gifted student-performers. What mountain-lover could resist?

This was a fitting next step for an institution that had already grown considerably beyond its original role. It was

170

founded in 1933 as a division of the University of Alberta extension department, funded by a $30,000 grant from the Carnegie Foundation. At first, in makeshift facilities, it offered undergraduate courses in theatre. Then it added playwriting, the visual arts and music and, after the school's move to its present site, opera, ballet and photography as well. Along the way it had to fight a lingering reputation as a summer playground for rich kids.

When Dr. David Leighton (named in the summer of 1982 to head the 1988 Olympic Winter Games organizing committee and replaced in Banff by Paul Fleck) took over as director in 1970 from Senator Donald Cameron, he and associate director Neil Armstrong saw the need for a professional arts school. Together, they began upgrading facilities, instituted tough auditions for students and recruited top faculty and guest artists. With two beautifully equipped theatres as showcases, the school began to draw an audience. Education became entertainment.

The Winter Cycle, introduced in 1979, was part of the long-range aim to turn the Banff Centre into Canada's foremost postgraduate school for professional artists, on a year-round basis. For the same reason, the summer season was expanded to run from mid-May to the end of August, with some kind of performance scheduled in the centre's theatres almost every evening. The festival is called "a celebration of young talent," but because some of the world's finest professional artists work with that talent (as well as perform their own solo and chamber concerts), the four-month festival has a spirit and quality all its own. Jamie Portman, Southam's roving arts critic, rightly calls it "an experience unavailable anywhere else in Canada."

Take the memorable 1981 festival, which marked the centenary of Bartók with several special concerts. Performing guest artist-teachers included cellist Janos Starker, German conductor Klaus Tennstedt, violinist Zoltan Szekely, who led the famed Hungarian Quartet for more than thirty years, pianist Menahem Pressler of the Beaux Arts Trio, the Canadian Brass, pianist Marek Jablonski, and violist Donald McInnes. The featured stage events were Douglas Campbell's production of Benjamin Britten's comic opera, *Alberta Herring*; the Brecht-Weill *Threepenny Opera*; Molnar's play, *The Guardsman*; and the Dance Workshop, with a new jazz ballet by Peter George.

The summer of 1982 celebrated Stravinsky's centenary with a production of his only opera, *The Rake's Progress*, directed by Brian MacDonald, the Canadian choreographer who also restaged his prize-winning jazz ballet, *Aimez-vous Bach?* Jazz musicians John Abercrombie and Davie Holland, trombonist Albert Mangelsdorff and vocalist "Big" Miller blew in to teach a three-week master class and jam at two concerts. Michael Bawtree, artistic director of the new musical theatre division, directed *The Music Man*; British actor-director Henry Woolf offered Chekov's *The Three Sisters*; John Cranko choreographed *Pineapple Poll*, a comic ballet set to Gilbert and Sullivan music.

The visual arts division sponsored nine performance-art shows featuring visual artists from North America, Britain and Germany, and exhibitions of Robert Rauschenberg prints and works by Ron Moppett. And, as usual, the music school's master teachers were at it again, providing a field day for name-droppers and an exhilarating time for both listeners and lucky students.

In 1979, when Dr. Leighton announced plans to turn the centre into a year-round arts conservatory, he predicted an immediate impact on the community. He was right. Not only has there been a marked increase in the pace of public performance with the start of the music school, but other Alberta communities start to benefit as students and their master-teachers tour and hold workshops. As the school phases in the other arts on a year-round basis, the cultural side effects continue to grow.

In 1981, the centre generated new excitement when Michael Bawtree, an energetic Australian producer-director who had been at the Stratford and Shaw festivals, arrived to start a unique pilot project in musical theatre. He promptly set up a training school which offers six-month sessions to young performers who have had professional experience. His goal is to turn musical theatre upside-down: not just by widening the range of student performing skills and encouraging their collaboration in staging and composition, but also by getting musical theatre away from the extremes of both tin-pan alley and abstract art-music. He wants to create a new genre out of the old, and Banff audiences are the first to see his creative experiments. Thomas Ralston, conductor and violinist who heads the music school, shares Bawtree's innovative ideals. He has said he hopes the school will be a catalyst, "an agent for change and discovery." To help creation along, the school is building a $500,000 artists' colony, providing studio and living space for professionals to work on their own projects while drawing on inspiration from artists of other disciplines.

All this adds up to year-round stimulation for professional artists—and for audiences as well. Take all of 1983—the Banff Centre's fiftieth birthday party—as the example. Witness the specially commissioned festival opera, new Canadian dance works, the spring international string quartet competition and the concert-studded April Homecoming Week.

But first, the Calgary winter sports crowd is advised to sharpen more than its edges: winter is as exciting now at the Banff Centre as is summer. The 1982–83 season has music school concerts or solo recitals scheduled every Friday night from October to May, with lunchbox concerts on Wednesday noons. Foreign films and Hollywood classics are shown two evenings a week. After Christmas, Bawtree's acting, dancing, singers offer a series of six weekend studio concerts ranging all through the musical theatre repertoire, plus two full-scale productions, including a new Canadian work. American violist Donald McInnes stars in an unusual musical drama written for him by writer Leofwin Luke and composed by Stephen McNeff, associate artistic director of musical theatre. And, just so no one has to turn out the lights in the Eric Harvie or the Margaret Greenham theatres, the Banff Centre's theatre events department sponsors an eight-concert big-name Celebrity Series and additional events, such as the Vienna Choir Boys, the Chinese Magic Circus, Dizzie Gillespie, and Theatre Beyond Words.

Non-skiing Calgarians desert their firesides in droves to catch the Banff Centre's winter concerts, but the skiers profit most. You may have to read Grove's *Dictionary of Music* in the lift lines, but at last you can have your Bach and eat it too.

The Insiders' CULTURAL BANFF

Cultural Banff, say the insiders, is three Banffs: Banff Centre, "indigenous" Banff and Banff National Park.

A cultural Banff National Park? Yes. A lot of work is going on in preparation for the 1985 centennial of this, Canada's first national park. Be sure to visit the ambitious **Cave & Basin** restoration project (already open) and learn more about our human and natural history the easy way. Another easy way: visit the **National Park Museum** on Banff Avenue. Established in the mid-nineties, it is the longest-running museum in Canada west of Toronto.

The **Banff Centre** draws people to its theatres year-round, but it spills over into Banff itself as well. Watch for the many freebie concerts put on by centre students year-round, in various locations throughout the town. In addition, the **Walter Phillips Gallery** (the art gallery located in the centre complex) should be on your list, especially if your tastes run to the avant-garde.

Ask about the cultural must-visits of Indigenous Banff, and you hear three main recommendations.

One is the **Banff Book and Art Den**. Start here, say insiders, because although Banff was a painters' town until World War II, it has now shifted cultural emphasis to become a major book-producing community (an average of ten to twelve publications a year means Banff has the impressive ratio of one per four hundred inhabitants). Browsing here can introduce you to the area's voices and help you decide where to focus your attention.

Banffites also urge you to visit the **Peter Whyte Foundation**, **Archives of the Canadian Rockies** and the **Peter Whyte Gallery**, all housed in one low, pleasant building along with the local public library. (Peter and Catharine Whyte were outdoors people, painters and collectors, whose donations provided the core for the institutions now named in their honour.) The art gallery shows many local contemporary artists, plus (more so in winter than in summer) a broad range of exhibits from across Canada and other parts of the world. As well: Sunday afternoon concerts in the art gallery, year-round; Wednesday afternoon tea and concerts on the lawn, summer only (obviously); and Thursday evening free films, September through May.

You can then go right next door and tour the two **Banff Heritage Homes**—the log homes of Peter and Catharine Whyte, and of Lieutenant Colonel Philip Augustus and Pearl Evelyn Brewster Moore. Open summers only.

Now for the unexpected recommendation: be sure to visit the pleasant little **cemetery** at Buffalo and Otter streets, for it is a walk through Banff history. All Banff's names are here, ranging from the "first families" (Brewster, Peyto, Wheeler, Wilson, Whyte . . .) to the Ukrainian miners who died in various mining disasters and the Chinese labourers who were the casualties of the railway's arduous push through the mountains. Take time to appreciate the thirty or so bronze plaques by Charlie Beil that mark some of the graves.

Finally, though, you get to know Banff the same way you get to know any place: by talking to people. Then you hear about "Nigger Bill" Davies (only Black man in town, at the time), who sassily named his restaurant The White Help Café . . . or learn that the town may be named for Banh, ancient Celtic goddess of swine. (Well . . . so the insiders say.)

Escapes

"Once beyond the city limits, travelling in any direction, you'll discover why the real old-time Albertans call this God's Country."

By Dave Greber

Visitors to Calgary are often struck by the fact that Calgarians love to talk about their city. Especially prone to this condition are the old-timers. (In a city with a growth rate and population turnover like Calgary's, "old-timer" generally means anyone who has lived here at least three years.)

"*Why?*" you might ask—especially after a day of being inundated by paeans to Calgary. It's simple, actually: no matter how small or peripheral the contribution any individual makes to Calgary's growth, we're building this city. It's an exhausting activity which, at times, can give us a distorted sense of time and space—we begin to feel that Calgary is Alberta and that Alberta has no past, only the present.

Those are the warning signals that it's time to escape Calgary for a day or two—anywhere, just for a change. In winter the best two-day escape is a weekend in Vancouver; a day or two on the ski slopes is a generally accepted second best. The truly brave try winter camping or hiding out at a secluded Alpine chalet.

But, come warm, sunny weather, escape can be had by picking a highway and heading out to where you can talk to small furry animals (or be chased by large furry ones), lean against a fence post out on the prairie and listen to the whisper of stalks of wheat caressing each other in the wind, visit a small-town rodeo, or wander around the landmarks commemorating the punctuation points of Alberta history.

Sometimes the drive—and you'll travel quite a bit on your escapes from Calgary—is in itself a relief from the pressure cooker.

Once beyond the city limits, travelling in any direction, you'll discover why the real old-time Albertans call this God's Country. Kilometre upon kilometre of unrelentingly beautiful scenery greets you wherever you go, whether it's the prairie—emerald green in wet weather; sere in hot, dry times; a desolate, rolling, blanket of white in winter—the badlands, the foothills or the mountains.

As for the history, it's everywhere and, because we're going off the beaten path (Banff is easy to find without our help, simply follow the other wild-eyed escapers), keep your eyes open; you'll find Alberta history began long before the North West Mounted Police came here in 1874.

One of the great natural beauties of central Alberta is also one of its best-kept secrets, probably because part of the trip to the **Ram River Falls**, tucked away in the **Rocky-Clearwater Forest Reserve**, is over gravel roads.

Travel north on Highway 2 past Red Deer and turn west on Highway 11 to Rocky Mountain House. Before going on to the forest reserve, stop at **Rocky Mountain House Historic Park**, about five kilometres west of the town. Here, at the junction of the North Saskatchewan and Clearwater rivers, you'll find a few pages of history. All that remains of the original trading post of Rocky Mountain House—four forts built by the Nor'westers between 1799 and 1886—is two stone chimneys from the 1846 fort, but a bit of imagination and the help of information and artifacts in the interpretive centre will give you the area's story in technicolour.

You'll be there during the three Indian attacks, when the forts were burned to the ground. Close your eyes. Imagine the tough Nor'westers coming out of the forest and the ruins of their old forts to rebuild the pallisades and get back to the business of sending bales of otter, fox and sable fur back to the East. And you'll meet David Thompson, the explorer who mapped a good portion of British Columbia. He was stationed at Rocky Mountain House before he left in 1807 on a four-year trek, establishing trading posts in the interior of British Columbia and exploring the Columbia River system, eventually reaching the mouth of the Columbia in Washington state in 1811.

Now, head back through the town and follow the gravel road numbered 752 past Strachan and into the forest reserve. Keep an eye out for the small bands of legendary wild horses—pony-sized animals now protected by wildlife legislation—that roam the reserve.

Bear right along the road and follow the signs to the Ram River Falls recreation area. Your ears will tell you when you're getting close—the glorious, elemental roar of that wild river as it tumbles over the gorge is a stirring and unmistakable sound. And the falls are even more beautiful than they sound. Camping facilities are available, and you might want to stay the night because, as breathtaking a sight as the falls may be in full daylight, watching sunset or sunrise over the falls is a humbling, almost religious, experience—fifty-story, man-made buildings can't even begin to compare.

When you leave the recreation area, you'll be on the Forestry Trunk Road. You can follow it to the road that leads to Caroline (#591), through **Innisfail**, and back to Highway 2, or continue your exploration of the reserve along the Trunk Road to the junction of Highway 1A outside Cochrane. Drive into **Cochrane** and stop for your choice of dozens of flavours of rich, thoroughly decadent, homemade ice cream at **MacKay's** on main street. Calgary is just a thirty-minute drive from here.

At 4:10 A.M., 29 April 1903, in the southwestern corner of Alberta, along what is now Highway 3, a piece of Turtle Mountain broke away and slid down into the valley of the Oldman River. One hundred seconds later 120 people were dead, part of the town of Frank, including an entire railway siding, was buried under thirty metres of rock, and the Frank Slide was history.

Take the scenic route to **Frank**, south on Highway 22, turn right at Lundbreck and keep going until you come to the site of the slide. There are highway markers that tell the story, but the location is impossible to miss. Great, white, tumbled limestone rocks—eighty-two million tonnes of them, as large as boxcars, as small as travel trailers—litter three square kilometres of the valley.

It's the kind of sight that makes you feel small, very small indeed, in the great scheme of things. **Turtle Mountain** is immediately identifiable, it's the one with the broad, gleaming white scar where that slab of limestone—915 metres by 640 metres by 150 metres—broke away. No one is sure what started the slide. One explanation is that an earthquake shook the slab loose; another is that water erosion, working with the freezing and melting of water in the fault lines of the stratified limestone, finally upset nature's balancing act. Whatever the explanation, the mountain itself is an interesting anomaly—a limestone outcropping among granite mountains.

Once you've clambered around the rocks and explored the site, turn around and go east to **Pincher Creek**, turn south and keep going until you hit the junction of Highways 5 and 6. If you want some camping and recreation, turn right, into **Waterton Park**, where you'll find five of the life zones of Alberta, from the glaciated arctic right down to prairie-parkland grassland. Sightseers turn left and continue to **Cardston**, site of the first Mormon settlement in Canada.

The town takes its name from founder Charles Ora Card, Brigham Young's son-in-law, who led the forty families that trekked here from Utah in 1887. You're here to see and tour Canada's only Mormon Temple. Ten years a-building (from 1913 to 1923), the temple is a white granite statement of faith, built from hand-shaped stones quarried from British Columbia's Kootenay Valley. Also in the town is Card's first home, a restored log cabin, which has been turned into a museum.

From the Prairie Temple go north to **Fort Macleod**, a town named after the original Mounted Police fort built in 1874. The pallisade at the edge of town is a replica housing a museum with displays of police weapons, uniforms and artifacts from the original fort. You can visit the blacksmith shop, chapel and medical centre—the primitive foot drill, which looks more like an instrument of medieval torture than a dental tool, should set your teeth on edge. The tepees and covered wagons within the walls give an added bit of visual historical authenticity.

Set up your accommodations at the nearby campsite and, if you still feel energetic, take a quick trip to **Head-Smashed-In**, about twenty-two kilometres west of Fort Macleod. Head-Smashed-In is a buffalo jump, the oldest in Western Canada. Before they acquired firearms, Plains Indians would drive buffalo between drive lines—rows of piled rock—and over a cliff where the lines converge. The drive lines at this site start eleven kilometres from the cliff.

The last stop on this little jaunt is the city of **Lethbridge**, which was originally called Coalbanks when it was built on a giant seam of coal in the 1870s. Here is exactly what you're looking for if you want respite from the bustle of Calgary— the **Nikka Yuko Centennial Garden**. Built in 1967 as a symbol of Canadian-Japanese friendship, it's an authentic Japanese garden, all trees and pavilions, pools and shrubs, bridges and paths, and no flowers. It's a peaceful place for contemplation among the delicate beauty of buildings—like the sixteenth-century-style cypress-wood pavilion—and bridges that were actually built in Japan and reassembled in the park.

On the west side of the city, in the **Oldman River Valley**, you'll find **Indian Battle Park** and **Fort Whoop-Up**. The park is the site of the region's last major Indian battle, fought in 1870. The Fort Whoop-Up located here is a replica of the real thing, remains of which can be found twelve kilometres south of the city in Whoop-Up Coulee. A whiskey trader's fort, Whoop-Up was named for the goings-on there—Indians and traders would gather to trade furs for liquor and whoop it up. The mounted police put the fort out of business in 1874.

Time to go home, you say? The fastest route is to backtrack to Fort Macleod and drive up Highway 2; the scenic route is up Highway 23.

If you take the #2, note the location of **High River**, for another great escape. Try to plan this one for the last weekend in May, time for the **High River Little Britches Rodeo**, when the cowboys in training get to show their stuff, their parents preen with pride over them, and everyone enjoys the hospitable atmosphere of a country fair. While you're in High River, take time out to visit the **Museum of The Highwood**—this was originally ranching country and the museum celebrates pioneer cowboy history.

In another direction, about 125 kilometres northeast of Calgary, is one of those sights everyone should see at least once in a lifetime, whether living in Alberta or simply visiting—**Drumheller** and the **Alberta Badlands**. The town is an agricultural and oil and gas centre, but it was another of the West's major coal towns until oil and gas replaced coal as a major energy source. It also sits among some of the most stark, arresting and raw scenery in the West.

You're driving along Highway 9, on the approaches to Drumheller. You've been travelling through rolling flatlands of mixed grain farming and cattle ranching—for as far as the eye can see, it's cattle and grain. Then, off to the left, one of those tourist-sight signs and a carpark catch your eye. Pull in, then walk over to the viewpoint.

The earth has just caved in, or so it seems, for before you a broad valley, dotted with tall hills glistening like raw gold in the sunlight, cuts through the prairie in a scene of windswept and primeval desolation. This is where the producers of *Quest for Fire* came when they wanted an authentic prehistoric location.

This is **Horsethief Canyon** (if you're adventurous, trails take you down to the bottom), part of the badlands created by erosion of the Red Deer River Valley. The land is sedimentary rock and soil deposited by rivers and streams that flowed into the prehistoric seas that once covered this area; it's been sculpted by the attack of wind and water during the thousands of years since uplifting created the Rockies and the Red Deer River. You could get in a canoe and ride the river from Drumheller to the Alberta-Saskatchewan border, where it joins the South Saskatchewan River. That's about a week's worth of leisurely paddling during the high-water season, but really, dead centre of the Red Deer River is the best vantage point for exploring the badlands.

The second best way is to drive the **Dinosaur Trail**, a fifty-kilometre loop that begins and ends in Drumheller. The trail takes you to the **Valley of the Dinosaurs**; the tiny, pink, **Biggest Little Church in the World**, which serves about twenty thousand people a year, six at a time; Horsethief Canyon; and **Drumheller's Prehistoric Park**, which has life-sized dinosaur models.

If the badlands catch your imagination and you want to see more, there's still **Dinosaur Provincial Park** about two hundred kilometres to the southeast. There's no direct route from Drumheller to the park, and the back country roads are dirt and gravel, so you might want to go back to Calgary tonight and travel to the park tomorrow by the easy route. It's 160 kilometres on the Trans-Canada Highway to Brooks, where you take a secondary road to Patricia, then a ten-kilometre dirt and gravel hop to the park, a huge museum of natural history.

The park was established in 1955 to protect land which by then had been ravaged for over fifty years by visitors indiscriminately digging for dinosaur remains. Some of their finds ended up in museums; others were simply taken to adorn private rock gardens.

Exploring this place is a trip along a timescape, whether on the self-guided walks or on one of the guided hikes that include interpretive programs. And don't miss John Ware's cabin, situated near the camping facilities. Ware is a fixture in Alberta history, a Black ex-slave who came to Canada on a trail drive in the 1880s and stayed as a rancher. The cabin, which was restored and moved to the park, tells a bit of his story and what life was like for the pioneers in Alberta. (You can learn more about Ware at the Glenbow Museum and by reading *Cowboy John Ware* by Grant MacEwan.)

This is only a short introduction to some of the escapes you can make from Calgary whether, as a visitor, you get tired of hearing us talk about it, or, as a resident, you decide you need a change. By no means assume you have to be the hardy pioneer type to escape—two days in the back country isn't quite the same as David Thompson's trek to the Pacific—but it does pay to plan and prepare a bit for these trips. And, as much territory as it seems we've covered, we haven't even *begun* to get away; we haven't even gone beyond a 275-kilometre radius of Calgary in our travels.

Whatever your reasons for escaping, enjoy the change and have a nice time finding out why the real old-timers call this God's Country.

The Insiders'
SMALL TOWN RODEOS

Cowboys have two legs, horses four, and there are five standard rodeo events everywhere you go: steer wrestling, calf roping, saddle bronc riding, bareback riding and bull riding. "The difference between the Calgary Stampede rodeo and small-town rodeos," says Winston Bruce, "is basically the atmosphere."

He should know. Bruce, who started helping at rodeos when he was five and (with his brothers) produced his first rodeo when he was twelve, is now rodeo division manager for the Calgary Stampede. It means he is in constant touch with rodeos of every size. "Here at the Calgary Stampede, we have a responsibility to maintain our western heritage and our rodeo heritage—so, along with the standard events and some new ones, like the Indian Buffalo Riding, we continue traditional events like the Wild Horse Race that aren't being kept up everywhere else. But every rodeo is produced with its own kind of audience in mind. Most people in the Calgary audience are not full-time rodeo-goers, they'll come and sit for two hours and then go on to enjoy other things in the Stampede. The rodeo is part of the entertainment package, so we have very high production values.

"In the small town, a rodeo is a neighbourhood gathering where people will sit for three to four hours and chat to each other while the events are going on. There'll be beer, and babies crawling around, and everybody knows somebody who's participating—and knows more about rodeo in general—and it's all very folksy."

For the best in big-time, professional rodeo, be sure to attend the one at the Calgary Stampede. Bruce adds only two more names to the list of top rodeos "to see before you die:" Cheyenne Frontier Days in Cheyenne, Montana and Pendelton Round-Up in Pendelton, Oregon.

The list for "folksy" rodeos is much longer. In July and August alone (though the season is practically year-round), in the Calgary area, you can choose from more than three dozen rural rodeos. Schedules that list most of them are available from both **Travel Alberta** and the **Calgary Tourist & Convention Association**.

As you look down those lists, you'll see just how thoroughly a part of western life the rodeo is. The same way communities anywhere in North America hold a town fair or exhibition, we hold rodeos and stampedes. The **rodeo** is the specific group of events; the older term, **stampede** (which used to cover rodeo as well) is now understood to mean the more general community fair that is often held at the same time. (Therefore, if you're not sure a straight rodeo would hold your attention for four hours, visit ones that advertise a stampede as well.) There are also **little britches rodeos**—as you might guess, rodeos for children. Here you can see four-year-olds ride sheep (the same event at the Calgary Stampede is called Wild and Woolly), six-year-olds struggle with colts and calves and mothers pray a lot.

There are also **chuckwagon races**. Again, these are often held in conjunction with a rodeo and a stampede, but not necessarily. You're sure to find them exciting, no matter how much you don't know about horses: in a chuckwagon race, the driver must maneuver his four-horse team and wagon around barrels, figure eight fashion, then belt (while trying to avoid penalties) for the racetrack and the finish line. Sometimes, to add to the melee, there are outriders and extra equipment as well. Want to know more? Call the office of the **World Professional Chuckwagon Association** in Calgary (287-3309).

There is quite a range of associations producing rodeos. You don't need to worry about that, since events and scoring systems are very similar in all cases. Even the names of the associations are interesting, though, because they demonstrate the grip rodeo has on all kinds of people: Foothills Rodeo Association, Canadian Professional Rodeo Association (CPRA), Chinook Rodeo Association, Southern Alberta Amateur Rodeo Cowboys Association, Indian Rodeo Cowboys Association, Canadian Girls Rodeo Association, even the Alberta High School Rodeo Association. Since most of these groups do not have permanent offices, your best bet is to call the CPRA office in Calgary (230-3407). They'll happily talk rodeo with you and give you the current contact name and number for any other association that interests you.

Now to decide which rodeo (or rodeos) to attend. There are some classics. Winston Bruce, who at first says he grew up with them all and therefore cannot possibly single out any one of them, finally names a favourite: "**Hand Hills**. It probably exemplifies the rodeo of forty years ago better than anywhere else around — they still have a lot of the old structures, wooden chutes, things like that."

The **Dogpound** rodeo has lots of fans, though they get a spirited argument when they claim that it's the oldest rodeo in the province. **Ponoka** gets high praise as well. One chuckwagon devotee loves it because it's a four to five-day event (depending on where the July first holiday falls), with rodeo and chuckwagon races all the way. She also singles out the **High River** event in August — what used to be a two-day chuckwagon show now has a rodeo section as well. If you too love the wagons, head for the **Grand Prairie Stompede** in early June: no rodeo, just the races with a midway and a few other attractions thrown in. The **High River Little Britches** rodeo, held in spring, is unquestionably the most famous of the children's shows, though there are many others.

In the end, though, don't worry about picking the "right" rodeo. Do what most of us do: go somewhere because the sun is shining, you want an outing, you'd like to get close — physically close — to rodeo action, and one of the places where a rodeo is taking place that day happens to be a part of the countryside you'd like to visit anyway.

As one very urban, pavement-loving Calgarian puts it: "What else would drag me out to Dogpound, Alberta? *And*," she adds in a surprised voice, "make me enjoy it when I get there?"

Shopping

Shopping

"Calgary has shopping areas, shopping complexes, shopping centres and districts for shoppers. You can find your own style of shopping here, no matter what it is."

By Tim Christison

Newsstands

Miss the old hometown? Or is it the old country? There are two newsstands in Calgary that specialize in out-of-town and foreign publications.

Billy's News & Smoke Shop (603 – 8th Avenue S.W.) sits stubbornly in a row of boarded-up stores, waiting to find out whether it will be moving or staying for another year. But wherever its location, Billy's will continue to specialize in magazines and newspapers from the English-speaking world with a few other publications thrown in as well.

Daily issues of papers from Vancouver, Victoria, Saskatoon, Winnipeg, Toronto, Ottawa, Montreal and Halifax are generally available the next day. The *Globe and Mail* and Calgary and Edmonton papers are today's issue.

The newsstand carries Sunday papers from Phoenix, Denver, Houston, New York, Seattle, Las Vegas, Miami, Los Angeles, San Francisco, Honolulu, New Zealand, Australia, Germany and Spain. Most people who take one of these papers regularly find it useful to reserve a copy. Ten British Sunday papers, ranging from the *Manchester Guardian* to the *News of the World*, are also available. Extra charges for the papers vary from an extra twenty cents for the *Edmonton Sunday Journal* to an extra $1.75 or more for the *New York Sunday Times*.

The magazines are primarily from the United States but

England, New Zealand, Australia and France are also well represented, especially in the fashion field. *Toronto Life* is the only city magazine carried regularly, other than our own *Calgary Magazine.*

Harry's News & Tobacco Shop is just east on the Mall (110 – 8th Avenue S.E.). Here the publications are in many foreign languages. Magazines and newspapers are received regularly from Germany, Poland, Italy, Hungary and Yugoslavia.

You'll find small-town papers as well—Red Deer, Medicine Hat, Lethbridge, and Kelowna, British Columbia, to name a few. Regina, Saskatchewan and St. John's, Newfoundland papers are stacked along with the papers from all the other major Canadian centres, including Quebec City.

Not as many American Sunday papers are carried here as at Billy's, but Harry's has some that his rival doesn't carry at all, and the British Sunday papers arrive here within a week of the publication date.

Both these downtown newsstands carry magazines on everything from pregnancy to darts, combat to the occult. Harry's also has a secluded alcove for those eighteen years and older—adult magazines, y'know. Finally, both shops carry racing forms, which seem to be the most popular papers of all with residents and visitors alike.

Shopping Malls

Calgary has shopping areas, shopping complexes, shopping centres and districts for shoppers. You can find your own style of shopping here, no matter what it is.

Even with the one category of malls, you have choices, especially if you consider the downtown buildings connected by Plus-15 walkways as a shopping mall.

In the dark ages (about twenty-eight years ago) when I first came to Calgary from Ontario, there were no shopping centres or malls. There was the downtown area and the north hill shopping areas. Period.

Downtown at 1st Street and 8th Avenue S.W., there was the **Hudson's Bay Company**, quite modern and large. It was the heart of downtown Calgary: one made appointments to meet at The Bay, probably in the Chinook Room for tea. At that time, part of the Bay building was given over to an oil company, with The Bay itself on only four floors (three for sales and one for administration). In the mid-sixties, The Bay took over the whole building. Some departments were expanded and new ones added such as the boutiques for high fashion, young fashions and lingerie. Over the years the fabric department has been taken over by the craft materials.

Eaton's was at 4th Street and 8th Avenue S.W., the outer edge of downtown in the fifties. This store was a big disappointment to me: it was dingy and not the type of Eaton's I was used to in the East. Since then, of course, it has changed considerably. As a matter of fact, it seems that Eaton's has been in a state of continual renovation for the past few years.

Now The Bay and Eaton's are more than two stores, they are the brackets for the main downtown shopping area. The enclosed Plus-15 walkways (named for the fact that they are built at fifteen feet above ground level) are a godsend when the winter wind blows, the chill sets in or the weather is wet. **Scotia Centre** and **T-D (Toronto-Dominion) Square** are connected by a Plus-15. Most motorists prefer to park in the Bay Parkade because the parcel pick-up is more convenient than at Eaton's (impossible to find and little used) and because it is easier to drive into and out of. The Eaton's exit is on a rise, and many shoppers find it too nerve-wracking to hold a standard-shift car steady while making change and then avoid backing into the car behind.

Parking is the hard part; walking around the interior downtown shopping area is easy. Many of the shops specialize in one way or another, but all concentrate on fashion. The unique feature of this shopping centre is the **Devonian Gardens**. A glass elevator takes shoppers or downtown workers up to the tropical gardens which were donated to the city by the Devonian Foundation. Here in the two-level green oasis, you can find a secluded bench on which to sit and watch or eat. In the main part of the garden, there are more benches and you can see art shows displayed on the walls or take children to the creative playground. In the winter, the exterior pool is frozen to form a skating rink. This whole area is free and open to the public seven days a week.

Another delight in this complex is the **Lancaster Building**. This old building has been restored and shops are installed in a third-level grouping called Lancaster Gate. These shops run to fragile and lovely decorating pieces, jewellery and silk garments from other parts of the world. On the second floor of the building you'll find a collection of food outlets that run the gamut from Oriental to French, via health food and regular old North American fast food. It's a good idea to buy a lunch or snack here to take to the Devonian gardens: you can remain indoors and the food will stay hot during the short walk.

A wander downtown on a Saturday will make you one of a few people on the streets, but the Fashion Four, that area from The Bay to Eaton's, will be packed as always.

And so are the suburban malls.

For many years a large segment of Calgary's population has been American. The influence of these Calgarians is evident in our shopping malls and stores.

If you have ever been to an American suburban shopping mall then you know what to expect in the suburbs of Calgary. The malls are huge sprawling places. Some have maps to help you find your way around, but others are indoor mazes that won't let you out until you've shopped all the stores. To give you an idea of the style and variety of malls in Calgary, we'll consider four of them in some detail, one in each quadrant of the city. Each has several major tenants (usually a department store and a supermarket), plus a number of chain boutiques, smaller independent stores and chain record and book stores.

Let's start our tour at **Marlborough Town Square** in the northeast. Several shops of the same type are bunched together here for easy comparison-shopping. Four jeans shops and six shoe stores come to mind. Bourne Shoes (located in this mall and in other locations) claims it is able to fit everyone. This means this is the place to fit your preteen's big feet with something that is suitable to her age. All the major jean store chains are well represented and virtually with shouting distance of one another.

The mall's eighty-plus stores are jam-packed, and there are kiosks as well, squeezed into the centre aisles. A food carousel invites anyone with a taste for ethnic fast food or health food to have a munch. This mall has a couple of import shops for clothing and small household items. Cinemas bring in people from all over the city, while other services—the laundromat and dry cleaners—are designed for tenants in the surrounding apartment buildings.

The major tenants in Marlborough Town Square are

Sears, Woolco, Boots and Safeway.

Thanks to the set-up of this mall, it should be possible to get good prices on most items since the competition is, in many cases, right next door and eager to win your custom.

Marlborough Mall (like a number of other malls) holds flea markets on Sunday. Individuals rent tables to sell antiques, collectables, imported Indian clothes and the like.

Market Mall is a well-established shopping centre in the northwest. The cinemas here draw people from other areas of the city as well, which greatly adds to the ability of Woodward's and The Bay to attract shoppers during the week. (Most malls are busy on the weekends and in the evenings but quiet during the day.)

This shopping centre faces townhouses and the backs of condominium units so the needs of single people and small families are reflected in the merchandise offered here. Woodward's meat market, especially, seems to be cognizant of the single eater, but case-lots of canned goods are still featured in their food sales.

Each year, The Bay has a large outdoor garden section to accommodate the fact that this is a newer area of Calgary where homeowners are house-proud and want a good garden despite the challenges of local weather.

Southcentre, in the far southeast at Anderson Road and Macleod Trail, was the first suburban mall to stay open until 9:30 P.M. on weekdays. This has a strong appeal in a two-job family neighbourhood. It also gives teens a chance to earn some money by working in the store at night.

The two major tenants are The Bay and Eaton's, with a myriad of little stores thrown in to attract every fashion dollar possible. Southcentre has wide aisles between the major department stores and an open mezzanine area. A number of fashion shows are regularly staged here and at Christmas a fantasyland fills in the centre area.

Chinook Centre, at Macleod Trail and Glenmore Trail in the southwest, was the first large suburban mall in Calgary. Here there are regular charity bazaars, art shows and other attractions to fill up the wide aisles between Sears and Woodward's. Food outlets are not grouped in this mall but pockets of fast food places exist, one in connection with Supervalu, part of a small Western Canadian supermarket chain.

One peculiarity of this centre is that you can leave Sears

without intending to and find yourself in the middle of the second-floor mall. To get to the second floor of Sears, it is necessary to use the escalator in the stationery department. (The escalator in the jewellery section will take you into the mall area and you will have to walk some distance to re-enter the Sears store.)

The city also has two small shopping areas that are not technically malls but are exciting shopping places.

At 16th Avenue and 8th Street S.W. sits **Mount Royal Village**. This brick building is new and only recently fully occupied. The rent is high and so are the prices of the items in the shops. What you get for your money is one-of-a-kind items.

Some of the stores are the only outlets for a given company west of Toronto—for example, Norma's (an exclusive sweater and knitwear shop), Ira-Berg, Ports for Men, 7 Flags Import and Magic Pan Restaurant.

Descamps de Paris, a French linen company, has only two North American outlets: one in New York and one in Mount Royal Village. A single sheet for an adult's bed costs one hundred dollars, while babies' things are priced to tempt doting (and affluent) grandmothers.

Another store for grandparents is Heffalumps & Woozels. A bridge takes you from the reality of the rest of the world into a child's fantasy of colour. Clothes are hung according to colour, not size. A variety of delightful bows, barrettes and sweet pieces of soft sculpture and handmade toys tempt child and adult alike. A herd of unicorns and other mythical animals decorate the store and are also for sale. Even the most mundane takes a decorative turn here: erasers come in shapes or in decorated containers. It's the type of store that would make one borrow a child just to have a reason to go inside.

On that same lower level stand two more temptations. One is Toute Sweet, which sells the most sinful candy in all shapes and flavours plus chocolate novelties in letter shapes and other shapes that give a giggle.

Your nose will help you find the Cookie Jar, where you can stock up on chocolate chip cookies the size of tarts and other homemade-type cookies. The selection is limited and quantities are usually gobbled up while still warm.

A door or two away is a bistro along the lines of a Parisian deli, called Blue Vinny. Baguettes, pâté and cheeses of all sorts are there to take out. So is a variety of coffees ready for the grinding. Potted, bottled and canned delights line the walls. Cappuccino and French pastries tempt one to stay—if a seat is available at one three tiny tables.

The displays in the forty-six shops in Mount Royal Village are imaginative and interesting enough to make window-shopping a satisfaction in itself. That is fitting in a building that won an urban design award for commercial buildings.

Design is the whole raison d'être at the **Devenish Design Centre**, located across the street from Mount Royal Village. This renovated apartment building at 8th Street and 17th Avenue S.W. is owned by interior designer Christopher Maier, whose furniture and design studio occupies a large portion of the building. But Maier has attracted other high quality interior design businesses, too, as well as those who supply furniture and other items for making space an individual expression.

Two art galleries deal in prints and one other gallery represents only Inuit artists. Both retail and wholesale dealers in furniture sell and display in this gorgeous building with its brass, leaded glass and thickly carpeted hallways. As you walk along the hallways, French doors beckon to shops that bring in handmade carpets, custom-designed furniture and objets d'art for every taste.

At the Devenish you will have an opportunity to compare styles, prices and fashions in furniture. It's a place for those who gradually build up their collections of art and personal belongings rather than redecorate every few years to suit the latest trend. Most of the shops cater to the traditional and classical, but there are trendy places as well.

To find a shopping area's location, just check the end of the Calgary listings in the white pages of your phone book. There you will find a list of all apartments, buildings and shopping centres in the city.

"Gently Used"

Used but not abused. Gently used. Fashion finds. Clothes with a history. Historically correct. These are phrases own-ers of secondhand stores use to describe still-fashionable garments with lots of life in them yet or those more eccentric clothes that help the enthusiast set fashion.

Most shoppers, however, take a less romantic view of secondhand clothing shops. For those who sell on consignment, it's a place to pick up a bit of extra cash; for those who have limited funds, it's a place to find bargains and give the tired old wardrobe a lift.

There are five secondhand places for adult clothing in Calgary and two for children's. The hours are almost uniformly 11:00 A.M. to 5:00 P.M. It's wise to check before going to the shop for the first time, though, since most of them are off the beaten track.

Let's start with the oldest established place of this kind, the **Cock-A-Too** (1433 - 17th Avenue S.W.). This business began with friends who wanted to exchange clothes. It moved out of the basement of one woman's home to 17th Avenue and 14th Street S.W., where it is now on the north side, a few doors up from the northwest corner of the intersection.

Antique furniture plus decorating odds and ends are for sale, as well as classy fashions. It's a shop with an air of selectivity: the owner has been known to tell more than one casually dressed visitor, "I don't have anything for you." The prices are hefty, but not out of line with the quality of genuine designer labels.

The contributors to this shop are in the upper social circles and discard garments, it would seem, after only one wearing. Italian wools, silks, Parisian and Californian designers are all found here. The owner will buy new or take on consignment pieces specifically for you once you have built up a rapport with her.

Though most of the clothes are secondhand, new pieces are also carried. Everything is selected with an eye to lasting fashion value. When a style makes a reappearance on the fashion scene, as tartan skirts did with the preppy look, the Cock-A-Too is the place to look.

Since the prices here are in the same range as those in better dress shops, it is not really the place for slim budgets trying to stay healthy. It's more the place to find designer fashions at old, preinflation prices.

Twice but Nice (1309 - 17th Avenue S.W.) sells men's clothing on consignment, as well as women's—a rare feature in a secondhand store in this town. The selling area is a converted house, each room devoted to a different type of clothing.

Men's clothing is tucked away in a room at the back of the house but despite the out-of-the-way positioning, there is a fairly wide range of suits, jackets, vest and pant combinations, shirts both dress and casual, as well as outer coats, ties and some shoes.

A good selection of maternity and lingerie items are well displayed, along with hats, purses and a large number of shoes.

Twice but Nice has a relaxed atmosphere, and everyone seems satisfied with the freedom to browse and compare within the store or with other secondhand stores.

Nearby is **Snooper's Clothing** (825 – 12th Avenue S.W.) where owner Audrey Gough, a former model, sells secondhand clothes on consignment and often wonders how there can still be so much good quality stuff coming into her store every day. Her own tastes run to the latest and trend-setting fashions, and this is reflected in her merchandise.

A large selection of shoes dominates one wall—some the sort that make you want to dance all night, while others look lovely but would probably be more suitable for a dinner date than dancing.

Quite a number of small sizes are carried, particularly in evening clothes, a boon for those who are tiny. Many women buy clothes, wear them for awhile and then bring them in here to trade for another set of sweaters, tops or skirts. Young women starting on their first job have also come here to trade in their warm, practical baggy cords for trimmer business suits.

Regular customers keep Gough supplied with items that were bought on holidays and were found unsuitable for the everyday life-style. This gives Calgary customers access to Hawaiian, Californian and Caribbean fashions, at half price. Some items find their way to Snooper's without even being worn.

New items are sold here as well and marked as such. The general rule is the price will be half the original price, but the styles are in the fashion forefront.

Another store with a fashion-conscious bent is **Peacock Boutique Dress Agency** (124 – 10th Street N.W.). A very large store, but every nook and cranny of the front of the store is packed with clothes bearing familiar fashion labels. Silks, blends and cottons, these secondhand clothes are half the original price or less and gently used. Most of them look fresh and new. Also displayed around the room are furs and fur pieces with reasonable price tags.

In the middle room are casual clothes, evening pants and dresses, swim suits, some delicate evening wear and attractive shoes. In the back room, a large open area, are suits, tops, sweaters, coats, slacks, jackets, and skirts. The styles are mostly classical and timeless. A few trendy things are on racks divided by size.

At **Pendulum** (1802 – 1st Street N.W.), the clothes are not arranged according to size but by colour instead. You will find, for example, all shades of red blouses in one place. (It makes putting your wardrobe together much easier.) As owner Anita Sereda says, sizes don't mean much any more to most shoppers, since one manufacturer's size 10 seems to be another's size 16.

Several local stores send their sales merchandise to Pendulum on a regular basis so there is an excellent selection of new as well as secondhand clothes. New designer jeans, for example, at half price. If the garment is new, it often still carries the original tag so the customer can compare values. Indian cotton imports are also new and reasonably priced.

In addition to new and slightly-used clothing, there are racks of what is termed "nostalgia." Granted they may not deserve the title "antique," but the charm of these elderly clothes is appealing. Prices are surprisingly low for both men's and women's clothes and accessories. Some pieces of older jewellery are also displayed, well protected in glass showcases.

The men's clothing here includes new, used and "nostalgia." There is a good selection of new jeans for men, and men's shirts and sweaters that would tempt some women as well.

It is possible to spend hours in this jazz-filled, incense-scented haven, picking your way through all the T-shirts, jeans, knickers, harem pants, gauze dresses, blouses, wedding dresses, men's suits, pants, vests, smoking jackets and dressing gowns, plus an astonishing variety of odds and ends. The dressing rooms are well lit and have good mirrors.

But if "nostalgia" isn't good enough, if you want truly period clothes, there are two other shops to know about. Each has its own sources and preferred fashion era.

Old Hat (116 – 10th Street N.W.) is owned by Anne Green, actress and theatre person. She seems always to be there, either helping someone put a gorgeous outfit together complete with hat, gloves and shoes or doing hand work on some precious piece that she won't trust to anyone else.

With her constant trips throughout North America and Europe, Anne is able to keep enough stock on hand to costume plays, films and TV productions. Though most of the clothes on the main floor are from the forties and fifties, on the mezzanine (guarded by a dated, or is it dateless, mannequin) are treasures from the Edwardian, Victorian and pre-twenties periods. Pieces that have been bought privately are often the choice pieces in the shop. These rare and valuable garments are Anne's pride and joy. Some of their value to Anne is for rental to theatrical companies. This allows her to hold out for what she believes the garment is worth.

Back to the main floor for the main portion of the stock. Several antique silk kimonos, satin lingerie with movie star glamour and nightgowns with old-fashioned virtue still evident on their white cotton-lace trimmed bodices hang on racks where the items for sale change constantly.

This is another place were items are bought with particular customers in mind. One customer with small hands and feet is the ideal recipient for sample shoes and gloves that come into the shop.

There's a good selection of rayon dresses, manufactured many years ago, and these have become popular with young Calgarians. Men's clothing here is strictly in the period category. Some delightful tuxedos and business suits are reasonably priced. Jackets and coats add inches to the shoulders and have slim waists. Prices on the main floor are very competitive with the prices of present-day clothing of similar quality.

Harlow (926 – 17th Avenue S.W.), as you might guess, concentrates on the era when Jean Harlow was all the rage. June Anne Simmons got her original stock from movie wardrobe department auctions. Some privately collected items also appear in the store from time to time.

The small shop is full of snapshots and posters of Mae West and other contemporaries of Harlow. A number of more recent photographs of models wearing clothes that have passed through the store give a real sense of the thirties and early forties.

A good collection of wedding gowns, both short and long, gives you the chance to wear a gown just like Mom's. Other nostalgic items are fur pieces, collars, capes and jackets.

Some bits and pieces of jewellery are also displayed in a small case.

At Harlow, the crunch of crinoline, the swish of silk and the formality of the clothes bring back a glamour that was first introduced by the movie stars of the thirties. This is a special shop for specific tastes.

Now for the children's-wear shops. Happily for mothers fighting the constant battle to find clothes at reasonable prices, there are two secondhand shops for children in Calgary. Both, as it happens, are in the northwest part of the city.

Children's Garden (318a – 10th Street N.W.) takes clothes on consignment. At the front of the shop are new handmade maternity clothes, some baby items, quilts (also new) and quilted floor mats for baby to play on. Also at the front of the shop are used Barbie dolls and clothes as well as other used toys. Occasionally there is even a bike.

In the large, well-filled room at the back are sweet little slips for girls, young men's and boys' corduroy or wool suits, diaper suits, jeans, T-shirts and cords. You could walk away with change from a twenty-dollar bill, even after buying shoes for a child here. Skates and boots are sold in winter and fall.

Mothers make a habit of bringing in their family's out-grown children's clothes and trading them in for the next size. T-shirts here are often a mere dollar.

Second Time Around (1804 – 1st Street N.W.), next door to Pendulum, started out with nine people consigning clothes. Now 154 consignees help to stock the store and buy or trade for different clothes for their growing children.

Again, at the front of the shop there are new clothes. Here the tiny garments are handmade for babies under a year old, and there are jumpsuits and pantsuits at reasonable prices.

The used clothes are the popular items, though. Diaper suits, tiny vests, cords, slacks, dresses for little and not so little girls, all the items a child needs and outgrows. The quality and size of the clothing determines the price. Here also, prices are less than half price, sometimes as little as one-quarter the new price. Tights were once on special at fifty cents.

Since it is possible at both these stores to pick up for very reasonable prices the dresses and fancy diaper suits that doting parents or grandparents lavish on their young descendants and it is also possible to sell outgrown clothes on consignment, I predict that it won't be long before there are more secondhand children's stores in Calgary.

There will also be more secondhand women's and men's shops when the success of the established ones tempts others to set up shops for customers who themselves want to be gently used.

Poke and Browse

If you are looking for a place to stroll, window shop, seriously shop, stop for a cool drink or have a chat over coffee, Calgary, alas, has only a limited number of areas to offer you. Even these you have to seek out.

But they are worth it. The charm of these strolling districts is their eclecticism—the mixture of staid, dark mysterious places next door to slick, modern, renovated stores still smelling of fresh paint and sawdust. Each time you open a door in these areas, it's like unwrapping a surprise package. Not every store will suit your tastes, but each has its own treasures to reveal. Each section has a distinct personality, too, but all of these quarters are mixed in period, quality, types of buildings and people who work or shop there. A visit to any one of them will bring you into contact with various cultures, classes and types.

First, the oldest area in Calgary for a stroll is a working man's neighbourhood: **Inglewood**. The shopping is mainly along 9th Avenue S.E. from 8th Street to about 13th Street S.E. and is on the threshold of becoming a place for Saturday strolling shoppers.

For some time Olivier's Candies has been attracting people to the area. You can watch candy being made in ancient copper utensils. The candies are sold elsewhere in Calgary, but the shop next to the factory is the place to pick it up still warm and at bargain prices.

A number of secondhand furniture stores dot both sides of the street. In one, you will get a political discussion along with a sales pitch on the new, upholstered furniture carried next to the used pieces; in another, the owner may tell you about her latest poem; and in another you find items bordering on the antique.

Shopping in Inglewood is like panning for gold. The nuggets are hidden in all the gravel of the light industrial shops, repair workshops, car lots and motorbike dealerships.

Waiting to be discovered are a genteel gift and framing shop, an art gallery that specializes in Plains Indian pieces (Westlands Art Gallery) and a couple of restaurants. Both of the new restaurants have used existing buildings to give something different to the character of the area. One, Pistons, is a converted service station now spiced to high-tech glamour with chrome and dark grey. The other, The Restaurant, is in a brick firehall renovated to traditional charm.

This area is obviously about to make it to the top of the stroller's checklist.

Another area that is still on the known-to-the-few list is **Bridgeland**. This is a small neighbourhood shopping district with strong German and Italian influences in the store signs along 1st Avenue N.E. from the 600 to 900 block.

The Italian Centre Shop and the Italian Centre Meat Market, two separate stores, both have excellent veal. Italian tomatoes, rows of pasta, baskets of Italian parsley, pungent cheeses and spices abound in the Italian Centre Shop. Pasta machines, huge wine jugs and other items necessary for authentic Italian meals are handy in this district, right down to the bread—fresh at City Bakery which makes European rolls, breads and pastries with fresh cream. Two bakings a day mean fresh hot goodies both morning and afternoon. Chocolates are also a specialty of this bakery.

There are other places that you'll enjoy discovering on your own in Bridgeland.

Louise Crossing, on the other hand (10th Street N.W., just north of the Bow River), has definitely already been discovered and is pointed to proudly by an increasing number of browsers as a place with character and interesting shops. This district has an air of "let's help each other get along and let's do it beautifully." Perhaps this comes from the concentration of craft outlets, secondhand stores, artists' works and supplies and other stores that smack of the back-to-basics attitude about life. There is also a definite sense of community and co-operation. The work of Prairie Textures, which doesn't have a street level location, is sold in the Children's Garden secondhand kids' clothing store. Steepleworks is a space operated by artists who fill the shop with a variety of art work from watercolours to dolls made from antique moulds. The works are done to order or from the artist's own inspiration.

Red Earth, Gallery Three, Freckles and the Galleria offer

a wide selection of craft items made mostly in Alberta but with some brass reproductions and sundry items from other provinces in some of the shops.

Used books and used furniture are available here. At Hunt's Bone Yard, mind, you will have to pass the inspection of the resident cat (Big Mo, who owns the place). Le Bistingo is a fast food outlet operated by the same people who run Le Cyrano Restaurant, both located in the small modern shopping plaza along with a games store (Ahead of the Game) that lists the favourite game of the week. (The secondhand clothing stores, Peacock Boutique and Old Hat, are described in the "Gently Used" section.)

The area has lately expanded in an interesting and welcome way along Kensington Road N.W. Restaurants and delis, the repertory movie house (the Plaza), clothing and sports equipment stores and a book bargain-hunter's delight (Book Warehouse) should all be enough to pull you around the corner for a side trip.

Be sure to take time to stop for a coffee and a sweet at Culinary Arts. Don't leave before you take in their large array of items for the kitchen and the cook. Practicality was never so esthetic!

When I think of the shopping area along **17th Avenue S.W. from 4th to 15th Street**, I think of a small town. Pedestrians dart from side to side, store owners visit each other and in the nearly one-mile stretch you can find almost anything you need or want.

The heart of this district is from 7th to 9th Street, which has been dubbed "Gallery Row" due to the concentration of art galleries. Nearby is a wonderful park with benches, trees and (cross your fingers) sunshine. Strollers buy food from any number of places nearby, then sit in the park to people-watch.

There are dress shops, hair dressers, food stores, kitchen shops for the trendy and the wealthy, bookstores for Christians and for the exploring reader, stereo and record shops, banks and trust companies, furniture stores, imported and domestic goods and much more. There are restaurants— Chinese, Greek, homestyle, workingman's café and, the undeniable favourite, Bagels and Buns. This Jewish bakery is the coffee-and-chat place on the south side of the river, especially on a Saturday or Sunday morning (when the Danish are hot and fragrant). A few small tables accommodate the early birds.

ABC Discount Foods (which, despite its name, is an ethnic goods shop) specializes in Eastern foods and spices, but it's the place to go if you need ethnic produce or spices for almost any cuisine. A couple of European delis carry fresh batches of foods made from old family recipes. The Chalet has paprika bacon and the next door bakery carries strudel that does an early disappearing act.

Neighbouring **Mount Royal Village** and the Devenish Design Centre combine to give this district a toney air which is reinforced by a few other nearby shops—three antique shops, interior design shops and a custom lampshade shop, for example. But, mostly, the area is a "just folks" place.

In all these strolls, you'll find the joy of dealing with an individual, who will deal with you as an individual in return and, given half a chance, will remember your name and your preferences.

Crafts

Sculptures all over North America are made from Alberta clay, so it's no wonder that ceramics and pottery enjoy great popularity in Alberta. They are ideal items to give as a sample of Calgary's indigenous crafts. You'll find pots, cups, mugs, dinner sets, coffee and tea pots, soufflé dishes, fondue pots, plant holders, salad bowls and servers along with novelty items and decorative items.

Now where do you find them? If you are buying in quantity, I would suggest visiting **J.B.K. Pottery** (3434 - 27th Street N.E.). The owner is a former art instructor who designs and makes dinner and tea sets and other functional items. Four potters work constantly to keep up with custom work and general orders for stores.

Most shops, like the **Croft** (1509 - 8th Street S.W.), carry the work of several artisans. This provides an ideal way for the uninitiated to do some comparison shopping. The Croft represents nearly thirty potters who will take custom orders but caution customers that each piece will be unique, even in a dinner set. This is handwork, not factory production, giving items their charm and artistic merit. The store carries other craft items as well, including wind sox—colourful strips of fabric designed to take the wind and bring cheer in the long Calgary winters. Tie one to a tree to attract birds and happy thoughts.

The **Galleria** (1116 Memorial Drive N.W.) is a constant

delight. This converted service station is tastefully used to display the works of over a hundred craft workers and designers. Fabric pieces give colour and warmth to the shop, but ceramics and pottery are also mainstays in the inventory. Shoppers also head for the patchwork items, napkins, jackets and quilts, all made locally. A good selection of knitted baby clothes and other baby-related items dominate one section of the store.

Gallery Three (104 – 10th Street N.W.) is a smaller shop but has a large selection of pottery. Wind chimes, bells and small clay pockets for holding dried flowers are ideal for gifts. Functional items such as mugs and bowls sell fast and come in glazes to appeal to a variety of tastes.

Steepleworks, farther north at 142 – 10th Street N.W., also handles the work of a limited number of potters. Ladles, tiny spoons and decorative pieces as well as mugs are attractively crafted.

Another craft bordering on art that is popular with Calgarians is stained glass work. If this interests you, visit the **Rubiayat Stained Glass Studio** (722 – 17th Avenue S.W.). The selection ranges from charming small pieces (including boxes of many sizes and shapes) to window designs (usually custom work) fashioned to catch the sun.

Since this is the West, Indian crafts seem an ideal souvenir or gift from Calgary. The **Wolf Den** (114a – 8th Avenue S.E.) on the downtown mall is the place to go for authentic Indian work, whether you are a casual shopper or a serious collector. Indian artisans come to the store daily to sell their works. Collectors' items include Navajo rugs, Indian dolls and turquoise.

Places to Eat, Drink and Stay

The Restaurateurs

" 'Calgarians have never had such a choice of good places to eat,' says restaurateur Sheldon Walker."

By Gillian Steward

During the past five years, eating out in Calgary has become as much an adventure as a quest for fine food and relaxation. The reason is the ever increasing number of restaurants—restaurants crying out for investigation and judgment. Gone are the days when Calgary was a steak and baked potato town and the best-restaurant list could be quickly narrowed down to two names: **Hy's Steak House**, and **Owl's Nest** in the Calgary Inn (now **The Westin**). Also gone are the days when Calgarians could keep up with the new restaurants and leisurely try each new one as it opened. Now the city boasts hundreds—everything from French to Vietnamese to Jewish delicatessen—and checking out one of the latest has become an obsessive sport practised by natives and newcomers alike.

The competition and the frenzied pace at which new establishments open has left many a restaurateur looking over his shoulder wondering who will open the next restaurant and try to capture more than just the familiar troupe of people who check out each new place and then move on to the next. They know Calgarians can afford to be fickle because there always seems to be someone trying to lure them away with a new menu or the latest in interior design. Calgary is full of people looking for the most interesting places to plug into, the restaurants and bars that have that extra hum, the ones that make you feel as though you have discovered what Calgary is all about. It's also a place where a restaurant can quickly die should it receive a negative review from the *Calgary Herald*'s prickly restaurant critic, Garnet Page.

As a result, the restaurateurs who have survived, who manage to keep their dining rooms full at lunch and dinner time throughout the week, have something they can indeed be proud of. And in many cases it is these established restaurateurs who have influenced and shaped much of Calgary's restaurant scene. According to Klaus Tenter, general manager of the Four Seasons Hotel and a keen observer of Calgary restaurants, the opportunities for a restaurateur to introduce new ideas and set trends are almost boundless. In other cities it's hard to break in, says Tenter, but Calgary is still so wide open a person can open a restaurant and succeed in a relatively short time. Tenter knows whereof he speaks, for during the last five years he has trained dozens of chefs, sous-chefs, maître d's and waiters for **Traders**, the Four Seasons' timeless and elegant dining room. Fortunately for Calgarians (and unfortunately for Traders), many only have to be in the city for a short time before they realize there's room out there for another restaurant — and off they go to open it.

As a result, the Four Seasons' old-boy network is an impressive one. Three of the city's top French restaurants, **Le Gourmet**, **La Chaumière** and **Le Cyrano**, were all started by former Traders' staff. Joseph De Angelis, owner of **La Chaumière** and former maître d' at Traders, took with him a concern for fastidious service and an extensive knowledge of food and wine. Even though his restaurant was hidden away in an inauspicious part of the city, only a stone's throw from Stampede Park and across the street from an auto body shop, it was soon setting the standard for all the other top of the line establishments. It also became a particular favourite of internationally travelled oil men such as Jack Gallagher, the suave chairman of Dome Petroleum. It seemed only natural that as **La Chaumière** basked in success it too would spawn its own little network, and that's exactly what happened. De Angelis' two partners left to open **Chez Remilio** and two of his waiters, Peter Christensen (also a **Traders** alumnus) and Otto Nielsen, departed some time later to open **Café Danois**, a classy, European-style fast food restaurant in the Chevron Building.

While the Four Seasons has done more than its share of providing Calgarians with new and intriguing places to eat, it would be misleading to suggest that only the Four Seasons loses staff to new ventures. In Calgary keeping good staff can be almost as challenging as providing good food and wine. No sooner is a waiter or waitress trained and familiar to the customers than another restaurant makes a better offer. So don't be surprised if one day you are served in **Cafe Calabash** by a waiter who, only a few days earlier, served you in **Kipling's**. The Calgary restaurant scene is much like a carousel, and a good chef, maître d' or waiter can get on and off almost at whim.

The fine art of chef-stealing, however, is nothing compared to some of the recipe-snitching that goes on. It was recipe-snitching that started *The Great Cheesecake War* which gripped Calgary for over two years and still has reverberations echoing throughout city restaurants. It all began in 1976 when Marvin Segal opened **My Marvin's** and started serving huge slabs of cheesecake, the likes of which had never before been seen in Calgary. Customers came in droves, lined up at the door, even outside the door in the middle of winter, to eat Marvin's cheesecake which—he claimed—was concocted from his grandmother's secret recipe. But then Marvin had a falling out with some of his partners and staff, and after they left one claimed it was actually *his* grandmother's recipe. By the time the argument had reached the rumours-of-lawsuit stage, Ken Lee (formerly of **My Marvin's**) was making his own cheesecakes, claiming they were the same as **My Marvin's**, and selling them almost as fast as he could turn them out. It soon got to the point that anyone who had worked at **My Marvin's** and claimed he knew the "secret" recipe was assured of a job making cheesecake in another restaurant. Lee eventually sold the "secret" recipe to Barb Warhaft, a young entrepreneur, who then started her own cheesecake business and started supplying the dessert to restaurants such as **Slack Alice** and **Cafe Calabash**.

In the meantime, no restaurant dared open or continue operating without cheesecake on the menu, the demand had become so intense. And cheesecake had become such a hot topic of conversation that it wasn't long before the most outrageous stories started circulating. The most preposterous was undoubtedly the claim by Harvey Cohen of **Ken-**

sington's Delicafé that a frantic customer had once paid one hundred dollars for a rush take-out order of one of his prized cheesecakes. Not that Harvey doesn't make a good cheesecake. He does. But the story seemed not so much evidence of culinary talent as of the lengths to which people would go when it came to one-upmanship in The Great Cheesecake War. Even the most refined restaurants couldn't resist. Joseph De Angelis at **La Chaumière**, for example, had no qualms about flatly stating that there was absolutely no comparison between his cheesecake and all the "others" in town. For one thing, his was the purest—no heavy crust, no jammy topping, just pure, lemony cheesecake with a thin layer of sour cream on top. His may indeed be the purist's delight, but The Great Cheesecake War and its insatiable appetite for gooier and gooier ammunition means that all kinds of variations are now available in Calgary restaurants. Everything from Piña Colada to Rum and Raisin to Peanut Butter. The war has subsided but it has guaranteed that there is one sure way to get a restaurateur so furious he'll kick the shin of his favourite waiter. Ask for a piece of his cheesecake, when it comes take a slow bite and then lean back in your chair and say: "But it's not as good as My Marvin's."

Of course, there were a few restaurateurs who avoided sullying themselves in The Great Cheesecake War. One was the eminently successful Witold Twardowski, whose restaurants have always been known for elegant desserts as well as intriguing appetizers and main courses. Twardowski started out with **Ambrosia**, a refined cafeteria that featured lots of bean sprouts, leafy vegetables, whole-grain breads and fish soups, all served to the sounds of chamber music. The restaurant was successful—despite the fact that it never served a single ounce of red meat in a city famous for its beef—that the young and esoteric Twardowski went on to open two other equally intriguing restaurants.

Since he has a keen interest in old buildings, all his restaurants have been carefully carved out of buildings that have seen better days but still have interesting architecture and detail. **Ambrosia** (which Twardorski has since sold) is located on the downtown mall in one of the city's prized sandstone buildings. His second restaurant, **Phoenicia**, is in a delicate, narrow, three-story building on 1st Street S.W. It has been renovated so it now features a large enclosed indoor-outdoor patio, but for the most part the building still retains its sense of warmth and history. Twardowski's third restaurant—**Divino**—is a small European-style café with black and white floor tiles, a huge espresso machine and inviting corners designed for long, languid conversations. Here again the setting is another historic building (and there aren't many left in Calgary), the Grain Exchange Building in the heart of downtown, kitty-corner from the Palliser Hotel.

Of all the restaurants in Calgary, Twardowski's seem best able to combine the history and tradition that is Calgary with the imported flair of fine foods and exquisite interior design. They are a good example of Calgary at the crossroads. And since Twardowski is a Calgarian who travelled extensively before settling into the restaurant business, it's not surprising that he's been able to blend the old and the new as well as he has.

Another world traveller who has made his mark on the Calgary restaurant scene is Brahim Oussif, owner of **La Fleur**. Ebullient Brahim, a Moroccan, began his restaurant career in Canada by working at a number of establishments in Calgary and Edmonton. But it wasn't long before he knew he had to have his own restaurant. He also knew that he wanted it French, but informal. At the time Calgary didn't have a French restaurant. He first opened near downtown, only a couple of doors away from an auto body shop. His restaurant was a success even without a liquor licence, but Brahim decided he wanted a better location, so he moved into one of Calgary's most vibrant inner-city neighbourhoods, Hillhurst-Sunnyside. He kept his theme of French-but-informal, got a liquor licence and became very strict about preparing French favourites (his brother actually did the cooking). He refused to keep ketchup or mint sauce, for example, even though **La Fleur** served rack of lamb and some customers insisted they couldn't eat it without those traditional accompaniments. **La Fleur** also became famous for its onion soup, soup so rich with cheese and onions that it was like a small meal in itself.

The move to Hillhurst-Sunnyside seemed to enhance the appeal of the small restaurant rather than diminish it, and it is now not only a lunch-time favourite for businessmen who work just across the river in the steel and glass highrises but has become a special dinner spot for local residents as well as those from other parts of the city. Its bar has become one of the few genuine, neighbourhood bars in Calgary and it's not unusual to see people in there like Alderman Elaine Husband, who lives only a few block away, winding down with friends after a week of politicking. It's been a long, uphill climb for Brahim (he had to sell his house to finance his first restaurant), but the young entrepreneur obviously enjoys his success and standing in the restaurant community. He also has to be given credit for being one of the first restaurateurs in Calgary to make the break from downtown and the suburban shopping centres. He helped pioneer the idea that sophisticated restaurants could be an integral part of the city's old neighbourhoods. The fact that he guessed right is reflected by the more than half dozen other restaurants that are now clustered nearby, including **Cafe Calabash**, **Don Quijote**, **Le Cyrano** and **Kensington's Delicafé**.

Despite the new tastes and trends, the old ways die hard. And since Calgary is in the middle of some of Canada's best cattle country, it only makes sense that the steak dinner is still alive and well and available for hearty eaters. One of the most interesting places to eat it in Calgary is **Ranchman's South** at 9311 Macleod Trail S. (**Ranchman's Uptown** at 1117 – 1st Street S.W. is under the same ownership and is as celebrated for its lounge as the original location is famous for its restaurant.) **Ranchman's South**, you see, isn't just a restaurant, it seems to be a state of mind, one that fulfills completely all the myths and legends about Calgary as Cowtown. Owner Harris Dvorkin planned it that way. And he didn't just use western props such as wagon wheels to create atmosphere, he made sure the *real* cowboys, the one who ride in the Calgary Stampede Rodeo and work on the ranches in the foothills just outside the city limits, came to his restaurant and nightclub. Dvorkin, who was selling real estate when he got involved in **Ranchman's** through family connections, was convinced that Calgary's cowboy heart was still throbbing beneath that cool exterior of steel and glass and acquired sophistication. He also knew that the cowboys were starting to feel a little left out, even though they were the ones who had made Calgary world famous in the first place. So he set about making **Ranchman's** into Calgary's cowboy headquarters.

He began by hiring Wayne Vold, a genuine singing cowboy with trophy saddles and prizes to prove it. Vold packed the place and began a tradition of country music at **Ranchman's** that has been carried on by performers like Ian Tyson. In

1975 Dvorkin added the Saddle Room and decorated it with trophy saddles, wagons and other horse paraphernalia donated for display by the cowboys. The Saddle Room is now the entertainment room, a place where cowboys of all kinds listen to the music, dance and drink their fill. As for Dvorkin—who proudly calls himself Calgary's best-known Jewish cowboy—the whole thing is like a dream come true. "I'm doing everything I want to do," he said once. "A relative recently told me that if there was a man living his fantasy it had to be me. I agree."

The restaurant scene in Calgary is so seductive it's managed to attract people who a few years ago would never have even considered getting into the business. Many find the glamour of being involved in your very own place, setting up your own little theatre with yourself as the star, just too irresistible. Others have seen that money can be made and welcome that challenge as well. **Kipling's**, for example, is owned by fifty investors—lawyers, doctors, accountants— who jumped at the chance to be involved in a lush restaurant with East-of-Suez decor and food. **Donahue's**, a San Francisco-style restaurant on 4th Street S.W., is owned by prominent real-estate lawyer, Jack Donahue. Another, **4th Street Rose**, is owned and operated by Barbara Beard who, after a career in marketing and sales, decided to take a chance on her real love—food. But perhaps the restaurateur with the most unusual background is psychologist Sheldon Walker, who decided that chicken soup was indeed just as important as psychotherapy and opened **Mr. Risty's**, a New York-style delicatessen.

Walker chose a thirties art-deco environment to go with his comforting food because he believes the design of that period is optimistic and bold, much like Calgary itself. He still has a little psychologist left in him because he gets great pleasure out of seeing people who come into his restaurant tired and irritable, leave relaxed and renewed. "In a way I'm still providing a nurturing atmosphere, only this way it's fun for me too," he says. And since Walker comes from a profession where analysis is an everyday affair, it seemed only fitting to ask him about his impressions of the restaurant business now that he's on the inside. "It's tough here, you have to be on your toes all the time, you never know when someone's going to copy you or come up with something better. But for the customers, it's great."

The Restaurants

"Today, little more than a decade out of the Tinfoil Age in Calgary, practically every taste can be catered to in the city's restaurants."

By Bernice Evans

When I first came to Calgary thirteen years ago it was a much smaller and much more conservative city. It was difficult to get to know people and so when in my second year here I was invited out to dinner by a charming if irreverent fellow, I was delighted to accept.

He took me to a favoured and locally famous steak house (now extinct) where I enjoyed the most delicious beef fillet I had ever encountered. It has a moist buttery texture and could be eaten with a fork; at the same time, it retained a hearty beef flavour. It could not have been more different from the beef with which I had been brought up—the almost gamey intensity of African grass-fed cattle, also tender, but deeper in flavour. I enjoyed the delicacy of the Alberta species but found I was unable to finish the large portion served.

A series of further invitations ensued from this (by now recognizably wicked) gentleman, but unfortunately they all culminated in steak dinners. I became restless. Was there, I plaintively asked, nothing but steak in Calgary? No, not unless you want Chinese food. There followed a spate of dreadful Western Chinese dinners, and finally, home cooking.

But all the while, a wondrous alchemy was at work.

All unawares, we were being infiltrated by "aliens." And, just as in a Ray Bradbury story, the invasion came silently and subtly. New waves of immigration brought Greeks, Italians, Hungarians, Yugoslavians, Spaniards, Lebanese and East Indians (from both the Indian subcontinent and the African countries of Kenya, Tanzania and Uganda).

These new Canadians were just as bored by the continual diets of steak and foil-wrapped potato as I was. Tiny holes-in-the-wall began springing up to cater to the new tastes. The demand for a varied, international sort of dining experience grew more intense as Calgary boomed and a more specialized European influx of newcomers arrived. And so, from small beginnings, grew sophisticated Italian restaurants, larger Greek restaurants, unabashed Indian hot-spots, specialized Chinese restaurants, a few superb Japanese houses and, finally, authentic French establishments. But wait—the process continues. the Japanese business input resulted in genuine sushi places, and Vietnamese and Thai immigrants have now launched serious operations in the culinary arena.

Today, little more than a decade out of the Tinfoil Age in Calgary, practically every taste can be catered to in the city's restaurants. Tour the world: begin in the north of Europe, work your way south, pass through the Middle East, on to Southeast Asia, India and the Orient, finally to return to Canada via Mexico. All this, without leaving Calgary.

Let us begin in *Denmark*. The **Copenhagen House** (1223A - 11th Avenue S.W.) will serve you traditional frikadellers with red cabbage and open-faced sandwiches. The **Viking Village** (7640 Fairmount Drive S.E.) is more elegant and offers sole, plaice, trout or salmon in various guises using mushrooms, onions, tomatoes, capers and spinach. The Danish pâté is smooth and pleasing, served warm, topped with sautéed mushrooms and the crispest bacon possible. There are cream cones with lingonberries and wonderfully satisfying rye bread made on the premises. Naturally, shrimp and marinated salmon have a large place on the menu, the shrimp appearing in many of the fish preparations. The Danish flavour in the menu is complemented by the incredibly courteous Danish flavour in the service. Anyone who has visited Denmark will recognize it at once—and will also appreciate the fine, clean lines of the restaurant itself with its patterned cotton cloths, wood trim and ceramic decoration.

Germany is next, in the form of **Franzl's Gasthaus** (2417 -

4th Street S.W.), appointed to resemble as closely as possible a German country inn with heavy dark beams and numerous ceramic beer steins and crests. This is always a jolly place, especially during Oktoberfest when beer and wine flow freely and the dirndl-dressed waitresses will happily dance a turn. The food is hearty and plentiful, from Biersuppe to bratwurst and sauerkraut. Enjoy fine steak tartare, well-seasoned rouladen, sauerbraten and full-bodied gamey hasenpfeffer. The Gasthaus is not the place for dieters, yet even now—when lighter food is in vogue—Calgarians still pack the restaurant, perhaps showing that they have not entirely forsaken their love of hearty rib-sticking fare.

It is not a large step from German cuisine to *Swiss*. At the **Chalet Heidi** (122 – 16th Avenue N.E.), though, you can treat yourself to the very special Swiss Bundnerteller (air-dried beef) served as an appetizer, or have the popular raclette, scraped and melted cheese, traditionally served with boiled potatoes. Swiss bread soup is an unusual specialty here, but the favourite veal dishes are also featured—with morels or with cream and cognac, a pork tenderloin sweetbread and liver combination served with Rosti—and, lest we forget, two fondues, one cheese and one beef.

From Switzerland we make a natural transition to *France*. French restaurants have been springing up in Calgary like the proverbial mushroom. One of my favourites is the **Ile de France** (5032 – 16th Avenue N.W.), which has a small menu, smaller premises, and a very sensitive chef. There is nothing on the menu I would not recommend. Everything is of prime quality, from the East-Coast oysters served with lemon wedges to the Nova Scotia smoked salmon. There is a lovely nouvelle cuisine vegetable terrine based on chicken mousse, and a most distinctive salmon mousse with a centre stud of scallop, served on a bed of creamy spinach. Beef is treated royally, but the rack of Alberta lamb reigns supreme—eight tender, succulent little chops come to your table pink and infused with garlic. Vegetables here are simple and varied, from little green beans to broccoli, all cooked *à point*.

Le Cyrano (201 – 10th Street N.W.) is another fine French place, again with simple offerings prepared with great clarity. A favourite of mine is the medallions of lamb in demiglace and cognac—a deep, richly-sauced plate of very tender lamb fillet. The snails in Pernod are popular, and there are always one or two sinful gâteaux and fruit tarts.

There are many other, rather grand, French restaurants from which to choose, but I find the simplicity that seems to me to be the hallmark of elegance is more prevalent in the smaller operations.

We push on now to *Spain* and the bittersweet flamenco. You can hear this lovely music professionally performed at the **Madrid Restaurante** (516 – 9th Avenue S.W.) while you are putting away your Paella Valenciana, complete with chicken and seafood; or the Bacalao a la Vizcaina (cod with tomato and pepper sauce); or the traditional Zarzuela (a Spanish bouillabaisse). For tapas (hors d'oeuvres), try the Gambas al Ajillo or the clams in white sauce. The Gazpacho or Sopa de Ajo (garlic soup) should also please a lover of Spanish fare.

Pizza parlours are easily found in every Canadian city; first-class *Italian* restaurants representing the many regional styles of Italy are much rarer. Two of our best are **Mamma's Restaurant** (308 – 16th Avenue N.W.) which takes an overall view, and **Lombardos Ristorante** (2111 Centre Street N.). You could easily spoil your appetite on the antipasta alone at Mamma's. The selection changes daily but I always go for one of the same three things: the fried eggplant, the marinated peppers or the scallop mélange. Most of the pasta is homemade and shown to its most tempting advantage in simple dishes like the fettucine al Alfredo. Fresh clams are used in the linguini with white clam sauce; the canneloni is a lush version; the milk-fed veal of superior quality. Fish is lightly treated and game is robustly sauced. Lombardos, for its part, has one of the best scampi preparations and does wonderfully aromatic things with chicken. You'll love the excellent Italian bread. The Italian love of the good life, the hearty and warm hospitality, are very much a part of Calgary's Italian restaurants.

Like the Italians, the *Greeks* are a vibrant people and this vibrancy is reflected in the dominant potent flavours of their cuisine. Visit **Orestes Restaurant Ltd.** (739 – 2nd Avenue S.W.) or the **Greek Korner Ristorante** (1212 – 17th Avenue S.W.), and enjoy garlic-infused roast lamb, lamb and rice-filled dolmas, moussaka, spanakopita, eggplant stew and baklava. There is usually much singing and music as well, especially at Orestes.

For a quieter evening, seek out a *Lebanese* restaurant. Lebanese food has much in common with Greek: the countries (in fact, Middle Eastern countries generally) share many of the same ingredients—olives, eggplant, spinach, chick-peas, lamb and mint. The lovely pita (pocket) bread they use is made right here in Calgary, and you can enjoy it with falafels or hommos bi tahini at either **Gotmy's Restaurant and Lounge** (3975 - 17th Avenue S.W.) or the **Olive Grove** (240 Midpark Way S.E.). The Olive Grove also offers the renowned and popular tabouli (bulgar with tomatoes, onions and mint), and dishes that the baby boom learned to love during their rucksack travels around the world: Kibi (raw lamb with bulgar, onions and spices), baba ghanoug (eggplant puree) and shish kebab.

Before quite abandoning Europe, have a *Hungarian* dinner. The **Tokay Restaurant** (331 - 8th Avenue S.E.) has goulash, of course, and chicken paprika at its reliable juicy best. There are also pork hocks, stuffed banana peppers, cabbage rolls and, for dessert, Dobos—that fascinating multilayered cake sandwiched with chocolate butter cream and topped with crisp caramel.

Similar in concept to Hungarian food is *Ukrainian* cooking, and many little outlets offer sturdy cabbage rolls (everyone seems to love them), pyrogis and marvellous breads and baked goods.

It is time, though, to move on toward the Orient. The first stop en route is *India*, and *East Indian* food is both well represented and extraordinarily popular in Calgary. You'll find restaurants here offering the Kashmiri style, Punjabi style and Southern Indian cooking. Lamb in all forms is the mainstay of both the Kashmiri and Punjabi kitchens, but the former also specializes in complex biryanis and the latter in fine wheat breads and tandoori preparations. The **Omar Khayyam Restaurant** (301 - 16th Avenue N.W.) offers the biryanis. At **Taj Mahal Restaurant** (4816 Macleod Trail S.), you will find pungent lamb and chicken curries, superb breads, tandoori chicken and a multitude of fresh vegetable dishes. Those irresistible snack foods, samosas and pakoras, are also on hand and can be enjoyed with a truly incendiary mint chutney. The **Curry Pot Restaurant** (4710 - 17th Avenue S.E.) offers excellent Southern Indian food. Coconut milk is used in many of the curries and there is a fish masala made with halibut. The chicken dishes use a fragrant (but still fiery) tomato base and there are lovely bhajias of deep-fried vegetables. These Indian restaurants are naturally much frequented by resident Britishers or visitors, who often outnumber the Indian patrons. A surprising number of native Calgarians, though, have fallen under the spell of this cuisine.

Should you prefer lighter and cooler tastes, however, there is nothing better than the refreshing delicacy of a *Vietnamese* meal. The best of the few Vietnamese restaurants in Calgary is probably the **Mekong** (207 - 4th Street S.E.). The charming manner of Vietnamese dining is in itself a pleasurable experience: take a piece of fine thin rice paper; lay on it meat, shrimp or shredded chicken; add fresh leaf lettuce, cucumber, mint leaves, bean sprouts, scallions, and fine noodles; roll up the package, dip it into a seasoned sauce, and enjoy a wonderful textural, flavourful sensation with the first bite. The spring rolls are deep fried in the same diaphanous rice paper, so that they are the crispest, most delicate morsels imaginable. These are only a few of the many alluring choices on the menu.

Chinese food can be found in any part of Calgary. *Chinatown*, of course, houses the most elegant restaurants, but some of the best are tucked away in the far-removed suburbs. One such example is the **Home Food Inn** (4B-340 - 17th Avenue S.E.). Its specialty is classic Peking-style food— prawn toast, spicy braised eggplant, matchless shrimp dishes, the lightest dumplings and noodles and, naturally, Peking Duck. Cantonese cuisine is widely available and well prepared. One of my personal favourites is the **Fantasy** restaurant, which produces inimitable pork shrimp and mushroom balls with softly succulent bean curd in the best rendering of this hot-pot dish that I have seen for years. The shrimp in black bean sauce is also superb, but then there are so many good dishes that one just has to follow the mood of the moment. (Calgary's Chinatown, located around Centre Street and 3rd Avenue S., is a fascinating place to explore, either from curiosity or a deep culinary interest in Chinese cuisine.)

A large plus in Oriental dining in Calgary has been the slow emergence of authentic *Japanese* houses (*not* American-inspired Japanese steak houses). The **Yuzuki Japanese Restaurant** (345 Heritage Drive S.E.) will not only provide the crispest tempura, the juiciest sashimi, and most elegantly artistic vegetable flowers, it will also allow you to savour those simple home dishes seldom seen in these parts: dishes such as Oyako Don (parents and children), combining chicken and eggs with rice, and a variety of family-style noodle dishes. There is also a specialized sushi house in Calgary, the **Sakura Tai** (3A – 3808 Morley Trail N.W.). You can sit at the bar counter and choose the particular raw fish or seafood you wish to have placed on your sushi, or you can sequester yourself in a tatami room and be pampered. Speaking as a sushi and sashimi freak, let me assure you that the quality of the fish will be every bit as good as that in Tokyo, even if the variety is not as great.

From Tokyo, it's a quick hop to *Korea* and the **Korean Restaurant Seoul House** (180 – 94th Avenue S.E.), where there is the traditional bulgogi (barbecued beef), the stir-fried cabbage, beef bean sprout dish, and as much kim chi as your heart could possibly desire.

Cross the Pacific via *Polynesia* (try the **Tiki Tiki Restaurant** at 718 – 8th Avenue S.W.) and touch Mexico on the way home—Calgary has plenty of outlets for tacos, enchiladas, burritos, quesadillos and chilli.

In other words, the Tinfoil Age has finally ended!

Specialty Supply Stores

"The natural parallel to more adventurous dining out is . . . more adventurous dining at home."

By Bernice Evans

The natural parallel to more adventurous dining out is . . . more adventurous dining at home. This in turn has led to a satisfying explosion in the foodstuffs available and in the places stocking them.   Traditional delicatessens are now bolstered by specialty supply stores catering to each national cuisine and by grocery outlets handling every conceivable fruit or vegetable. An excellent example of the latter is **Mother Nature's** (Macleod Trail S. and 70th Avenue S.W.), where you can find such fresh fruits as figs, granadillas, tamarillos, prickly pears, kiwi fruit, kidney mangoes, gooseberries, pomegranates and persimmons. And, if you simply *must* have fresh shitake mushrooms for that special Chinese or Japanese dish, you can find them here as well, together with parsley root, fresh tumeric root, topinambours, salsify, daikon, black radish, coriander leaves, mint, and every kind of lettuce imaginable. Wonderful news, specialty stores are no longer the only ones to stock reasonably varied produce: places like **Foodvale** (803 - 49th Street S.W.) and even those mass outlets—**Woodward's, Safeway** and **All-West**—now offer shitake, spaghetti-squash and Japanese eggplant along with the carrots and onions.

Chinatown is the obvious place for Chinese ingredients, but these days it's the place for Japanese and Vietnamese items as well. The lovely, delicate white cloud ear fungus and black tree ear are both available—together with fermented black beans, fresh Chinese spinach, "yard-long" green beans, sni choy, daikon, sweet potatoes, bitter melon, winter melon, fresh lotus root, incredibly fresh snow peas and bean sprouts, and all the wonderful essences, stocks and cooking wines that the imaginative cook desires. Nuoc nam, a fish sauce essential to Vietnamese cuisine, is easily found: so is every type of Oriental rice, from long grain to glutinous to sweet. There is a profusion of noodles in a vast range of textures, sizes and tastes. Delicate spring roll wrappers and Japanese and Vietnamese rice paper share shelf space with rare items such as black moss, golden needles and seaweed.

You can become even more specialized and esoteric if you visit the places catering to one particular national cuisine. There have long been fine delicatessens offering all manner of salamis and cheeses, specialty French mustards, wine vinegars, canned marrons, pâté, truffles, snails, green peppercorns *et al*; not to mention German anchovy and sardine pastes in tubes, pickled herring and other Teutonic mainstays.

But how do you find mastic, rose or orange blossom water if you want to make your own lokum (Turkish Delight)? Easily. Just pop down to **Middle East Imports** (4202 - 17th Avenue S.E.) and you'll encounter Greek, Lebanese, Egyptian and Moroccan foods. Fat green olives are marinated with hot peppers, spicy pickled eggplant comes in large jars, and of course there is homemade lokum, phyllo pastry and fine honey for the baklava enthusiast. For a wider selection of Greek goodies, try any one of the many small outlets stocking meaty black Greek olives, feta cheese, basturma, red mullet, tarama, and grape leaves.

Curry fiends can indulge themselves at **A.B.C. Discount Foods** (1110 - 17th Avenue S.W.)—which is also a great place for unusual fruits and vegetables. A.B.C and **Dattani Foods Ltd.** (4710G - 17th Avenue S.E.), an exclusively East Indian outlet, both sell garlic, lime, lemon and mango pickles (to name a few); chutneys of impressive variety; and an incredible line of herbs and spices and complex mixtures intended for particular dishes. There are dried legumes of every description, different varieties of rice (among them the superb Basmati and Patna), spicy lentil snacks, nuts, and more *et cetera* than one could list.

I still find it amazing that no matter what I wish to cook, in whatever cuisine, I can find virtually everything I need. Years ago when I first ventured into Japanese cooking, for example, few of the necessary ingredients were available and wholesale substitutions were the order of the day. Then **Sato Foods** (2901 – 34th Avenue S.E.) opened, offering all those items needed to make the dishes authentic: mirin, wasabi (that scaringly hot horseradish for sashimi and sushi), somen, shirataki noodles, sheets of nori, kombu or kelp, rice vinegar, and togarashi. Lovers of Korean food can also rejoice. The store carries Korean items as well, including the volcanic kim chi, the cabbage pickle so dear to Korean hearts (and, presumably, stomachs).

Interest in other, more familiar, cuisines has become more sophisticated. The advent of Italian restaurants serving rather more ambitious cuisine than the ubiquitous pizza or spaghetti Bolognese has increased consumer demand for Italian cooking ingredients. Why use bacon when you can procure pancetta? Real Parmesan, Sicilian olives, prosciutto, Parma ham and fresh ricotta are to be had for the asking at the **Italian Centre Meat Market** (824 – 1st Avenue N.E.) in "Little Italy." There are also enterprising operations producing fresh pasta—everything from fettucini to agnoletti.

Another growing influence: Calgary's new-found passion for fish and seafood. As a result we now have numerous stores selling nothing but: **Boyd's Lobster Shop Ltd.** (3808 Macleod Trail S. and 1511 – 14th Street S.W.), for example, for live lobsters; and **Billingsgate Fish Co. Ltd.** (630 – 7th Avenue S.E. and 3700 Blackfoot Trail S.E.) for fresh shrimp flown in from Vancouver, fresh Malpeque oysters and squid, and the day's selection of fresh fish (sole, cod, red snapper, trout).

And Other Specialties
by Peggy Weddell

Bakeries
In 1904 Calgary's biggest and best bakery was City Bakery. After two ownership changes it is still a grand bakery, but there are now many others that compare favourably with it

and it would be impossible to choose *the* best, because each has its own specialty. Here, then, is a rundown on some of Calgary's best bakeries.

City Bakery is located near the General Hospital at 906 – 1st Avenue N.E. The baked goods are the best you'll find anywhere, but what is really outstanding is their cakes ... glorious, gooey, rich cakes (some twenty varieties) and heavenly pastries. (City Bakery's Black Forest Cake is usually singled our for praise and it certainly deserves the kind words, but the other varieties are fabulous, too.)

If you live in the southwest part of the city and would like to try something closer to home, visit the **Britannia Pastry Shop** (819A – 49th Avenue S.W.). It whomps up a very special Gâteau St-Honoré, which is a heavenly, creamy booze cake. Their petits fours, pastries and croissants are served at plenty of the classier dinner parties in town.

Calgary, compared to Montreal and Toronto, is a little shy on Jewish bakeries, but you'll find that **Bagels and Buns** at 807 – 17th Avenue S.W. and in the Mayfair Shopping Centre (6511 Elbow Drive S.W.) has a selection of bagels (made fresh daily) and cream cheese (flown in from Winnipeg) that equal the best. (One of life's major challenges, apparently, was to adapt the bagel recipe appropriately for the Calgary altitude.)

Try the **Parthenon Bakery** (1330 – 15th Avenue S.W.) for brown, crusty (Greek-style) rolls and bread and Greek pastries to complement your Horiataki (Greek-style), and read the grocery section to find out where to buy the feta cheese and Greek olives.

Glamorgan Bakery (3919 Richmond Road S.W.) sells current buns that are positively addictive. Get there early, though, because they often run out of things by noon.

For ordinary items like bread and hamburger and hot dog buns, the **Riverpark Bakery** (3503 – 14th Street S.W.) and the **Stadium Bakery** in the Stadium Shopping Centre (1907 Uxbridge Drive N.W.) are both excellent. The Riverpark isn't strictly "ordinary," though: it also makes a very authentic-tasting French croissant.

Sweets

City Bakery (906 – 1st Avenue N.E.), mentioned in the bakery section, carries an excellent selection of praline truffles and fine chocolates. They have a good year-round supply, but the largest selection is offered at Christmas, Easter, Valentine's Day and Mother's Day. The champagne truffles are a must, and the unique Calgary Souvenir chocolates are a lovely gift to bring to your hostess or send off to a friend. (They are already gift-wrapped.)

Olivier's Candies (919 – 9th Avenue S.E.) has been around Calgary almost since the turn of the century. It has changed hands, though, and is now run by the Jensen family. They have carried on the traditional candymaking processes from the good old days, and you'll find an unbelievable selection of candies and chocolates. Especially good are the Jensen Mint Sandwiches, the peanut brittle and the candy canes (which you can order in almost any size or flavour).

Ice Cream Parlours

There are four shops that carry up to thirty-one flavours of ice cream. All use Palm ice cream, which is top quality ice cream, and all charge about the same for about the same size of cone. So if it is simply ice cream you want, you can try **Little Deuce Scoop** (17th Avenue and 27th Street S.W.), **My Favourite Ice Cream Shoppe** (42nd Avenue and 20th Street S.W.) or the **Sweet Tooth Sundae Palace** (10019 Elbow Drive S.W.). For atmosphere while you enjoy your ice cream, the **Rainbow Patio** across from Western Canada High School (17th Avenue and 64th Street S.W.) is the place to go. It is set up in the old-fashioned ice cream parlor style, complete with wrought-iron chairs, little round tables and a soda bar.

Want to combine an excursion with an ice cream treat? There are two more places you should know about.

It has often been said that Calgarians like nothing better than touring show homes on a Sunday afternoon, but whoever said that hasn't stood in the lineup stretching all the way around the block in Cochrane waiting to get one of Scotty **Mackay's** ice cream cones. Mackay's is the only place that makes its own ice cream (using Palm's mix but adding its own fruit and flavours) and going out to Cochrane on a Sunday afternoon is an entrenched Calgary tradition.

The Frontier Candy and Ice Cream Store in Bragg Creek (west of Cochrane) is a charming old-fashioned-looking store in the new mall. Again, you'll find Palm ice cream but, for a change of taste, Frontier offers special crushed candy dips. On Saturdays there is frequently a singer or musician around to entertain the children.

Tea and Coffee

We have already mentioned **Mother Nature's** (70th Avenue S.W. and Macleod Trail) and **Foodvale** (Britannia Shopping Centre) for their fresh produce. Both these shops also carry an excellent selection of fresh coffee beans and teas. Or, you can trek around the Louise Crossing shopping district (just over the bridge on 10th Street N.W.) and discover the supplies at the **Culinary Arts Shop** (there's a second outlet in Roxboro Mall). You can even enjoy a fresh cuppa while you wait for them to grind your choice. As a matter of fact, the aroma as you walk through the door is irresistible. Or, another option, you can tempt yourself with one of the many varieties of teas (they've got just about everything) at **Earth Harvest**, right on the corner of Memorial Drive and 10th Street N.W. They will even brew you a cup to sample before you buy.

Deli Meats and Meat Markets

Rupp's Meats and Delicatessen (37 – 4th Street N.E.) for German, Hungarian and Yugoslavian smoked meats and sausages.

Chalet Meats (1303 – 17th Avenue S.W.) for Hungarian sausage and fancy pâtés at Christmas and Easter.

European Delicatessen and Imports (2712 – 14th Street S.W.) for sausages and salamis. The specialty is double-smoked bacon and beef jerky.

Alpine Sausage (3919 Richmond Road S.W.) has the best pepperonis in town—great frankfurters, too.

Mountain View Meats (2137 – 33rd Street S.W.) for Bavarian-style sausages and salamis. Especially good are the Bavarian-style wieners. Excellent fresh meat.

Mark's Delicatessen (4212 – 17th Avenue S.E.) supplies many of the smaller shopping-centre delis. Largest selection in town. Corned beef and pastrami are recommended.

Danish Smorgasbord (1221 – 11th Avenue S.W.) is Calgary's only Danish deli. Specialty is the Spegepolse, an attractive rosy salami. Danish-style wieners and liver paste are big sellers.

Schaier's Meat and Kosher Delicatessen (340 – 17th Avenue S.W.) has kosher meats and poultry.

Excelsior Meats and Imported Foods (629 – 1st Avenue N.E.) understands Italian cuts of meat, will butcher to order and makes its own true Italian sausage.

The Enchanted Palace

"The Alberta Liquor Control Board (or Enchanted Palace, as one grateful employee once dubbed it) was established as the almighty governor of ethanol in the province. . . . "

by Todd Cristall

It is dreary day in Calgary. You have had a day at the office that makes any mere world statesman's itinerary look like a picnic. So, you brave the gale-force chinook winds and make it to the local liquor store (hereafter referred to as the people's libation outlet). Having felt the width of your wallet, you realize that your spectrum of choice must be just as slim, so you grab your old standby, Beaujolais (or perhaps a cheaper style of California Zinfandel), pay the cashier and scurry on home.

Such a transaction is hardly unique—it is acted out thousands of times daily in every city right across the country. Even so, there are some uniquely Albertan aspects to the way you are going to do it here. The Alberta Liquor Control Board has its own markup procedure, its own "regular" and "specialty" lists and, perhaps most important, its own attitude toward drinking.

The ALCB (or Enchanted Palace, as one grateful employee once dubbed it) was established as the almighty governor of ethanol in the province, with a mandate to control consumption and prevent alcohol from passing the lips of those not eligible (currently all human beings under the age of eighteen). Whether or not your political posture leads you to approve of this monopoly is irrelevant: the Enchanted Palace is as entrenched in Albertan society as any charter of rights provided by those pundits in Ottawa. There has been talk of allowing the larger and maybe even smaller grocery stores to sell wine and beer, but it remains talk. So—to the chagrin of many Canadians and the confusion of many American visitors—the ALCB outlets continue to be the only legal places in the province to buy wine and spirits.

Still, one may note a certain amount of progress. The selection of wines, for one thing, has improved very handsomely. I am told by colleagues who reside in other regions of Canada that our board's list of wines is to be envied.

Part (but only part) of their envy has a financial base, as a rudimentary comparison of wines on the ten provinces' regular lists shows. This list is brief, of course, but it does allow you to compare some standard brands. (These prices may now be heart-breakingly outdated but the price variations they illustrate are still true.) For example, take that well-known staple, Black Tower. A one-litre version of this E.E.C. blend, at $5.35 in Alberta, was cheap when compared to the prices in other provinces. Another example, Christian Brothers nonvintage Cabernet Sauvignon: when it was $5.40 in Alberta, it was $7.65 in British Columbia and $7.95 in Quebec. So, perhaps life in Calgary is not all that bad—with or without the Alsands project.

What the above figures imply is that each province's Enchanted Palace employs a different markup procedure. And "procedure" is indeed the word, when you consider all the variables that must be brooded over before the retail wine price is finally determined.

According to reasonably reliable sources within the trade, the wines we Calgarians buy are subjected to a sixty percent markup after duty and excise have been paid. This compares very nicely with the other provinces. Indeed, all things being relative, it begins to look like a blessing. P.E.I.'s markup, for example, is a whopping 140 percent, which means that about sixty cents out of every dollar you spend on wine there goes to the provincial coffers. In Calgary, we have the somewhat dubious comfort of knowing that the figure is around the forty cent mark per dollar.

But the markup policy is not just a straightforward matter of percentages. Those variables I mentioned earlier make it impossible to offer a comparison of certain wines and the prices they command. Most provincial boards seem to scrutinize two factors more carefully than the others: alcohol content and sugar content. In Alberta, the over-riding concern of Enchanted Palace officials seems to be focussed on alcoholic content. The rule, I am told, is that wines of less than fourteen percent alcohol/volume are subject to a lower markup then the rest. If you are a port drinker, or fond of some of the heavier California wines, this is bad news. Other provinces have their own variations on the game: they employ a lower or higher alcohol content threshold than does Alberta and may combine it with an emphasis on sugar content.

I suppose, though, it really doesn't matter what the other provinces charge. If you have made the decision to visit or move to Calgary, you're not about to drive to Saskatchewan to pick up—for example—a bottle of 1971 Dom Pérignon, even though you know that the 1975 edition available here is from a poorer year and costs about ten dollars more! Anyway, this is the exception not the rule: Alberta usually comes out ahead in the price comparisons.

Price is only part of the good news. The next thing you should know is that the ALCB maintains a group of "specialty shops," which carry items above and beyond the regular listings. There are six such shops in Calgary.

Mount Royal	1140 - 17th Avenue S.W.
Southcentre	#95, 100 Anderson Road S.E.
Market Mall	3625 Shaganappi Trail N.W.
North Hill Centre	1598 - 14th Avenue N.W.
Trans-Canada Mall	1440 - 52nd Street N.E.
Palliser	140 - 11th Avenue S.W.

(Note that the Market Mall outlet carries a limited selection of specialty items.)

Specialty store selections change fairly often. This can be both a pleasure—since it keeps giving you the chance to try new wines—and a frustration—since it sometimes removes one of your personal favourites from the shelf. (But even then, all is not lost: see below for some comments on the special order system.)

The frequent turnover also makes it hard to name ALCB "best buys" with any assurance that they'll be available when you go looking for them. Still, certain generalizations apply—the ALCB has its recognizable areas of strength—and if some of the specific examples are not to be found, so what? Think what a good time you can have filling in the specifics for yourself!

The Enchanted Palace offers a good variety of French clarets and Burgundies. There are no fewer than ninety or so

Château-bottled listings. Most of these are classified wines that are young and (unfortunately) from lesser vintages, but nonetheless the ALCB has bought well. Examples of this group are 1977 Ch. Beychevelle, 1976 Ch. Pichon La Lande, 1977 Ch. Palmer and 1976 Ch. Montrose. The Burgundy array is more limited yet there exist about twenty selections, mostly from the heady and powerful 1976 vintage. Examples here are 1976 Beaune, Clos des Mouches by Beaune; 1976 Pommard Rugiens by Henri de Villamont; and 1976 Fixin La Mazière by Bouchard Ainé et Fils. I am sad to report to the white wine enthusiast that the French specialty listings are, in the main, red, although some recent purchases by the ALCB indicate a cautious move toward more whites from all countries.

The Germans are well represented in the specialty listings and are, of course, almost exclusively whites. Examples: 1977 Bernkasteler Doktor Kabinett, 1979 Erbacher Marco-brunn Riesling Spatlese; and 1979 Niersteiner Kranzberg Riesling Kabinett. All told there are about sixty-five special-ty German wines, most of which are in the affordable six to nine dollar range.

Sadly, the ALCB has only a handful of Italian specialty listings, most of them red. One of my personal favourites is Castello di Nippozzano Chianti Rufina 1977.

In addition to importing wine from the conventional sources, the Enchanted Palace has played ambassador for wines from some lesser known countries. Examples? Israeli 1976 Carmel Cabernet Sauvignon; a South African 1978 Cabernet Sauvignon by Nederburg; and Reynella Australian 1978 Cabernet Sauvignon. Recently, there has been a small expansion of the South African and Australian listings to perhaps a dozen between the two (well, I *said* it was small . . .).

Last but by no means least come the California wines. Here the Palace officials have indeed done their homework. In the early spring of 1982, evidence hit the shelves of an ALCB buying spree that had resulted in a grand total of some seventy listings. The array is well chosen and, for the most part, offers good values. Examples include Fetzer 1978 Mendocino Zinfandel; 1978 Spring Mountain Cabernet Sauvignon (remember that nighttime TV soap, *Falcon Crest*?; the Spring Mountain winery provided the setting) from the Napa Valley; and Dry Creek 1978 Cabernet Sauvignon from Sonoma County. The selection is enormous, with at least a couple dozen wineries represented—Château St. Jean, Clos du Val, Chappellet, Veedercrest and many others have all made their way to the shelves of Calgary's specialty shops.

If swilling your way through the wide variety of listed wines isn't enough for your taste buds, you may want to consider placing a special order. To do so, you must drop into a people's libation outlet and ask for the logically named Special Order Inquiry Form. Fill in this form, stating the details of each wine (or other alcoholic beverage) you are after, and in due time you will receive an answer by mail from the Enchanted Palace's main fortress in Edmonton. This letter will include the price per case of the requested item(s) and another form to fill out and return with a twenty-five percent deposit. In time you will be notified that your order has arrived and that you may pick it up at your convenience—as long as you bring a certified cheque or cash for the balance owing (not even the government trusts you these days).

This procedure works well enough, but I must caution you against ordering wine for a specific occasion. The ALCB is careful to point out that while they will *estimate* the probable time delay involved, they will not *guarantee* it. I made the mistake of expecting an order of California champagne to arrive in time for my university graduation— after all, I had allowed four months for delivery. Fourteen months later, the shipment arrived. Start planning now for any special wines you would like to have for the 1988 Olympics.

The nonwine products in the Enchanted Palace are much the same as anywhere else, though the prices may be a little lower. One general tendency: western tastes dictate that the beer selection has a heavy bias toward lagers, as opposed to ales. This allows you to identify the regional origins of the person next to you in a tavern, without having to ask. The only other interesting thing about beer in this province is that you buy it at the ALCB outlets. Alberta, unlike some other provinces, does not have a system of separate brewers' retail stores.

There you have it. Whether you intend to settle here or are just passing through, there should be enough on the shelves of the people's libation outlets to keep you properly occupied. And to convince you that all is not oil in Calgary.

The Bars

"We have bars to suit the relentlessly trendy, pseudo-cowboy, sports-fan macho, three-piece-suited and just plain thirsty."

By Catherine Ford

The first thing you notice about bars in Calgary is the number of men. The Wild West, after all, is one of the few places in the country where men outnumber women. At some stand-up bars, they are three deep. (No, of course I am not going to tell you which bars. Find out for yourself.) This can make drinking in Calgary either a pleasure or a pain for women, depending on what they are looking for. Stampede Week is something else entirely, with which we will deal later.

The second thing you may notice is what we drink. The pattern, like everything else in Calgary, is changing, and these days you can get whatever drink you want in whatever kind of bar you want. Still, traditional preferences (and the attitudes that go with them) haven't disappeared and—depending on where you do your drinking, of course—you may reach the conclusion that Calgary floats on a river of rye. Not true, Our rivers contain cold mountain water, and it only seems that whiskey is the sole liquid consumed within city limits.

We drink beer, too.

And we drink it anywhere. Anywhere we can find a seat and, barring that, on the banks of the Bow and/or Elbow, at the feet and on top of mountains, in vans and RVs, on lawns, in parks, under trees and on the street. Sometimes in our cars, which may account for the plethora of blue uniforms and flashing lights around the main city streets each week-end night.

The Alberta government is not only fuelled with oil, it runs on the proceeds of the booze business. It's lucrative enough that there is no sales tax, no gasoline tax and bargain liquor in Alberta. (Of course that's not the sole reason, it just seems that way.) Where else but in Alberta—and specifically in Calgary—would one of the "leading" citizens of 1902 come out in favour of Prohibition—as long as the drink prohibited was water? The man in question was Bob Edwards, usually referred to as "colourful" (a euphemism for "alcoholic") and the editor of the *Eye Opener*, a newspaper, not a drink.

The eye-opener as a drink is actually a raw egg, drop of tabasco, slosh of Worcestershire, sprinkle of pepper and tightly closed eyes. It is ingested in the kitchen the morning after and will keep the worst hangover at bay until 10:30 A.M., when the bars open.

It's probably only coincidence that the most famous local drink is the Calgary Red-Eye. Even the thought of this combination of beer and tomato juice makes Easterners gag—but then, they haven't gone through a couple of lengthy beer strikes when the only Canadian beer to be had came from a Red Deer brewery and was loved more for its availability than its taste. Tomato juice, we felt, helped immeasurably.

Certainly some of the more shirty residents will sniff at beer and good ol' rye whiskey, preferring the more esoteric Campari and soda, or white wine, but *real* Calgarians don't have much time for them. As a matter of fact, ordering a Campari and soda in some of the seedier establishments in the city will cause the locals to raise loud questions about your manhood. The women who orders such an effete drink will be instantly identified as a ball-breaking eastern Libber and thereafter shunned.

No sir, the most effete you can get out here in the West is to order a light beer, and it had better be an Alta 3.9. Real men don't drink American light beer, opining that American full-strength beer is light enough without further adulterating its taste. Real men when they can't get beer (or whiskey) will also drink a vicious concoction known as The Para-lyzer—vodka, milk and Kahlua. It tastes like a chocolate milkshake and has the effect of paralyzing the vocal cords along with the rest of your anatomy.

Ah, but Calgary is changing. The old beverage room, long the favourite of university students, sleazy hookers, winos and rubbies is vanishing. Gone the way of the ten-cent draught. Gone the way of Ladies and Escorts. The city now has as wide a range of places to drink as you could wish for (some of which I'll eventually get around to describing). Why, even the roughest beer parlours are changing: these days they contain increasing numbers of braless women in nipple-tight T-shirts, ordering such drinks as a Brown Cow (a vile mixture of Kahlua and milk).

The roughest beer parlours, however, are not places to frequent. Not without a very large escort wearing a Caterpillar hat and carmel-coloured workboots with steel toes. It helps if he's ugly. It helps more if he's really big. Forget all the beer commercials; there isn't a beer parlour in Calgary where anyone looks like that. The real Calgary beer commercial would show five guys with pot bellies lolling about a tiny terrycloth-covered table, itself covered with draught beer. They are all wearing some variety of hat—visored caps with brand names such as Caterpillar or Case just visible though the oil and grease; brown or black cowboy hats (never white, that's for girls and tourists), preferably showing a sweat ring; hard hats in yellow or red (white is for the suit-wearing engineer or the architect). They wear very old, very dirty blue jeans, and plaid shirts, also dirty. This is a sign of extreme masculinity.

So is the use, in every possible part of speech, of the most overworked of all four-letter words (yup, the one that starts with F). Preferably repeated every second word, and extra points are scored if you can recognize the past pluperfect subjunctive. The guys are all watching a hockey game. Or a football game. Or anything else on the colour television set (or super-sized screen) in which a bunch of men attempt to move a small object into, around, past or through a goal-tender or goalpost.

Unless you really enjoy the local colour, beware the hotel beer parlours in east Calgary. Especially the ones with blue and white cruisers parked outside.

Please do follow these instructions: it will mean an available seat in the place for us natives, who are really tired of waiting in line for a drink. You see, life in Calgary is life in a lineup, and never is that more obvious than at the bar. If you really want to go to the newest pine-panelled, plant-smothered bar and stand around looking mellow, go about 3:00 P.M. Stay put. If you leave and return at 8:00, there will not be a seat and the doorman will make you wait, thirsty, on the stairs and occasionally outside the door, until someone leaves.

Why the eternal lineup? Do a little math...and the question is still a puzzler.

At the last "official" count, at the end of 1981 (and the count changes rapidly in Calgary), the ALCB had issued licences to 279 dining lounges, 179 cocktail lounges, two nightclubs, one racetrack, four stadiums (although there aren't four stadiums in the city), three theatres and two educational institutions. The private clubs got thirty-four annual licences, five seasonal, twelve recreational and fifteen canteen. The drinker doesn't have to worry about the ALCB breakdown: the only difference is hours of operation and the presence or absence of music.

The total licence count of around 575 means there is one bar for about every thousand Calgarians. Half of those may be underage, bringing the total down to five hundred. Half again—you think—aren't going to want to get into *your* bar on any given night, cutting the total to 250. Half again will change their minds about heading for the bar and go to the mountains instead. So now we have only about 125 people trying at any one time to get into any one bar.

Logical mathematics, in other words, says there should be no lineup. Hah. Logic be damned, it is obvious that every able-bodied person over eighteen in the city is trying to get into the same bar at the same time. Hundreds of Calgarians in dozens of drinking establishments across the city brave the lineups each weekend and the occasional lineups during the week to drink, mingle, pick-up, put-down or dance with another warm body. And they can do it in any style they like. We have bars to suit the relentlessly trendy, pseudocowboy, sports-fan macho, three-piece-suited and just plain thirsty. There are quiet bars and bars with entertainment. You can find music from fifties rock to eighties mellow, live and canned. There's middle-of-the-road, outta sight, jazz, and country and western.

For the newly arrived, finding *your* bar can take some serious drinking for a few weeks. Here are a few entirely personal suggestions, broken down into main categories to get you started.

Three-piece-suit Bars

Hy's (316 – 4th Avenue S.W.)—Here is where the Calgary myth lives. Huge steaks in the dining room next door. Bar has the ambience of the usual waiting-for-a-table detour. Every visiting fireman from Texas or Denver of where-have-you takes his lady to Hy's for dinner after getting liquored someplace else, so they don't seem to pay too much attention to the bar.

Owl's Nest, Westin Hotel (4th Avenue and 3rd Street S.W.)—An established Calgary bar, always packed during the weekdays with out-of-town businessmen (particularly visiting oil company executives). Appeals to the three-piece-suit and briefcase crowd (male and female). Only blue jeans seen are the latest designer variety. One of the few places in town (**Delmonico's**, at 1121 Centre Street N., is another) that knows how to make Kir and has the ingredients. Service great. Discreet and quiet. No canned music.

Trendy Bars

Charlie's (213 – 10th Avenue S.W.)—Opened early in 1982 and became an instant success because of the dance floor right in front of the smoked window, loud canned music and long stand-up bar. Attracts a young crowd willing to wait on the stairs for hours. (Oh, all right. I'll tell you. This is one of the three-deep-in-men bars.) Bartenders can be surly because they're so busy, but the bar itself is bright, friendly and crowded. Be prepared to dress with flash, if you want to be noticed. Lots of thighs and cleavage, open shirts and gold chains. Be young, not-too-bright and smile.

Donahue's (2500 – 4th Street S.W.)—Smack in the "trendy" part of downtown, encourages games such as backgammon, as well as the video variety. Seems to attract lawyers but lawyers are a fickle bunch so some nights it's packed and some nights it's nearly deserted. As in some of the other "trendy" places, such as **Phoenicia** (1315 – 1st Street S.W.) or **Divino** (817 – 1st Street S.W.), the not-regular customer may feel he has wandered into somebody's living room. Everybody seems to know everybody else. They can all occasionally have the charm and warmth of an ice cream freezer.

Quiet Bars

Damiens, Esso Plaza (410 – 2nd Street S.W.)—Very elegant touch of New York, and an authentic one at that. One of the most pleasant and quiet places to drink in town. The great decor makes you forget that the building surrounding it is a steel and glass horror.

Pardon My Garden (435 – 4th Avenue S.W.)—Started out relentlessly trendy a few years ago, when Calgarians weren't used to being able to see out a window onto the street while imbibing. Has settled into a more peaceful atmosphere.

Standing Room Only Lounge, QR Centre (830 – 9th Avenue S.W.)—Since the QR Centre also houses Theatre Calgary and radio station CHQR, the SRO is definitely media and theatre-oriented. Don't go on a theatre night before the 8:00 P.M. curtain, because you won't get in. Be prepared for another "living-room" atmosphere, this time full of clubby radio types. It's a great bar, though, if you'd like to escape the din of other places and relax.

Traders, Four Seasons Hotel (110 – 9th Avenue S.E.)— Trader's is strictly for the leather armchair, hello-I'm-rich (or want-you-to-think-I-am) crowd. Open fireplace goes winter and summer, lots of turn of the century bordello touches. Ideal place for a rendezvous, rarely crowded. Peaceful, elegant and pricey.

Bars with Music

Horned Toad, on the mezzanine level of the Delta Bow Valley Inn (209 – 4th Avenue S.E.)—Features not only a stand-up or sit-down bar but also a sitting at or leaning counter facing the bandstand. Has a dance floor and some of the best music in town, if you are over twenty-five and like to dance. Relentlessly New Mexican in decor with fake cactus and Hopi Indian motifs. Saturday afternoon from 2:00 to 5:00 P.M. it's the only place to be in Calgary, as a twenty-two-piece jazz band (made up of musicians from around town) blasts the walls off for an enthusiastic crowd. Other places in town are just discovering jazz, but this is still the best bargain. No cover charge and you can listen to some of Calgary's top musicians jam for three hours. The hotel also has the best—and one of the few—lobby bars in town. Pianist tinkles a grand piano for the after-work crowd.

The Scotch Room, on the main floor of the Four Seasons Hotel (110 – 9th Avenue S.W.)—One of the veteran singles, stand-up bars in town. Always has great entertainment— none of the one-guy-with-a-guitar stuff. Huge, usually packed, and they'll soak you three dollars to get in the door. But they're nice about it, although on a busy night the service is slow to nonexistent. Has a mixed crowd of suits and polyester double-knits who've wandered in from the Convention Centre. Try not to become preoccupied with reading the *Hello! My Name Is . . .* tags.

Sports-fan Macho Bars

Lonnie's (306 - 4th Avenue S.W.)—Across the street from Damiens and across the world in style. Features enormous television screen for the sports fans, but the sound is usually turned off. This should give you the first clue that this is a place where they don't need the commentary on a hockey game, because the patrons are already sports experts. Lots of room to stand around and make eye contact. Definitely not for the suit-wearing crowd. Macho with the honesty to admit it. Waitresses great, bartenders ditto.

The Unicorn (304 - 8th Avenue S.W.)—The first Irish Rovers' tavern and the first one in town to offer a wine bar. The stand-up bar featuring draught beer in pints was an instant hit the year it opened. Piano in the corner out of tune, but anyone willing to entertain the patrons usually finds the management buying the beer. Initially attracted expatriate Irish, Scotts and English hungry for an almost-authentic touch of "over-'ome." Has been taken over by the soccer and rugby crowd and has changed accordingly. Now only for rugby players, "rugger-huggers" (as their girlfriends are known in the U.S.A.) and the like.

Cowboy Bars

Mad Trappers (602 - 11th Avenue S.W.)—This bar has saddles instead of seats, which should tell you exactly how *cute* this place is. Attracts the young oil company and associated types and equally young women who are expected to wear blue jeans so they can straddle the bar saddles. Obviously not for the high-heel and slim-skirt set.

Ranchman's South (9311 Macleod Trail S.) and **Ranchman's Uptown** (1117 - 1st Street S.W.)—This is *the* Calgary bar (at both locations) for the cowboy crowd, ersatz or otherwise. Jeans, boots, cowboy hats and country and western music. Impossible to get in on a Saturday night. One of the features of the uptown location is "ladies night," which should tell you immediately that this is macho country, pardner.

There is one period a year when even people who normally wouldn't be caught dead in Ranchman's are either there or doing their best to look like they belong there. I'm talking about the Calgary Stampede, of course, and sometimes it seems that all our year-round drinking is only practice for this main event—Stampede is ten days of solid, unremitting, unexcused drunkenness.

Do not attempt, under any circumstances, to get into *any* bar in Calgary during the Stampede unless you: (a) own it (b) are married to the manager (c) are willing to stand in a lineup for at least three hours or (d) have a secretary/wife/ girlfriend (or the male equivalent thereof) willing to head for the bar of your choice at 11:00 A.M. and *stay put*. The Chosen One will have to guard enough seats and a table. The rest of the party should be there by noon or forget it. Also forget work. During Stampede Week, nobody expects work to be done. Not to "dress Western" is to be a freak. Expect to see fifty-year-old executives in jeans, plaid shirts and neckerchiefs. Do not laugh, one of them may well be your boss. Try to last out the full ten days, because you are expected to Have Fun. Try not to run down any of the drunks in the street. Resist the temptation to serve your husband or wife with divorce papers during Stampede Week, no matter the temptation.

After all, life—and drinking—will be back to normal for another year next week.

The Insiders'
CALGARY HOTELS

The hotels are impossible to rank, since each has its own personality. Here are some character profiles, though, to help you decide for yourself.

The first hotel you'll see—if you arrive by air—is CP's **Chateau Airport**, right within the airport complex. Location alone tells you what to expect—a bright, new hotel favoured by businessmen for stopovers and quick meetings. "It has unusually soundproof rooms," adds one Calgarian, enigmatically.

If you come by train (does anyone?), you'll meet CP once again—this time in its original incarnation as the CPR—and **The Palliser Hotel** (133 – 9th Avenue S.W.). Train stations aren't what they used to be—this one, in the basement of Palliser Square, is as bland as a sixties public washroom but not quite as functional. Neither, alas, is the hotel what it used to be, namely, Calgary's landmark. Never mind, locals still love it for the home-baked bread and revere it as the site of the year's (any year's) rowdiest Stampede Breakfast, the one thrown by the Calgary

Ad & Sales Club. (Is this why the hotel is nicknamed The Paralyzer?)

Across 9th Avenue and slightly east you'll find **The Four Seasons Hotel** (Calgary Centre). Definitely one of the city's leading hotels (though perhaps slighty edged in the prestige sweepstakes by the newer Delta Bow Valley), it has an excellent dining room and very popular lounges. Lots of convention-goers here, thanks to the adjoining Convention Centre.

"Hotel Row" is on 4th Avenue S.W. and S.E., just south of the Bow River in the city core. Farthest east on the row—and a pioneer in the general upgrading of the city's east end as a whole—the **Delta Bow Valley Inn** (209 – 4th Avenue). A relative newcomer, it quickly attracted not only top-status visitors but jazz-oriented Calgarians as well. The Hotel is now an established part of the local music scene.

Oil people have tended to stay faithful to **The Westin Hotel** (320 – 4th Avenue S.W.), perhaps because it is closer to oil industry offices (clustered nearby in the city's Oil Patch) — or perhaps because it houses their favourite restaurant, the Owl's Nest. Most Calgarians still call this hotel "The Calgary Inn" (which it was, for decades) and look on it as a local institution.

The International Hotel (220 – 4th Avenue S.W., is the standard, dependable sort of place that one woman calls "a Howard Johnson kind of hotel, but without the ice cream." It is cheek-by-jowl to the **Sheraton Calgary** (202 – 4th Avenue S.W.), dwarfed these days by all the newer buildings round about and known mainly as the site for many charity casinos.

Moving off hotel row and further south, we come to the **Lord Nelson Inn** (1020 – 8th Avenue S.W.). Oil execs head for the Westin; the industry's roughnecks head for the Lord Nelson instead. Very different places.

Farther south again, **The Elbow River Inn** (1919 Macleod Trail S.E.) — a basic, cinder block hotel with a beautiful location on the (what else?) Elbow River. It is also right across Macleod Trail from the Stampede Grounds, which means it is usually full of horse trainers and people from the various shows and exhibits that fill the Grounds all year long.

As Calgary itself pushes busily south (down to Midnapore and still moving), almost a whole new city and a second centre of gravity are taking shape. What used to be a modest, straggling motel strip on the way out of (or into) town is now dominated by several full-fledged hotels. **The Stampeder Inn** (3828 Macleod Trail S.) is one; another is **The Hospitality Inn South** (135 Southland Drive S.E.), which even draws folks from north of the Bow River to its Sunday brunch.

Finally, back north and west to **Motel Village**, some seventeen or so motels are clustered in one convenient package just off the Trans-Canada Highway (16th Avenue N.W., by its city name) at Crowchild Trail near the University of Calgary campus. It's close to the city centre, but its position on the Trans-Canada means it also gives you your quickest exit to Banff.

CALGARY EMERGENCY NUMBERS

FIRE, POLICE, AMBULANCE		911

24-HOUR SERVICE STATIONS

Northeast

Calgary Husky Car-Truck Stop	3010 Barlow Trail N.E.	285-2555
Crossroads Shell	2020 – 16th Avenue N.E.	277-6307
Edmonton Trail Esso	1701 – 3rd Street N.E.	276-5505
Mohawk Auto Square	401 – 16th Avenue N.E.	277-0758
Mohawk Gas Hut	1530 – 48th Avenue N.E.	275-2211
Thorncliffe Gulf	5004 Centre Street N.	275-0777

Northwest

Brentwood Shell	3919 Morley Trail N.W.	282-5677
Mohawk Montgomery Service	4639 Bowness Rd. N.W.	288-5080
Stadium Esso	2320 – 16th Avenue N.W.	289-6707
TransCanada Shell	4647 – 16th Avenue N.W.	288-4130

Southeast

Macleod Trail Esso	4303 Macleod Trail S.	289-6707
Mohawk Auto Square	5505 – 17th Avenue S.E.	272-9793
Mohawk Blackfoot Trail Stop	1840 – 9th Avenue S.E.	269-1636
Mohawk Village Service	7123 Fairmount Dr. S.E.	252-3166

Southwest

Bow Trail Shell	37th Street & Bow Trail S.W.	246-2634
South Trail Gulf Service	7603 Macleod Trail S.	255-6411

DRUG STORES—OPEN UNTIL MIDNIGHT

Penley Drugs	187 Chinook Centre	255-7731
Tucker Drugs	3505 – 14th St. S.W.	243-0785
Telstar Drugs	1437 Kensington Rd. N.W.	283-0741
Town Square Drug Mart	105-4909 – 17th Ave. S.E.	273-7656

(In emergencies after midnight, use the number on your local pharmacist's door—it's usually the home number.)

DENTIST

Emergency Services	108 – 4616 Valiant Dr. N.W.	247-2713

(after regular dentists' hours and on weekends)

HOSPITALS—EMERGENCY RECEIVING
Northeast
General Hospital	841 Centre Avenue E.	268-9111

Northwest
Foothills Hospital	1403 - 29th Street N.W.	270-1315

Southeast & Southwest
Rockyview Hospital	7007 - 14th Street S.W.	252-7511

Downtown Southwest
Holy Cross Hospital	2210 - 2nd Street S.W.	266-7231

LOCKSMITH
Parry Bros. Lock & Safe	1302 - 11th Avenue S.W.	269-2222

PLUMBERS—Emergency Service (plumbing & repairs)
Northeast
Bow River Plumbing & Heating	916 Moodie Rd. N.E.	277-9107

Northwest
Jack Dish Plumbing & Heating	2320 - 22nd Street N.W.	282-2601

Southeast
Bondy's Plumbing & Heating	3704 - 47th Street S.W.	242-6260

Southwest
McGowan Plumbing & Heating	3-6029 - 3rd Street S.E.	252-3121

24-HOUR CONVENIENCE STORES
Mac's Convenience Stores	all over Calgary
7-Eleven Food Stores	all over Calgary

SEVEN-DAYS-A-WEEK ALTERNATIVE FOOD STORES
Mother Nature's	Macleod Trail & 70th Avenue S.
Alternative Food Stores	Memorial Drive & 36th Street N.E.

EMERGENCY GAS SERVICE
Canadian Western Natural Gas	(24-hour—365 days)	245-7110

EMERGENCY SEWER
City of Calgary	sewer emergency only	268-1155
Waterworks	emergency only	268-1155

HANDY NUMBERS
AID (Advice Information Direction)	268-5211
Alberta Government Telephones	231-2111
Alberta Motor Association	246-7900
Alpha Milk Company	276-9661
Calgary Board of Education	268-8211
Calgary Catholic Schools	264-1610
Calgary Public Library (main)	266-4606
Calgary Singles Council	269-3346

Canadian Western Natural Gas   245-7110
City of Calgary Electric Dept. (water, too)   233-2121
City of Calgary Garbage Inquiries   268-4925
City of Calgary Transit—schedules   276-7801
Consumer & Corporate Affairs—Alberta   253-0909
Consumer & Corporate Affairs—Canada   231-5601
Time and Temperature   233-2222
Travel Alberta   261-6574
Palm Dairies   272-3366
Weather (Environment Canada) recording   275-3300

HANDY NUMBERS FOR THE MOVING-IN PROCESS
(listed as one thinks of them not as they are listed in phone book)
1. General Information about Calgary
    (community services, social assistance)   268-5211
2. Gas (utilities)   245-7110
3. Light & Water   233-2121
4. Phone   231-2111
5. Garbage collection   268-4925
6. Transit Information   276-7801
7. Parks & Swimming Pools & Golf Courses   268-5211
8. Schools—Public   268-8211
         —Catholic   264-1610
9. Dairies—Alpha   276-9661
        —Palm   272-3366
10. Motor League (Alberta Motor Association)   246-7900
11. Consumer Information—Provincial   253-0909
                      —Federal   231-5601
12. Library (Main) Information   266-4606
13. Time and Temperature   233-2222
14. Weather Information   275-3300
15. Road Condition Information   246-5853
16. Singles Group (Calgary Singles Council)   269-3346

The Insiders

LOUISE BRESKY is a writer-broadcaster who first came to Calgary in 1953 and settled here for good in 1962. She writes and hosts TV documentaries; regularly covers the arts, particularly film and theatre, for CBC radio and television; and is arts columnist for *Calgary Magazine*.

TIM CHRISTISON arrived in Calgary in 1954 and confesses she "hated it at first but now remains here by choice." She does regular consumer commentaries for CBC radio, writes and performs for local television and acts professionally so "I need to know all the cheap good places to go."

ALLEN CONNERY is a Calgary native who "grew up in Hillhurst before it was fashionable." He went east long enough to work for *The Globe and Mail* and *The Beacon-Herald* in Stratford, Ontario and came back to join *The Calgary Herald* in 1968. He now writes four columns a week for the paper, frequently recording the pontifications of The Man On the Bus. He compiled *As Reported in the Herald*, a collection of articles from the paper's first century.

TODD CRISTALL is an Alberta native who discovered wine at age fifteen during his first trip to France—"I bought a fifteen-cent bottle of rosé in Le Drug Store in Paris and staggered back to my hotel." He now runs his own wine investment business (Chardonnay Equities Ltd.), works from Edmonton for a wine agency and makes regular trips to the wine-growing areas of Europe and California.

FRANK WESLEY DABBS has lived in Calgary since 1966, working as a journalist, increasingly specializing in business issues. He has been a reporter for both *The Albertan* and *The Calgary Herald*, exploration editor of *Oilweek* and editor of *The Daily Oil Bulletin*. He is now a freelance writer and consultant and the business columnist for *Calgary Magazine*.

ERIC DAWSON came to Calgary from *The Ottawa Citizen* in 1977 to become music critic of *The Calgary Herald*. He also writes for *Opera Canada* and *Performing Arts in Canada* and does commentaries for CBC network radio.

ELAINE DIXSON, a Calgary native, works freelance in advertising and public relations and as a freelance writer. Since 1979 she has been a volunteer member of the creative-living committee of the Calgary Stampede.

BERNICE EVANS was born in Rhodesia and came to Calgary in 1968 from Europe. She spent five years as restaurant reviewer for CBC radio and several years as food columnist for *Calgary Magazine*. She is now a freelance writer and southern Alberta editor for Ann Hardy's guide, *Where to Eat in Canada*.

C.D. (CHRIS) EVANS, Q.C. is a marathon runner, criminal lawyer ("I know the seamy side of the Calgary scene") and regular contributor "of uninformed commentaries" to Calgary newspapers and to CBC radio and television.

CATHERINE FORD was raised and educated in Calgary and Edmonton; worked with various newspapers in Eastern and Western Canada; in 1979 received a Southam Fellowship and spent one year at the University of Toronto before becoming the Toronto-based Ontario correspondent for Southam news. She returned to Calgary in 1981 as an editorial writer and columnist with *The Calgary Herald*.

DAVE GREBER left London, Ontario for Vancouver in 1974, determined to be part of the lost generation, but stopped short in Calgary instead. "Ambition caught up with me," he says, and he accepted a job with *The Medicine Hat News*, moving back to Calgary in 1976 to work for *The Albertan*. Now a freelance writer/broadcaster and devoted outdoorsman, he had criss-crossed the province in his explorations, "camping and tramping, wandering and visiting."

PAUL HEPHER grew up in Regina and Lethbridge and has lived in Calgary since 1960. He was entertainment writer and critic for *The Albertan* and now works as a musician and freelance journalist, contributing to *Calgary Magazine*, the CBC and *The Calgary Herald*.

DANNA LEAMAN left Ames, Iowa for Calgary in 1977 and immediately made art-gallery hopping part of her routine. She is a scientific and technical writer and contributes to *Calgary Magazine*, ACCESS Alberta and the CBC.

GORDON LEGGE is a born-and-bred Calgarian who, as a youngster "bicycled the city from Nose Creek to Fish Creek, from Bragg Creek to Chestermere Lake, long before bicycle pathways were invented." As an adult, he has worked as a journalist in Calgary, Yellowknife, Ottawa and Toronto; he is now back in Calgary as Alberta bureau chief for *Maclean's*.

CAYT McGUIRE is native Calgarian of "an old Alberta family—my grandfather homesteaded in southern Alberta." Now a freelance writer and filmmaker, she draws on her "jock" upbringing whenever the topic is sports.

GEORGE PARRY is originally from Morrin, Alberta but has been a Calgarian since the early seventies. He has, among other things, lived on the Blackfoot Reserve (as part of a research project for Indian Affairs) and taught Alberta history at University of Calgary ("Indian history, taught by a white man . . . "). One of Calgary's longest-running independent booksellers, he is now president of Westlands Book Express Ltd. and Westlands Art Gallery.

JACK PEACH, born when Calgary itself was still new to the white man, is now the city's unofficial grandfather, thanks to his devoted chronicling of its history. Over the years, he has expressed this fascination in regular broadcasts for CBC radio, a weekly column in *The Calgary Herald*, and in three books (*Peach Preserves*, *Peach Cordial* and *Peach Melba*). He is also nightly weatherman for CBC-TV.

GILLIAN STEWARD was brought up in Saskatchewan and Alberta, and has been a Calgary journalist since 1968. She writes for (among others) *Canadian Business*, *Maclean's* and *Calgary Magazine*, where she is also city columnist. An article of hers sparked The Great Cheesecake War.

ALISTER THOMAS is a relative newcomer who left southern Ontario for Calgary in 1979, convinced the job opportunities were here. He was right: within weeks he was assistant editor of *Calgary Magazine*. Since then he has worked for *Alberta Report* and *Canadian Petroleum Magazine* and is now a freelance writer specializing in the areas of business and sports.

PEGGY WEDDELL is a Drumheller native who moved to Calgary in 1965, later worked in Montreal for three years and moved about before settling here again in 1975, along with "husband and pool-playing springer spaniel." She has done public relations work for the Lake Louise Ski Area and for the Pontiac Ski Circuit and was ski columnist for *The Calgary Herald*. She is now a freelance writer and is foodstuffs columnist for *Calgary Magazine*.

JON WHYTE, a Banff native says, "Calgary? Oh yes . . . gateway to the prairies." He returned to Banff with two M.A.'s from Stanford University and is now curator of the Banff Heritage Homes of the Peter and Catharine Whyte Foundation. He is also a columnist for the weekly Banff *Crag and Canyon* and author of two volumes of poetry (*Gallimaufry* and *Homage, Henry Kelsey* and several books of prose, including *Lake Louise, a Diamond in the Wilderness*, *Rocky Mountain Madness* (with photographer Ed Cavell) and *John Davenall Turner, Painter of Sunfield*.

THE EDITOR
PENNY WILLIAMS, Montreal-born and Toronto-raised, has worked in both the field of international development and in journalism. Because of the former, she lived in Peru and Indonesia and travelled throughout Pakistan before ever setting foot in Western Canada. Because of the latter, she followed her curiosity west in 1977 (after working for *Maclean's* and for the original CBC radio *As It Happens* team) and became assistant producer of the local CBC morning radio show. She was editor of *Calgary Magazine* from 1979 to 1982 and has prepared numerous CBC network radio documentaries and translated ten books (French to English) for publication. She is now a freelance writer/broadcaster/translator and is, among other things, translations editor for *The Canadian Encyclopedia*. "There are," she says, "two interesting cities in Canada: Montreal and Calgary. They are interesting for the same reason—something is really happening, really changing, in each."

INDEX

254